T0029163

IRREVOCABLE ENDORSEMENTS

It has been my distinct privilege to have known John Espy for nearly 35 years. I first met John while working with a Connecticut-based educational software company. I oversaw content development for training users of large-scale mainframe computers, while John created instructional materials for students in the K-12 education market.

Over the years, I become increasingly impressed with John's work ethic, keen wit, memory recall, and, most of all, his remarkable intelligence—coupled with humility and basic humanity; characteristics which are exceedingly rare to find in one person. For these and other reasons, as John moved to Kansas and I moved-on to other companies, I recruited him for writing positions in each.

Years later, when I heard that John's wife, Pam, was undergoing surgery for a suspected brain tumor, I felt compelled to be with him as he awaited the results at the Johns Hopkins Hospital in Baltimore. While the tumor proved benign, its extraction resulted in several other complications, most significant of which was a stroke caused by a brain bleed. It was then they each entered an on-going struggle to reclaim Pam's life.

To that point, I had yet to experience the depth of John's spirituality. It is a side of him that bespeaks a great inner strength, and not something to be paraded casually for public consumption. Pam's condition offered an opportunity to expose that internal fortitude, in facing the trials of recovery for both the stroke patient *and* the patient's most personal support system: the loving spouse. It shoulders the fear, anger, despair, loneliness, confusion, loss—as well as hope and the potency of prayer they each experience.

Knowing John as I do, I'm absolutely convinced his retelling of Pam's tale will be of compelling interest to the millions of stroke patients and their families and loved-ones—and reaffirm the amazing power of family, faith, and friendship in overcoming the obstacles they confront.

— **Jim Howe,** Friend

When everything suddenly seems insurmountable, and we have no grasp on where to go for help in the deepest sorrows and associated fears brought on by a sudden diagnosis and the ensuing difficulty of stroke and its recovery, we find our first steps in desperately reaching out to God, our dear friends, and those who have traveled the journey before us.

Irrevocable is the story of a couple who courageously faced a seemingly impossible journey, reaching into the deepest depths of the human spirit, relying on their deep faith in a healing God who miraculously brought them through to the other side.

Their story will inspire your journey through the sometimes-dark valleys of life, draw you to into a deeper walk with God, and offer tangible hope and helpful insights for stroke victims and their families.

— **Cheri and Pat,**
friends who were given the opportunity to walk alongside
at times and to witness first-hand the presence
of God in the lives of those who trust and believe in Him

Here is an opportunity to see not only see persistence and resilience in the face of challenge, but also to see how music and music therapy can play a valuable role in one's health and life. Pam's story is an opportunity for each of us to learn and grow.

— **Bill Matney,** Ph.D., MT-BC

I have had the privilege of knowing and serving alongside women and men from around the globe; few have the depth of wisdom, insight, humility, and grace that I have seen and experienced in the life of John and Pam. Their nearness to Christ in suffering has produced an intimacy with Him that is raw and real and that draws in anyone who will pause to listen and to learn. When told using John's truly God-given gift for the written word, this story of pain and Presence can't help but call us out into the Deep and leave an imprint on our hearts.

— **Katie Toop,**
Director of Transformational Development,
World Concern, worldconcern.org

Irrevocable is tremendously powerful and moving. It's also wonderfully funny and uplifting, despite the fact—or maybe because—it's such an intimate and unvarnished journey through a tremendously challenging ordeal. This is Corrie ten Boom for the 21st Century. I'm unlikely ever to be sent to a concentration camp, but it's not at all unlikely that I or someone I love will someday have to face rebuilding a life after a traumatic brain injury.

— **Mark MacGougan,** who also offers this one:
This is a book that I'm proud to be seen with.
[Name Withheld By Request]

Pam's story is a faith-building jewel. When it comes to suffering, believers and unbelievers both ask, "Where were You?" Unbelievers ask in accusation. Believers ask in confusion.

John, Pam's devoted husband and partner in her suffering, dives into their confusion (and mine and yours) with honesty and transparency. The splash-over is glorious. Readers will emerge soaked in the love of a Savior that also suffered. Don't wear a raincoat. Let their story wash over you. You will cry, sigh, and smile—more a believer than before!

— **Dr. Jeff Barclay,**
Lead Pastor, Christ Community Church,
Lawrence, Kansas

John's uplifting account of navigating the trails of stroke recovery should be required reading of stroke victim family and friends. I have witnessed my mother, Pam, recover steadily over the past 10 years, beyond the expectations of most physicians. John's steadfast patience, support, and humor have no doubt greatly contributed to this recovery. John's description of my mom's recovery is both cathartic and inspirational to the loved ones of stroke victims.

— **Brian,** Son

IRREVOCABLE

IRREVOCABLE

A Story of Human Aphasia and Divine Grace

BY
JOHN M. ESPY

Deep River
BOOKS
Sisters, OR

FOR PAMELA,
With love and bugglegun
Day by day, I remember you

CONTENTS

PROLOGUE

His arms are full of broken things.

— Charlotte Mew[1]

"I remember you!" The young man's eyes shine; his face strains with the excitement that we feel when someone's story has captured our imagination and stirred our compassion. "Hey, how ya doing?"

He is, of course, oblivious to me, and addressing my wife Pam. And I, like any loyal husband, am standing by, silently rolling my eyes, and thinking, *Gee! What did she do now?*

We are leaving a busy restaurant, her hand grasping my arm because she still has a narrowed field of vision and is apt to bump into people and chairs. Now we stop, right in the midst of the bustle, and turn to face him. I am becoming used to these encounters.

At first we don't recognize him. He is just a busboy here, he explains, but it's a much better job than the one he had when he last saw us (okay, saw *her*), well over a year ago. Then he worked in the food court of a large grocery store. I parked Pam there, with a salad, while I shopped for fruit and cereal. Each time I circled back, she had a conversation going.

[1] Charlotte Mew, "Madeleine in Church" (1914), in Robert Atwan and Laurance Wieder, eds., *Chapters into Verse: Poetry in English Inspired by the Bible* (Oxford and New York: Oxford, 1993), 2:233. (Hereafter *Chapters into Verse.*) Also at *Poetry Foundation*, accessed December 19, 2021, https://www.poetryfoundation.org/poems/55330/madeleine-in-church.

The young people who staffed the food court would come round to ask, "Would you like a refill of soda?" And Pam would take this as a cue to tell her story: "I had a stroke! I was in a coma!"

The first response was always bewilderment: "So you don't want more soda?" But Pam has a disarming smile, and her recitation, once launched, is difficult to derail: "The God I believe in is able to heal! I'm learning to talk all over again." And then, more plaintively: "Do you have any mustard—sorry, wrong word—to go on this?" Soon they would sit, to "help" her. And I would return to the aisles with a lightened heart.

"Your story moved me," says the busboy. "I couldn't forget it. I've told it to other people."

He seems to have forgotten a climactic moment in the tale, or perhaps he's embraced it only too well. Flashing a grin, pointing at me if I'm nearby, Pam announces proudly, "And John was deleted from the brain!" Sometimes I step forward, offering my hand: "Hi, pleased to meet you. I'm Deleted From The Brain. You can call me Dell."

Recovery accounts tend to be solemn, even somber. This one is less so. I keep reaching upward, aspiring to Emily Dickinson and John Donne, and I still come out sounding like Edward Lear or "Weird Al" Yankovic. Or, a better analogy, since I used to fancy that I could deliver a punchline too: George Burns was a funny guy. But when he teamed up with Gracie Allen, he became a straight man. There was something about Gracie: with all of her talent, with all of the writers and scripts and rehearsals, somehow, as the delighted listener, you always felt, when she opened her mouth, that you had no idea what would come out of it. George said:

> The character she plays has what we call "illogical logic." She
> is completely earnest about what she is doing and saying,
> and I think it is the fact that she is so kind to the rest of the

world for its lack of understanding of what is perfectly clear to her that makes people love her.[2]

See how little George has to do in this excerpt from one of their routines:

George: Oh, what beautiful flowers!

Gracie: Aren't they lovely? And if it weren't for you I wouldn't have them.

George: Me? What did I have to do with it?

Gracie: Well, it was your idea. You said that when I went to visit Clara Bagley to take her flowers so when she wasn't looking I did. . . . Isn't it good that they're carnations, dear? I'll put them in the refrigerator and we'll milk them later.[3]

That, in a nutshell, is the story of my marriage. Pam has had a hard life; she has walked by faith; she has persevered through pain. The sappy among us might describe her story as a triumph of the human spirit— although one of these, after being on the receiving end of an angry outburst, amended this verdict slightly, muttering, "I think it takes a wooden stake or a silver bullet to stop her kind." Yet it is her utterances, with their endless capacity to surprise, that captivate people. Who better to tell that story—using her own words as often as possible—than her eternally upstaged husband?

---

[2] George Burns, *I Love Her, That's Why!: An Autobiography* (New York: Simon & Schuster, 1955), 106. See also David C. Tucker, *The Women Who Made Television Funny: Ten Stars of 1950s Sitcoms* (Jefferson, NC: McFarland, 2007), 8, 11, 12.

[3] This and other routines are posted at the *George Burns and Gracie Allen* blog, accessed December 19, 2021, https://georgegracie.wordpress.com/category/comedy-routine/.

Pam has three children and, at this writing, ten grandchildren. She has four siblings, two ex-husbands, and many friends. They all have their own takes and memories, which they alone can tell. They will not figure largely in these pages, though their contributions to Pam's life (and mine) have been incalculable. I hope one day they will write their own accounts, sharing their best snapshots of a subject who has never held still for long. This chronicle chases only one trajectory of mingled shadow and glory.[4]

When I first met her, some twenty years before the revelation in the restaurant, Pam was a member of a church worship team. She was a musician, but also something more: a person of deep feeling, with an expressive face. She could help those of us who still had hearts of stone, who got trapped inside our heads, to open a door to joy and humility, grief and repentance, anger and forgiveness, shame and consecration.

On this day, three years after her stroke, she no longer leads worship. She rarely picks up her guitar. There are outbursts of rage, and long lonely stretches. She struggles to order food.

But as I see her chat with this young man, I admire again how vigorously she "strengthen[s] what remains" (Rev. 3:2). There is an openness about her that draws people in, and an energy—an unquenchable joy, even when it manifests as rage—that inspires hope. She is still inviting people into the presence of God.

And so this story falls into the illustrious genre of "funny stuff my spouse has said" books—while, at the same time, perhaps subversively, it tries to trace God's handiwork. It tells of recovery and spiritual growth. At least, Deleted From The Brain hopes so.

---

[4] Compare David Talbot: "During my recovery, I have found that some survivors' change-of-life stories thrill me, while others send me spinning downward to the pits of gloom. . . . But I always find myself responding to personal accounts that have a truthful mix of shadow and light." *Between Heaven and Hell: The Story of My Stroke* (San Francisco: Chronicle Prism, 2020), ebook, chap. 16.

1

WEAKNESS

I do not know why God should strike
But God is what is stricken also: . . .

— Archibald MacLeish[5]

MAY 28, 2010

It is 2:00 p.m. In my cluttered office on the second floor of our home, I am busily plying my craft as a Bad Instructional Writer. I have just finished editing a lesson about evolution, and I need to notify my supervisor, Jenny, that it is complete and posted on our website. Since I firmly believe the subject line of an email is an invitation to a wisecrack, and since I award myself extra points whenever said wisecrack mocks our boss, I title this one, "Is That Jim on the Left Side of the Picture?" The body of the email reads:

> Probably so, since we're looking at one of those classroom charts of "Evolution," now published. You gotta give the guy credit for crawling all the way out of the primordial slime just to get a doughnut.

---

[5] Archibald MacLeish, *J.B.: A Play in Verse* (1958; Boston: Houghton Mifflin, n.d.), 89.

After I click *Send*, Jenny writes back that she was chuckling at this, sitting at her desk in the Connecticut office, when Jim walked by in the hall. (The only life lesson the guy gleaned from *In Search of Excellence*, back in the 1980s, was that, if you're the boss, you can get away with being an antsy busybody so long as you call it "management by wandering around.") Of course she reads my email to him. A master of self-defense (if not of managing projects, balancing budgets, or evolving toward the right side), Jim quips, "Yeah, well, at least in my case we're talking about HUMAN evolution." So now everybody's happy, and we're having a pleasant if not particularly productive day.

When the phone rings, I'm expecting more of the same. Instead, a man with a tone of practiced authority, speaking in clipped sentences, informs me that he is a state trooper. He is with my wife Pam. (He pronounces her full name, and I breathlessly confirm that she is my wife.) She is all right. She has been in a single-vehicle car accident. Apparently she swerved to miss something and then lost control. The car hit a concrete barrier, glancingly, scraping along it for a short distance. The airbag didn't deploy, but the seatbelt bruised her chest. She's having a little trouble breathing. She may have a slight concussion. Although she is almost to Kansas City, where she was heading to babysit the grandkids, she has asked that the ambulance bring her to the hospital in Lawrence, where I am.

The rest of the day we pass at the peculiar pace of an emergency room. It is the way I picture the trench warfare of World War I, or London during the Blitz of World War II: we hunker down, waiting, as bombs of illness and injury explode around us. We hear the cries of pain and the engines of counterattack, but we are powerless to intervene. We pray silently, holding hands, all the while in suspense concerning our own safety. We seek to draw reassurance from the more muffled sounds, the periodic attentions we receive, and even the mundane drabness that whispers hoarsely, *This is no place to die*; but mostly it is our breathing that steadies us, and our hands' touch.

The story unfolds in reports from the lab, like a series of telegrams.
No sign of internal bleeding. Good. But the X-ray shows a small mass,
not in the chest but up in the brain. Oh, no! It could be the ticking
time bomb of an aneurysm. Let's get a CT scan, and then an MRI.
Whew, it's almost certainly not an aneurysm. But it probably is a
brain tumor.

Sometimes it seems as if we are marked for catastrophe, for
judgment. "It is as if a man fled from a lion and a bear met him" (Amos
5:19, Ampl). God as Lemony Snicket! We have tried hard to turn this
combination of irony and inevitability into low comedy, to imagine a
black-and-white silent movie of slapstick comeuppance, in which no
one escapes a pie in the face. But the Bible doesn't say that all we can
do is laugh and resign ourselves. Its tone is urgent: "Seek good, not
evil, that you may live. . . . Perhaps the LORD God Almighty will have
mercy . . ." (Amos 5:14-15).

God's mercy and kindness often appear against a backdrop of
severity (Rom. 11:22). In the shell-shocked days that follow, we tell
ourselves and others that the accident was a blessing in disguise. The
car is totaled, but Pam is not. The tumor has been discovered before
it could grow larger. We now know why, in recent years, her left eye
gradually has become painful and light-sensitive—symptoms her
ophthalmologist dismissed without recommending further tests; he is
suddenly polite and deferential. *Brain tumor* is a scary diagnosis, but
God has made us aware of the nature of this trial, and He will lead us
through it.

In the evenings, we stroll hand in hand—like children entering
the Valley of the Shadow, like Hansel and Gretel in the dark woods.
Because we live only a block from the hospital, our walks take us
around it. In some ways, we have never left the ER.

AUGUST 5, 2010

Once again, I'm at the computer. I have rewritten a case study about
a classroom that uses my company's software. As an experiment,

administrators asked every school employee to greet each student with positive, encouraging words. It is an uplifting story. Still, as I send it back, I type in the subject line, "And Then the Lunch Ladies Sang 'Climb Every Mountain.'"

Pam comes into my office. Much as I welcome her intrusions, I have learned to be downright suspicious. In large measure, this stems from our conflicting philosophies of pest control. A few years back, when there was a mouse in our kitchen, I purchased glue traps, fully intending to drive the captured rodent far out into the woods and free it by anointing it with oil—while, no doubt, several of its relatives hopped aboard my car for the ride back to town. Pam felt no such stirrings of humanity (or, in her native language, wussiness). After waiting a mere three days for the glue traps to work their magic—not without hampering their spell through steady mockery—she obtained old-fashioned, spring-loaded, snap-and-break-its-neck mousetraps. In one night, she achieved an undeserved success.

The next day, although I was on the phone with a customer when she handed me the brown paper bag, I was touched by the gesture. *She is bringing me a treat,* I thought. *Maybe a raspberry Danish.* True, she murmured, "Don't be alarmed," but I ignored that. She has lots of strange impressions about me: that I'm a wuss, that I don't work all that hard, that I'm nervous and excitable, . . . And so I was somewhat surprised when I opened the bag and glimpsed a long, hairless tail and a trap. I exclaimed "Oooo!" right in the client's ear, and almost jumped out of my stupid and anti-ergonomic rolling office chair. As usual in this marriage, I was left holding the bag.

Say what you will about Pam, but she's a good mouser.

Today, though, she is holding a cordless phone in her outstretched hand. There's no sign of a hidden corpse. She wants me to talk with a neurosurgeon.

In the weeks since the accident, she has mounted a tremendous research effort. Additional tests have confirmed that her tumor is a *meningioma*—located in the meninges, membranes on the outskirts of the brain. This is a good placement: the further into the brain a tumor lies, the less likely it is to be operable. But hers is pressing against the optic nerve—the most sensitive part of the brain—and wrapped around the carotid artery. Because these vessels are so close to the tumor, there's no way to do a biopsy, blindly sticking a needle into her head. So, although 80 percent of meningiomas are benign, we can't be sure about hers. But even if it's not malignant, it is affecting her left eye and beginning to influence the right eye as well. Doing nothing doesn't seem like an option.

We have asked for prayer at several local churches, and at a home group. We pray together. Pam traveled with a friend to a healing conference, while I fasted and prayed at home. There have been words of encouragement, but no bold declarations, and no abatement of symptoms.

I have heard Joseph Prince say that sometimes, after we are divinely healed, symptoms persist as a test of our faith. We are to stop praying and simply believe that we have been healed. But I find no biblical warrant for this. When the blind man touched by Jesus still saw imperfectly (people like "trees walking"), Jesus did not rebuke him, or urge him to resist the symptoms; He laid hands on him a second time (Mark 8:22-25).

My brother and his wife come to pray with us. He says, "I have the impression that you'll have to go through this, but you'll be all right in the end." Later, he writes me these words: "It is surprising that sometimes we touch others' lives by our vulnerabilities rather than our sufficiencies."

And so we have also proceeded with doctors.

A neuro-ophthalmologist has told Pam that meningiomas are slow-growing; hers may have been there for fifteen years. He calls her ophthalmologist a fool for missing the signs. He is able to measure the effects: she has lost 70 percent of the visual field in her left eye.

We have met with a neurosurgeon at the University of Kansas Medical Center. She wants to operate, but doesn't believe she will be able to remove the entire tumor; she recommends following up with a course of radiation. But her hospital's Tumor Board overrides her and proposes stereotactic radiation instead of surgery.

Resourcefully, Pam has found a website called *Meningioma Mommas* that has discussion threads.[6] Through those, she obtains contact information for a half-dozen neurosurgeons around the country. Several of them volunteer to look at her scans. None of them likes the idea of stereotactic radiation, which will inevitably kill healthy tissue along with the tumor. I can't help feeling that our medical center is eager to find opportunities to use the new tool they have purchased. Yet when I ask, if we get the operation, what decisions I need to be prepared to make for Pam during surgery, one doctor answers, "Life and death." We have continued to look further afield.

> It seemed you needed to study brain science before you could actually select a brain surgeon. — Lauren Marks[7]

The neurosurgeon on the phone this afternoon is at Johns Hopkins Hospital in Baltimore. He believes he can remove the whole tumor, with no need for radiation. Pam is enthusiastic, and I am cautiously hopeful. It is good to soak in his confidence. But what makes him so sure? "We do a thousand of these procedures a year," he tells me.

I will wonder later whether I should have discerned a touch of arrogance, a reckless hubris. Such speculations circle back upon themselves: How arrogant is it of me to think that I could discern another person's spiritual attitude?

A few Christians will argue afterward that the outcome is proof that we must have erred. We prayed, but not with perfect faith. We sought prayer for healing, but not from the guy they like. We didn't

---

[6] *Meningioma Mommas*, accessed December 19, 2021, http://www.meningiomamommas.org/.
[7] Lauren Marks, *A Stitch of Time: The Year a Brain Injury Changed My Language and Life* (New York: Simon & Schuster, 2017), 201.

fast enough. We didn't rebuke the right demon. We could have been spared all that follows.

Perhaps they are right. I know and understand only in part (1 Cor. 13:9, 12). I have often strayed or run ahead. On the other hand, even the Good Shepherd sometimes leads us out of the green pastures, away from the quiet waters, and into the Valley of the Shadow of Death; and this too is one of the "paths of righteousness" that we walk "for his name's sake" (Ps. 23:3, NIV84).

We decide to go to Hopkins.

AUGUST 6 – 20, 2010

Pam and I both draw up simple wills, but she balks at any sort of Do Not Resuscitate or Advance Directive form. In the end we agree that, if a medical decision must be made and she is unable to participate, I will confer with her daughter and one of her sisters.

We book a one-way flight to Baltimore, since our return date depends on variables outside our control.

She continues to make plans for life after the operation. We visit a local community college where she may take some classes.

I call my boss. Jim and I have similar senses of humor, much to the annoyance of others. Two decades ago, he approved my request to move to Kansas and work from home—but he took some convincing. "I'll be a dedicated resource," I argued; "without the office noise, and all the meetings, I'll work more efficiently." "Maybe," he allowed. "Well, how about this?" I persisted: "with me out of the office, everyone else will be more efficient." A master stroke: "Now *that* I believe," he said.

Today we begin with the customary exchange of insults. "Is this the great man?" I inquire. A slight pause, then: "Yes," he replies. (The guy's either a marvelous straight man or a pompous ass.) "Well," I say, "my grate is broken; you'll have to come over and fix it."

Eventually, I tell him that I need to ask for a leave without pay. Pam and I will fly to Baltimore, settle in, meet the doctor, and have a day or two to sightsee. We hope to enjoy a fleeting second honeymoon. Pam likes to quote God's promise in Joel 2:25: "I will restore to you the years which the swarming locust has eaten" (RSV). Following the surgery, we've been told to expect about five days of recovery time in the hospital; then, after her discharge we're to stay in Baltimore to have the same medical team remove the staples, perhaps an additional five days later. On a conservative estimate, we anticipate being gone for two weeks.

Jim's response astonishes me. "Take the time you need," he says, "but it won't be without pay." On the spot, he commits the small company to paying my full salary for as long as we're gone.

Next thing I know, he has made arrangements to travel to Baltimore at his own expense, just to sit with me in the surgery waiting room. "No one should have to go through that alone," he tells me.

It is my first look at a truth I will see demonstrated again and again: When someone suffers a severe misfortune, it brings out the best in a great many people. It's not only strangers who are drawn to Pam through her affliction. Some family members, friends, and acquaintances connect with her at new levels. Pain can open doors.

AUGUST 21 – 24, 2010

We sit in one of the departure gate waiting areas in the Kansas City Airport. The seats are comfortable but packed too closely together. As in a theater, everyone studiously ignores one another to concentrate on the main story—except here there is no focal point, no troupe of actors; we have only our separate impending journeys.

Although it is a cloudless summer day, we are delayed. The airplane we were scheduled to board has a door that won't close properly. The airline's nearest available plane is seven states away; the delay will drag on for five hours. I have read enough of the business press to recognize Just-In-Time Inventory: a great concept on paper, but messy to implement. Too often, it becomes one more excuse for valuing profits over people. A more accurate name might be Out-Of-Luck Service.

Pam is sitting in an airport wheelchair, wearing dark glasses. Her eyes remain super-sensitive to light, so she has been riding, letting me push her. She is sobbing. She rarely travels anymore, and is not as used to flight delays as I am. But that's not really it. Her busyness has been halted in its tracks, and the strain has caught up with her.

I marvel again at her strength, the mysterious combination of physical energy and supernatural faith that propels her through life. And I see again that all human strength is brittle, liable to snap in an instant.

We have both leaned more than a little on gallows humor to carry us through the past weeks. I suggested to Pam that, since the surgeons won't be too far away from the brain regions that control personality and mood, I may put in a requisition to turn her into a Stepford wife. She retaliated by coming home from the library and handing me a mystery novel entitled *Mad Cow Nightmare*.

The jokes keep us going until—as now—they don't.

Late in the day, we arrive at our lodgings in Baltimore. Pam isn't happy with them, and we spend a good part of the next day, Sunday, finding a different hotel, and moving. Our luggage, lost by the airline, is at last delivered.

A couple of days before our flight, the hospital informed us that they'd scheduled a pre-op visit on Monday, plus new scans on Tuesday. Our sightseeing time has effectively been taken away.

We have one good moment as we are filling out forms at the hospital. Pam has asked me to hold the insurance card and dictate while she writes; soon she becomes annoyed at my slow and methodical reading. "You can give it to me faster than that!" she says. "Oh," I quip, "so this is like our sex life: 'More, more! Faster, faster!'"

Pam only gives me a tolerant smile, rolling her eyes, but behind us we hear a huge guffaw: "Haw-HAW!" I thought I had spoken in soft and muted tones; apparently not. The receptionist is collapsed across her desk, laughing. She was bored when we arrived, but is bright and cheerful when we turn in the forms: "How y'all doing? Do you need anything?"

On Tuesday morning we are back at the hospital so technicians can stick markers all over her scalp to guide the surgical team. They look like the bolts on the neck of Frankenstein's monster. Pam accepts them with good grace, but I can see she has experienced the procedure as one more indignity. When we leave she steps a bit more gingerly, as if she senses that she is now visibly marked out as a special case, a patient, someone slated for an ordeal.

In the afternoon we take a long taxi ride to meet our neurosurgeon at his private office. He shows us the previous day's MRI, and for the first time we see the tumor. To me it looks huge, but he says, "It's only about the size of a grape. Just last week I removed a tumor from exactly the same location in a woman, only it was considerably larger."

He exudes confidence, and we drink it in.

On the ride back, I muse that this surgeon, like all the others who bid for the work, has promised to shave very little of Pam's hair. Perhaps my own wide open spaces of baldness make me sensitive, but I keep thinking, *This is brain surgery! She could be paralyzed; she could die! And the best assurance these bozos can come up with is, "Hey, at least you won't look like Chrome Dome over there"?*

This is my way of whistling in the dark. At least I know to keep it to myself, and leave Pam to her own thoughts.

We haven't seen much of Baltimore other than the hospital, the doctor's office, and the block around our hotel, but on this last night we've planned an outing to a restaurant that specializes in local seafood. But Pam is self-conscious about the surgical markers on her head, and the waiter is rude. We don't have much appetite. Fear flavors our food.

Back at the hotel, I reach out to a prayer warrior friend through email, summarizing my requests for tomorrow.

> As for our prayer concerns going forward, here's what I am thinking (Pam's list might be different):
>
> - I would love to see her sleep well tonight and go in rested.
> - That Jesus would be with her going through the dark valley, and that His presence will comfort her.

- That she will come out of this with a stronger assurance of God's love for her, and also a clear sense that He still has things for her to do in this life.
- That there will be no infection, no stroke, no damage to healthy organs or tissues.
- That the surgeon can remove all the tumor.
- That Pam will not lose further sight, and, indeed, that some sight will be restored.
- That the tumor will prove to be benign.
- That her recovery will be both swift and restful.
- I think she is also concerned about my ability to care for her. She says sometimes that I am "too nice"—she would like to see me fight for her in some situations. I am asking God to show me how I can be the support she needs—or rather, I am saying, "God, I CAN'T do this in my own strength."

We need to get to bed early so as to rise at 3:30 a.m. for surgical prep at 5:30 and surgery at 7:00. The second honeymoon has been a bust. Later, we say; in a week or so. At least we're together.

But it feels as if the locusts are still gnawing.

AUGUST 25, 2010

I sleep like a rock, as I have for several nights now. Maybe it is a coping mechanism. I am slow to go to bed, but when I do, I'm out almost at once. I think of the disciples in Gethsemane, "sleeping for sorrow" (Luke 22:45, RSV) while Jesus prays in anguish. Not their proudest moment, and yet that sorrow was genuine—in their broken way, they truly loved Him. One paraphrase (Living) says "exhausted from grief." Were the disciples really worn out from the Supper and the events of Holy Week? Or did they dimly sense the draining agony that lay ahead? It's the shadowy apparitions that paralyze the soul.

Up early to ride fasting through the sleeping city. Then we are part of a process, guided along by hospital staff. We keep being separated, then reunited, as if rehearsing for some longer severing. At last an orderly has Pam give me her wedding ring to hold, and tells us to exchange a parting kiss.

At such a time, the words "I love you" sound like resignation, a sigh of letting go. They hang in the air with all my tentative hopes as she is wheeled away.

In my last vision of her, she is in fine form, pointing at me, joking with a nurse that, if she winds up needing a brain transplant, they can use me as the donor—or at least rummage in me for spare parts.

She is the bravest person I know.

*   *   *

Fortunately I am adept at keeping busy, filling time. I've brought Pam's laptop so as to send out email updates—but I've been parked in a waiting room close to the cardiac unit, and big signs warn that electronic devices must be turned off. It's just as well; I feel disconnected anyway. I read.

At length I am ushered into a neurosurgery waiting room. True to his word, Jim joins me. We embrace, and I give him a quick progress report. I thank him profusely for coming, but he says it counts toward his court-ordered community service. Then, as guys will, we sit and talk about everything except the elephant in the operating room. We plan work projects, castles in the air. He steadies me.

"I already had the rod and staff to comfort me," I tell him (referring to Ps. 23:4). "I guess God thought I needed the cattle prod as well."

"Yeah, well," he says, "you're supposed to walk *through* the valley, not settle yourself on your keister." He pokes me. "Move along, there."

"Jim, have I ever told you that you remind me of Samson?" He is flattered, but suspicious: "Why, because I always bring down the house?" "No, because your favorite weapon is the jawbone of an ass."

The surgical team is an hour late in getting started. After our travel experience, I'm ready for anything, I think—I'm prepared to hear that the OR door won't close, that they may have to bring in a new surgeon from seven states away, or that they've lost the tumor during handling.

But they send me word every hour or so; and, though yesterday the neurosurgeon said the procedure should take five hours, they're done in three and a half. He appears in his scrubs and tells me the tumor came out cleanly—he compares it to scooping out pudding with a spoon—and he got it all. For the first time, he expresses hope that she will regain some of the sight lost in her left eye.

Pam is moved to the Neurosciences Critical Care Unit (NCCU). No flowers are permitted because of the risk of infections—and bees! At last I am allowed in to see her, just for a moment. The bandage seems massive, but what gets my attention is her posture: eyes down, rocking slightly. She keeps repeating, "I am so sick." After a little coaxing, she is able to get out that her pain is a "ten" on a one-to-ten scale. I pray over her, and then consult a nurse. I'm told the brain itself has no nerve endings, so this is not "deep" pain but incision pain, kind of a giant headache. They are giving her pain medication every ten to fifteen minutes, but they can't knock her out because, unfortunately, one of the key cognitive function tests following brain surgery requires them to keep checking in with her, asking questions. They also rely on the flashlight-in-the-eyes test, which doesn't work well if the pupils are already dilated by medication.

This is the stuff they don't warn you about ahead of time. Mercifully, she falls back to sleep.

Jim and I go to supper, but I am poor company, thinking about her pain. She is like a cord stretched tight; I am far away, detached, a frayed end.

Back at the hotel, before sending a last email to family and friends, I call the hospital. The nurse says that Pam keeps drifting into sleep but, when she wakes up, she is more agitated and disoriented than they like to see.

Thankfully, I have just a bit of context for this news. A month ago, Pam and I watched a documentary about brain surgery. One of the doctors commented that they often restrain the patients, physically strap them down, because for some reason they tend to wake up abruptly, raring to go. And Pam has always been restless. Ideally, that reaction should subside fairly quickly.

> Most brain surgery is simply the creation of a new injury
> to avoid the potential effects of a more significant injury.
> — Michael Paul Mason[8]

As I switch out the light, alone in the too-big bed, I pray that "the peace of God, which passes all understanding, will keep" her heart and her mind "in Christ Jesus" (Phil. 4:7, RSV). If God's peace can bypass our understanding, it can certainly outpace her comprehension following brain surgery. Perhaps it can even silence my anxieties.

AUGUST 26, 2010

The ringing phone jolts me awake at 6:00 a.m. An ICU doctor is telling me that, when Pam didn't settle down, they ran a head CT. It shows bleeding in the brain; more precisely, there may be a clot in the large veins responsible for draining excess blood from the brain. *Sinus thrombosis*, they call it. Blood thinners might reduce clotting, but they're not a good idea so soon after surgery. They want me to come in early, now, to discuss treatment options.

"I don't want you to think she's at death's door," says the doctor. Consequently, in the taxi, that's all I can picture. Or if not yet at the door, then on the gurney, being wheeled down the hall, still pointing back, cheerful. Receding.

---

[8] Michael Paul Mason, *Head Cases: Stories of Brain Injury and Its Aftermath* (2008; New York: Farrar, Straus and Giroux, 2009), 153.

Once I'm at the NCCU, they want me to sign a form giving them permission to open Pam's chest and put in a *central line*. This will be a wider, more effective conduit for medications and fluids than a simple IV line. More than that, it delivers a saline solution. For most of the body, ice is the best way to prevent or reduce inflammation, but sodium must be used in cases of brain swelling. This is critical, because the brain is trapped inside a confined space, the bony box of the skull. If the brain continues to expand, the doctors will have to apply the drill and remove the back of Pam's skull, temporarily, to make room. Another intrusion, and one that increases the risk of infection.[9]

I sign the form without even reflecting on my agreement with Pam: that, in the event of a medical emergency requiring a decision to be made on her behalf, I will consult her sister and her daughter. In the heat of the moment, this doesn't feel at all like an open, deliberate choice. It is simply the only option, the next right thing to do. It is almost the only thing I can do for her: to sign my name.

Visiting hours don't start till noon, but they let me see her for a moment. She is resting, but it is a fitful sleep. I think of her last words to me: "I am so sick." Cast down, a cry of pain. Where is the heavenly Father who loves her, the Jesus who stands by her side? Does He not say, "I will never leave you nor forsake you" (Josh. 1:5)?[10]

The NCCU waiting area begins to fill with families: anxious, hopeful, silent, restless. We swapped stories yesterday, said "That's good" at any sign of progress in our loved ones. They are kind people.

---

[9] Some patients, particularly those who have suffered traumatic brain injuries, do need to have part of the skull removed to manage swelling, an operation called a *craniectomy*. The skull fragments are frozen; eventually, they are either reinserted or replaced with a customized implant. See, for example, the accounts of Gabrielle Giffords and Mark Kelly with Jeffrey Zaslow, *Gabby: A Story of Courage and Hope* (New York: Scribner-Simon & Schuster, 2011); Lee and Bob Woodruff, *In an Instant: A Family's Journey of Love and Healing* (2007; New York: Random House, 2008); Katherine and Jay Wolf, *Hope Heals: A True Story of Overwhelming Loss and an Overcoming Love* (Grand Rapids, MI: Zondervan, 2016); and Lu Spinney, *Beyond the High Blue Air* (New York: Catapult, 2016), 26, 42, 51.

[10] Indeed, this is the very heart of God: compare Deut. 31:6, 8; Heb. 13:5; Matt. 28:20.

Today, though, I am the object of averted eyes, everyone's worst fears realized.

Jim arrives. There are no jokes today. Somehow I know that I don't have to maintain a false front with him. I can worry, and fall silent.

The neurosurgeon stops by to say that Pam's latest CT scan shows three areas in the brain—one on the left side, two in back—where blood is not draining properly. It doesn't appear to be a hemorrhage, nor a full-blown clot. When a tumor is removed, the brain tends to "settle," expanding into the cavity, and so the sinus veins may be stretched, unable to drain the blood properly.

"This is a one-in-five-hundred outcome," he tells me. Small comfort. Later, I recall his over-the-phone assurance: "We do a thousand of these procedures a year." So every year this happens twice? I can't tell confidence from arrogance in doctors, and I don't like their odds. I want to take a flight—even a delayed, lost-luggage flight—back to the life we had.

Ninety minutes later, a nurse practitioner announces that Pam has suffered a seizure. It was caused by pressure in the brain, but it's not the body's preferred method of relieving pressure. In fact, it has the effect of increasing the pressure even further.

It will be four months before I learn from a neurologist that "seizure" is, in this case, a hospital euphemism for "stroke." Four months during which I am terrified of seizures.

The day is rapidly unraveling. As if reflecting the intricate connections inside Pam's brain, my cell phone dies. Too much activity, and I left the charging cord at the hotel. Voices and messages slip past, unheeded. I cannot catch them.

More bad news: It turns out that putting in a central line involves some tricky maneuvering. Something slipped up, and they have punctured her lung. Not life-threatening, but one more complication. They have to insert a chest tube to re-inflate the lung. How much pain does all of this entail? I can't tell.

Jim needs to leave, but he lingers till Pam's sisters arrive to keep me company. As a last thoughtful gesture, he goes down to the hospital gift shop and comes back with a stuffed toy: a dog with floppy ears. It will sit by Pam on her bed for many weeks, mostly unacknowledged—a symbol of innocence or childlike comfort, or maybe an unspoken hope for the return of playfulness.

Pam's sisters bring a bustling and capable energy—and a cord to charge my phone. They set up an iPod in Pam's room to play music. When flowers from one of Pam's sons are delivered, they persuade a nurse to waive the rules and set them up where Pam will be able to see them, outside her room but visible through glass.

AUGUST 27 – 30, 2010

A new word is introduced by the doctors: Pam is "unresponsive." This one I can decipher: she is in a *coma*. It is not the coma I have always pictured—Sleeping Beauty slumbering peacefully, framed by a flock of chirping Disney birds; this is the collapse of a crushed body and a bludgeoned mind. She is not simply "out." At times she is more wakeful, but her eyes don't focus or track. She doesn't respond to our voices or touch. Always there is agitation. "We can't really know how 'aware' she is right now," the neurosurgeon tells me.

And then he says something surprising: "We have to assume, when we're in the room, that the patient knows we're there. We have to believe, when we speak to them, that they can hear and understand."

"We have to believe." These doctors and nurses are people of science. Yet they have witnessed marvelous things, recoveries beyond their skill or understanding, brains healing mysteriously while they could only watch and wait. They testify with Hamlet,

> There are more things in heaven and earth, Horatio,
> Than are dreamt of in your philosophy.[11]

---

[11] William Shakespeare, *Hamlet* (1599-1602), 1.5.167-68; available at *The Folger Shakespeare*, accessed December 19, 2021, https://shakespeare.folger.edu/shakespeares-works/hamlet/.

And what of me, the Christian? The apostle Paul says, "[W]e walk by faith, not by sight" (2 Cor. 5:7, RSV) but, every time I step into Pam's room, my senses overwhelm me. I have the faith of a weather vane, spinning wildly with every wind that blows, even if I am nailed to one spot. When I take her hand and there is no responsive squeeze, I am forlorn.

I talk to Pam. I pray aloud. I declare over her that nothing in all creation—not trouble, hardship, persecution; not hunger and nakedness; not danger, brain tumors, bleeding and swelling, seizures and strokes; not medical errors; not sword or scalpel; not death nor vegetative life; neither angels nor demons, present nor future, height nor depth—will ever be able to separate her from the love of God that is in Christ Jesus her Lord (see Rom. 8:35, 38-39).

Paul says at one point that faith is believing and therefore speaking (2 Cor. 4:13). So I speak, but my voice sounds thin and strained; it reverberates in silence, answered only by the beeping of Pam's heart monitors.

We had said that we would go through this valley together. But she has been swept away by an avalanche, and I am far behind, picking my way carefully down the bunny slope. She is somewhere out in the depths of the ocean of God, while I only wade in the shallows.

It occurs to me that, on the night when He stood in our place, Jesus went to pray in a garden called Gethsemane, the Olive Press. The name calls to mind a machine with a stone roller, so large that it took two men to work it,[12] crushing the olives to squeeze out precious oil. Jesus went often to this pressure zone (Luke 21:37; 22:39); on this night, "he was in such agony of spirit that he broke into a sweat of blood, with great drops falling to the ground as he prayed more and more earnestly" (Luke 22:44, Living). The living Christ understands what it is to be hard pressed, on and inside the head. He

---

[12] R. K. Harrison, "Oil," in J. D. Douglas, ed., *The New Bible Dictionary* (1962; Grand Rapids, MI: William B. Eerdmans, 1975), 906. (Hereafter *NBD*.)

walks with her, not I; He holds her hand, He knows her pain. She can still hear His voice, wherever she has gone. His life is light, "and the Light shines on in the darkness, for the darkness has never overpowered it" (John 1:4-5, Ampl). Her eyes, that cannot meet mine, still see that light. And somehow "it was the LORD's will to crush him and cause him to suffer" (Isa. 53:10): good will come from this, though now we see only the merciless rollers. If Pam should descend to the depths of the pit,

> ... even there your hand will guide me, your right hand will hold me fast. ... [E]ven the darkness will not be dark to you; the night will shine like the day, for darkness is as light to you. — Ps. 139:10, 12

With scattered thoughts and faltering lips, I wage my puny battle at her bedside. I sling my little stones in the general direction of the giant. Then I retire to the waiting room.

Already the nurses are learning to "read" Pam's expressive face. They can see when she grimaces in pain. Before visiting hours end at 10:00, I ask one about some agitated twitches; she watches with me, and then suggests that Pam is laboring to breathe. Sure enough, when the nurse administers oxygen, Pam settles right down.

One of the counterintuitive points of human anatomy is that the left brain, the site of Pam's tumor and stroke, controls the right side of the body. So she has some right-side paralysis. A nurse describes the response in Pam's right hand as a "flicker," and adds that the periods of agitation are probably good, as movement may prevent a blood clot from forming in the right leg. So all my prayers and wishes for peaceful repose are misdirected. She is, after all, in a battle.

I am becoming a basket case. I stumble through each day, haunting the hospital, hanging on symptoms. Pam's sisters sustain me, as do Pam's ex-brother-in-law and his wife. They come to visit even though the wife must face down painful memories of her own hospital stay.

Emails and phone calls remind me how many people care for Pam. Some share wonderful, biblical, articulate prayers, steeped in a settled faith I cannot muster. Despite all our hurts, our feelings of insignificance, Pam and I are part of the body of Christ. Now we are being carried along by the prayers of others.

After visiting hours one evening, rather late, I get back to the hotel. A desk clerk calls me by name as I walk in, and asks how Pam is doing. This is a busy place with heavy turnover, and we got a discount hospital rate. But this kind man has made a point of learning our names and filing away somewhere the fact that Pam was going in for surgery.

I am not very reserved these days; when he asks, I blurt out the whole story, seizure and swelling and unresponsiveness. He has the best reply: "I remember her." I can't help smiling. I say, "Yeah, that's Pam—everyone who meets her remembers her! She always makes an impression." And still does, and always will.

The weekend passes; the family members who have gathered and lent their strength must return to their lives. I keep vigil alone—although, in a sense, I am more like an astronaut, standing sentinel in one module while my partner goes round to the dark side of the moon, into radio silence. Many listen and watch with me, even if they don't breathe quite the same rarefied, weightless air.

One evening, as I pause outside the hotel, it suddenly occurs to me that I should flee. Just hop on a train, on a plane, going anywhere, and then keep moving, not look back. It is only an impulse, too unspecific and frivolous to qualify as a temptation. Where would I go, away from her?

Later, I read this:

> My heart is in anguish within me;
> the terrors of death have fallen on me.
> Fear and trembling have beset me;
> horror has overwhelmed me.

I said, "Oh, that I had the wings of a dove!
I would fly away and be at rest.
I would flee far away
and stay in the desert;
I would hurry to my place of shelter,
far from the tempest and storm." — Ps. 55:4-8

Fight, flight, or freeze. I have been running away from things most of my life. And I have been frozen: even now, I get through the day by numbing out, dissociating, attempting to boil down all that is happening around me to facts and words as I lurch through the hospital offering my stumblebum prayers. But my wedding vows lie like a line in the sand. Will I fight for her? Will I stop pining for the wings of a dove, and storm heaven demanding the talons and beak of an eagle?

I am willing to settle for slow progress, however reluctantly. But I'm finding it hard to bear with her evident pain and frustration. Her eyes, when open, are wild, ranging the walls; she is like a majestic animal brought down by its enemies, held in captivity. At times she thrashes violently; her left hand is swathed in a mitt and kept on a leash—what the hospital calls "light restraints"—because she tears at the chest tube and the catheter. But all on one side: on the right there is no spontaneous movement, only feeble responses to prodding. She looks uncomfortable. And trapped. She struggles with breathing.

Are these just messy indicators that she is fighting to become fully awake? I cannot tell. One of the nurses suggests that consciousness doesn't simply toggle between *Off* and *On*; it's like a dimmer switch, and, if it's turned by a restrained and patient hand, you pass through many intermediate states.

I manage best in the mornings, back at the hotel. I wake up thinking of Psalm 3:5: "I lie down and sleep; I wake again, because the LORD sustains me." Prayer follows simply: "Lord, let her sleep. Sustain her. When she's ready, wake her up."

Our pastor emails me Romans 8:11: "And if the Spirit of him who raised Jesus from the dead is living in you, he who raised Christ from the dead will also give life to your mortal bodies because of [or "through"] his Spirit who lives in you." And faith rises up in me, assenting. If the Lord God can speak life to dry bones (Ezek. 37:1-14), assuredly He has ways to comfort a bruised or clouded spirit.

A friend directs me to Psalm 91, which I find highlighted in Pam's Bible. I rewrite part of it, altering "him" to "her":

> She who dwells in the shelter of the Most High
> will rest in the shadow of the Almighty.
> I will say of the LORD, "He is my refuge and my fortress,
> my God, in whom I trust."
> Surely he will save you from the fowler's snare
> and from the deadly pestilence.
> He will cover you with his feathers,
> and under his wings you will find refuge;
> his faithfulness will be your shield and rampart. . . .
> "Because she loves me," says the LORD, "I will rescue her;
> I will protect her, for she acknowledges my name.
> She will call on me, and I will answer her;
> I will be with her in trouble,
> I will deliver her and honor her.
> With long life will I satisfy her
> and show her my salvation." — Ps. 91:1-4, 14-16, NIV84
> (modified)

My spirit feeds on this; my mind agrees. Yes, Pam's life, like that of every believer, "is now hidden with Christ in God" (Col. 3:3). We still are joined, for in Christ "all things hold together" (Col. 1:17).

And we are tiny parts of a great body of believers, that is being stirred to "weep with those who weep" (Rom. 12:15, NRSV); beyond that, we belong to a vast creation that is groaning for redemption

(Rom. 8:22). The prayers of many are rising on Pam's behalf to the One who "heals the brokenhearted" and "sustains the humble" (Ps. 147:3, 6). In my mind's eye the veteran prayer warrior, adorned with scars and medals, kneels side by side with the rawest of recruits, who rejoices heaven by stammering, "God, if there is a God, help Pam . . .". And Pam herself participates with "groanings which cannot be uttered" (Rom. 8:26, NKJV; NRSV "sighs too deep for words"). The loving Father accepts her very agitation as a prayer—even as, when the Israelites were slaves in Egypt, "God heard their groaning" (Ex. 2:24). It doesn't take an eloquent, articulate prayer to move the heart of a God who knows what pain is. "In all their affliction he was afflicted" (Isa. 63:9, RSV). He gathers up our tears (Ps. 56:8).

Another friend writes me about his grandfather, who for a time was "unresponsive." As he described it later, in his spirit he was taken to a place like a post office. His own box was filled with letters—other people's prayers—stacked up very high, like a ladder. A voice told him, "Climb up on these; they are your strength, and your way to healing."

I try to clamber up on all the prayers, and to stay there. I try to lift up Pam. And then I close my Bible, rise from my knees, and ride in a cab through clotted streets to spend as much time as I can in Pam's room. I am trying to fight for her—the very thing she feared I wouldn't do, or couldn't. I persuade nurses to give her pain relief, to help me adjust her position in bed.

Beyond this, I am at a loss. How do I fight for her spirit, her emotions, her mind, her will?

The view doesn't help. Her facial expressions convey frustration, forlorn discouragement, and sometimes pain. She has a bandage on her head, a catheter in her leg, a chest tube in her side, a central line in her chest, a feeding tube down her nose, and a BiPAP mask on her face. She is propped up in bed; her head may still hurt from the surgery; she can hardly move her right arm and hand. The collapsed lung has led to pneumonia, and she has been given three units of blood. She may be disoriented, confused, and frightened—even though, every day, I and others tell her the surgery went well, explain where she is, and emphasize that she is healing and this situation is temporary. I worry that her days are long and bleak.

Also, I don't quite trust my powers of observation; I am leery of imagining what I want to see. If I take her hand and she squeezes my fingers, does that indicate recognition? Some of our visitors are convinced that Pam knows, but I am skeptical. I agonize over what I should say in emails sent out to a group that includes her kids. It's difficult to say, "She turned her head toward my voice" without raising false hopes. It invites the conclusion, "She's listening!"—when, really, it's ONLY "She turned her head."

She isn't obeying instructions; the neurosurgeon's "Can you cough for me?" elicits only a blank stare. Still, five days after the surgery, she's definitely more communicative and alert, even feisty. At one point I'm standing beside her, touching her right arm. She lifts her left leg, swings it up and over, and kicks my arm—twice!

Once I would have joked that here we have two irrefutable proofs that Pam is alive and well: she won't follow directions, and she's kicking her husband. But now I don't know what to think. Perhaps she was only trying to get my attention. (She did.)

A bit later, though, she keeps moving her mouth, shaping the same sounds again and again. We remove the BiPAP mask for a moment, and bend low.

We hear "What?" and then "Please—," only sometimes her sentences are longer. The nurse hazards a guess: "She's saying, 'Please let me go.'"

Even more chilling, to me, is the look on her face. At last we are making eye contact, but these aren't the eyes I know. There is no softening, no stopping to make allowances, nor even the summoning of old resentments. No history at all; no fire.

She doesn't know me.

We are severed—and she is awake in a world of strangers.

2

MENDING

On my bed I remember you;
I think of you through the watches of the night.
Because you are my help,
I sing in the shadow of your wings.
My soul clings to you;
your right hand upholds me.

— Ps. 63:6-8, NIV84

AUGUST 31, 2010

Yesterday she didn't know me; there was no light of recognition in her eyes. It was good to see her alert and fully conscious, but not really—not if she has awakened only to wild agitation. She let me take her hand, but I did not soothe her spirit or her mind.

We have always met through words. She lived in words. What remains to us if those are taken away?

I don't know what to expect on this Tuesday, as I arrive at the hospital at the start of visiting hours. To my surprise, Pam is sitting up in a chair! A physical therapist is now working with her each day, and has her out of bed for a little while.

Better yet, she smiles at me—halfway; the right side isn't working well—and clearly says, "I love you." The nurses tell me that earlier today she got out, "What happened to me?" and something like, "I want to go home." To me, she says, "It's done!"—which I take to mean that she knows she has come through the surgery.

Unfortunately, most of her speech is not this intelligible. She starts well, with "Please" or "Come on" or "Okay," but then it trails off into what anyone present hears only as gibberish. Nor does she seem to understand anything we say. This is clearly frustrating to her. She is fifty-three, but suddenly lacks the communication skills of a two-year-old.

Back in bed, she takes a long nap. I have her laptop set up now, and keep worship music—songs she knows, or knew—playing in the room while I'm there.

Waking up, she seems agitated again. And then she begins to sing. It isn't the tune I have playing, so I rush to mute the computer, and listen to Pam. She has no words at all, but the melody is unmistakable:

> "WAH wah-wah-wah WAH wah-wah-wah WAH wah-wah-wah WAH wah."

She is singing one of my favorite hymns, written in 1739 by Charles Wesley. We don't have it on her laptop; I haven't been playing or singing it. So this is purely her memory at work.

I am astonished. I want to believe she chose this song *for me*, knowing that I love it, and recognizing I'm by her side. Maybe, maybe not. What is undeniable is that it's Pam—still there, and remembering; still using her voice to honor God.

In her repertoire there are songs of lament, and prayers for immediate change, and even complaints, but this is a hymn of praise. Some of its lyrics are remarkably appropriate for a person who can't find her words:

> O for a thousand tongues to sing my great Redeemer's praise!
> The glories of my God and King, the triumphs of his grace! . . .
> Hear him, ye deaf! His praise, ye dumb, your loosened tongues employ!

Ye blind, behold your Savior come, and leap, ye lame, for
joy![13]

Pam leads me in singing this song over and over, me adding the words
to her "wah wah" sounds. She smiles and relaxes; she lifts her good left
arm and circles it through the air, as if conducting. We have no music,
and my voice could grate cheese; the heart monitor beeps, and her
leg compression sleeve (to prevent blood clots) makes sighing sounds;
occasional traffic noises drift in from the world beyond; discarded
gloves and plastic caps litter the floor; yet this is by far the best worship
service I've ever attended.

She takes my breath away. She lacks even one working tongue;
still, the longing of her heart is that she might have a thousand so as
to devote them all to praising her God. Even if He hasn't saved her
from every distress—though she's confused and disoriented, hooked
up to tubes and in several kinds of discomfort—she is grateful, determined to give thanks. She has faith to see abundance in the midst of
ruin. She is like the prophet Habakkuk, who rattles off the checklist
of his desolation—no figs, no grapes, no olives, no crops, no sheep, no
cattle—and then draws an illogical conclusion: ". . . yet I will rejoice in
the LORD, I will be joyful in God my Savior" (Hab. 3:17-18).

This is the mark of a true worshipper of God. And so this is still
Pam: her identity is secure. I am hugely comforted and relieved. I am
not at all certain that she recognizes me, but she still knows God.

And at my waking hour I find
God and his love possess my mind. — Isaac Watts[14]

----

[13] See all eighteen verses of this great hymn at *Wikipedia*, accessed December 19, 2021, https://
en.wikipedia.org/wiki/O_for_a_Thousand_Tongues_to_Sing.

[14] Isaac Watts, "Psalm 139 Part 2," in *The Psalms and Hymns of Isaac Watts* (1719-48, com-
piled 1806), 449; available at *Christian Classics Ethereal Library*, accessed December 19, 2021,
https://ccel.org/ccel/watts/psalmshymns (Hereafter *Psalms and Hymns*).

After she tires, a nurse practitioner takes me aside to tell me they now suspect Pam has *mixed* (or *global*) *aphasia*. Her "seizure" (stroke) affected her brain's two left-side language centers. Some stroke and brain-injury survivors suffer only *expressive aphasia*: they can understand what is said to them, but can't find their own words to speak or write. Others experience *receptive aphasia*: they may express themselves clearly, but have trouble taking in others' words. Pam is showing signs of both.

This news is delivered with caveats and cautions. It's early yet; things come back; the brain heals itself. And I'm given a helpful metaphor: Pam's brain isn't like a blackboard that has simply been erased. It's similar to a computer that has crashed. All the information—everything she knows—is still there on the hard drive; we just can't tap into it, bring it up on the screen. Over time, though, the brain creates new pathways. Consequently, her progress won't be a steady upward slope. There will be a long plateau, followed by a sudden breakthrough as some old words and knowledge come back, and then another plateau.

Alone in the evening, reflecting on all I have seen today, I marvel at the evident distinction between Pam's mind, which has taken a hit, and her spirit, which remains fully alive. I have always tended to equate the two, to assume they develop together. Pam's awakening suggests something different.

The apostle Paul writes:

> Do not be deceived; God is not mocked, for you reap whatever you sow. If you sow to your own flesh, you will reap corruption from the flesh; but if you sow to the Spirit, you will reap eternal life from the Spirit. — Gal. 6:7-8, NRSV

Here one may read either "Spirit," meaning the Spirit of God, or "spirit," meaning the human spirit. In Pam's case it doesn't much matter:

by spending time in intercession and worship, she devoted herself to opening up her own spirit to God's Spirit. She has sown there, and the crop coming up can withstand even hail and blight. In contrast, I have cultivated mostly my intellect—my mind. If I suffered a stroke, would there be anything left?

We live in a culture that prizes the functioning mind and the able body. I start to wonder how many times each year we pull the plug on someone still strong in spirit, because they are damaged in mind.

I am also reminded of a great New Testament promise:

> For God's gifts and His call are irrevocable. [He never withdraws them when once they are given, and He does not change His mind about those to whom He gives His grace or to whom He sends His call.] — Rom. 11:29, Ampl[15]

His blessings are "never canceled, never rescinded" (Msg). He made Pam to be a worshipper, and now she is singing praises again. This encourages me to believe that every one of Pam's spiritual gifts, every part of God's calling on her life, will be restored. She will again lead others (besides me) in worship. She will again introduce outcasts and strays to Jesus. She will again speak prophetic words that strengthen, encourage, and comfort (1 Cor. 14:3). She will again pray for people. She may not serve in exactly the same ways; the gifts may find new forms. But not one of God's good purposes for her will fall to the ground.

I will pray and declare this over her each day.

And I will pray, echoing Charles Wesley, that the great Redeemer will loosen her tongue to sing His praise.

---

[15] Compare Michael Paul Mason: "Their brains have undergone irrevocable change, but their humanity abides." *Head Cases*, 279.

SEPTEMBER 1 – 8, 2010

Early in the morning, I call the night nurse for an update. Pam didn't sleep much overnight, but was mostly calm. Her vital signs are all stable, though her temperature is up a little. She is breathing well without the BiPAP, but has some congestion.

Then the nurse adds a comment that makes me smile: "Most times when I went in, she seemed to be humming a tune."

We sing again today, starting with "O For a Thousand Tongues." Pam manages to get out, quite clearly, the words "Come, Thou Fount," the opening of a hymn written by Robert Robinson in 1758:

> Come, Thou Fount of every blessing, tune my heart to sing Thy grace;
> Streams of mercy, never ceasing, call for songs of loudest praise.
> Teach me some melodious sonnet sung by flaming tongues above!
> Praise the mount! I'm fixed upon it, mount of Thy redeeming love. . . .
>
>
> Jesus sought me when a stranger, wandering from the fold of God;
> He, to rescue me from danger, interposed His precious blood.
> How His kindness yet pursues me mortal tongue can never tell;
> Clothed in flesh, till death shall loose me I cannot proclaim it well.[16]

---

[16] See all five verses at *Wikipedia*, accessed December 19, 2021, https://en.wikipedia.org/wiki/Come_Thou_Fount_of_Every_Blessing.

It seems to me that Pam is recognizing, in her spirit if not her mind, that human language always falls far short in describing and praising the grace of Jesus, and that she has the bold faith to ask now for a heavenly tongue.

At the healing conference Pam attended in July, she had an opportunity to receive prophetic ministry. The word she was given was simply Nehemiah 8:10: "[T]he joy of the LORD is your strength." When she told me about it, she was disappointed: "I already knew that." I offered lame encouragement from Samuel Johnson about the value of reminders, and the suggestion that she might be entering a time when she'd need to apply this knowledge in a new way. Now here she is, strong precisely in her joy, and growing stronger.

> Men more frequently require to be reminded than informed.
> — Samuel Johnson[17]

A nurse points out that we can submit a request for a visit from a hospital chaplain, and I do so, not knowing what to expect. An African American woman comes, small but regal, with white hair. Pam composes herself contentedly as the chaplain offers a marvelous prayer, asking that, out of the rich treasures of His glory, God would strengthen Pam with power through His Spirit in her inner being (Eph. 3:16). Then she joins us in singing, rousingly, "Amazing Grace." I ask her to stop back whenever she can.

Pam's body, like her mind, is struggling. She has a bacterial infection, resistant to antibiotics, and chest congestion that needs to be suctioned out every so often. She coughs a lot, and isn't sleeping much. Brain swelling is still a concern, although it's holding steady. The chest tube and the sodium are our remaining milestones, the only two things keeping her in intensive care.

---

[17] Samuel Johnson, *The Rambler* #2 (March 24, 1750); available at *Samuel Johnson's Essays*, accessed December 19, 2021, http://www.johnsonessays.com/the-rambler/no-2-the-necessity-and-danger-of-looking-into-futurity/.

She still isn't following verbal instructions, even simple ones. There's no indication that she understands our words, even the answers to her own occasional questions. It's possible that all her speech so far is *automatic language*, phrases she's able to find without having to think about them or match them to a thought she wishes to express. And sometimes there's agitation. Once she manages to yank out her feeding tube. Sometimes her left hand and foot must be restrained.

And yet her room is a peaceful place to be. It's like visiting my father during his last years: time slows down. I sit by her bed, holding hands, listening to music, sometimes exchanging smiles. Most of the time, no words. We have gone down and back to a layer that's younger, more rooted; a place before stories, and from which all stories arise. Simple touch and togetherness. We sit as the light shifts around us, as day moves toward night. She smiles at anyone approaching her.

Sometimes she offers a melody, unknown to me and yet persistent, haunting. I take it as an invocation, and join words to it:

> Come, Holy Spirit,
> in Jesus's name;
> settle here.

Sometimes I sing over her a song she likes, a peaceful song of trust and surrender:

> We bow down and confess You are Lord in this place,
> We bow down and confess You are Lord in this place.
> You are all I need; it's Your face I seek.
> In the presence of Your light we bow down, we bow
> down.[18]

---

[18] Viola Grafstrom, "We Bow Down" (Thankyou Music, 1996).

Sometimes we listen together to songs she once knew, stored on her laptop. I gravitate to simple affirmations:

> Though I feel alone I am never alone;
> You are with me, You are with me, oh my Lord.[19]

Each day I pray with her, or declare over her, Psalm 23. It's the psalm of the little sheep, a wordless animal that opens not its mouth (Isa. 53:7), yet leaping up with an unerring and wholehearted joy at the sound of the Shepherd's voice; simple but knowing, foolish yet trusting, greatly beloved:

> Lord Jesus, You are Pam's Shepherd. Guide her, gather her, call out to her. Summon her whole being back from the pit with the sound of Your voice.
>
> Jesus, let her want for nothing. Enter into her, breathe in her; bring Your resurrection life into every part of her being:
>
> Fill this bed, and this room, these instruments, and these caring hands; let them serve as Your green pastures. As Pam lies here, nourish her body, strengthen her brain, speak to her spirit and mind and emotions.
>
> Call to her, lead her out beside quiet waters. Restore mobility to her limbs. Even while she is confined, give her dreams and visions. Raise her to heaven; let her sip from Your river of delights (Ps. 36:8). Calm her anxieties and fears.
>
> Restore her soul, the life in her. Create new pathways in her brain; dig again the ones that are blocked; bind up the ones that are severed. Tear down every stronghold, but do not leave her defenseless; be a wall of fire around her, and her glory within (Zech. 2:5).

---

[19] Don and Lori Chaffer, "Though I Feel Alone (Psalm 63)" (Hey Ruth, 1999).

Jesus, lead her on from here. Don't let the enemy gloat, mocking that You were unable to save one who bears Your name.[20] For Your name's sake, raise her up. Carry her through the fire, and burn away every idol; wash her with water, and cleanse her thoughts; change her desires, and give her an undivided heart; strengthen her in the inner being. Lead her in paths of righteousness and holiness, even now.

Jesus, as she walks through this valley of darkness, stay by her side, closer than ever, calling her by name. Overcome every fear. With the rod of Your strength, keep back the enemy. With the staff of Your Word, gather her up and draw her close. Comfort her; speak peace to her. Let her come forth from this wilderness, this place of death, with a renewed intimacy—not even limping like Jacob (Gen. 32:31), but "leaning upon her beloved" (Song 8:5, NRSV).

Jesus, You have spread a table for Pam. You are the Good Shepherd who has laid down His life for His sheep (John 10:11). Your broken body is her bread of life; Your spilled blood is her cleansing stream, her covenant cup. Whenever we come to Your table, we come to Your cross. Guide her there even now; frustrate her enemies, and vindicate her trust in You.

Jesus, anoint her head with the oil of Your Holy Spirit. Your own head was beaten and pierced by thorns; Your face was disfigured and spat upon; Your brow sweat blood. Sustain her and heal her; shield her and save her. Lift her up from the lowest place to shine in Your presence with the oil of Your gladness. Fill her afresh, to overflowing; let Your goodness

---

[20] See Ex. 32:12; Num. 14:13-16; Deut. 9:26-29.

and comfort to her be a blessing to others. Make her a noble vessel, holy and useful (2 Tim. 2:21); a cup of cool water to refresh discouraged spirits.

Jesus, appoint Your goodness and Your steadfast love to watch over Pam, every day. You have already prepared for her an eternal home (John 14:2-3), now strengthen her hope. "In Your presence is fullness of joy" (Ps. 16:11, NASB); even now, since You go with us, light and joy are strewn along our path (Ps. 97:11, Ampl). Open her eyes to see tokens of Your presence. Open her mouth to sing Your praise. Write a new song in her heart.

Several times, standing by her, I paraphrase Mary's words: "Behold, here is the handmaiden of the Lord; be it unto her as You desire" (Luke 1:38, modified).

When Pam talks, it isn't clear what degree of comprehension stands behind the words. "Oh, thank goodness!" when released from restraints and settled more comfortably. "I love you so much!" when I enter; then "Last season sucked!"—although there is no television. Sometimes we sit in silence, and both doze off. I write to myself, "Aphasia's not as scary as we feared."

Back in July, I had a dream: Pam was turning to speak to me, and she said, ". . . baffle falderoh." This shocked me awake—and, next to me, I heard Pam say, ". . . razzlepraz." She was talking gibberish in her sleep! This was troubling enough to be memorable, but still there was a connection too deep to be disrupted by it. I stayed beside her and drifted back to sleep. Has that dream become our life, and should we simply sleepwalk through it?

We suffer setbacks. For a couple of days, Pam's infection leads to "isolation" status. Everyone entering her room, staff and visitors alike, must wear a disposable gown and gloves. I can't carry in the computer with her music. At least no face mask is required, so we still can smile.

Then I catch a cold—the first of many warnings that this new life is a marathon, and I must learn to pace myself. I doze a lot, wear a mask while I'm with Pam, and cut my visits short a couple of days.

At last Pam allows me to put on her glasses without resistance. She doesn't see well without them, so I hope that now she can take in more, and her world will seem less strange.

But the glasses have been the least of it. Throughout these first days, Pam's natural sense of modesty is simply gone. She pulls off whatever is uncomfortable: leg compression sleeve, diaper, even her hospital gown. I keep trying to cover her, but she doesn't understand, and at once throws the extra layer aside. One nurse says sweetly, "Aw, honey, don't show the world your booty!" Pam just smiles at her and doesn't move.

Another nurse, Ken, tells me as I arrive one day, "I think I recognize the song your wife is singing. I'm in the choir at a Methodist church, and we sing it, only we use a different tune."

I stare at him, at another unexpected gift. "Please come in with me," I stammer, "and let's sing it to Pam's tune." Pam smiles and waves her left hand as the three of us sing "O For a Thousand Tongues" and then "Amazing Grace," Ken taking the lead with his marvelous voice.

There seems to be a growing division among the hospital staff who tend to Pam. Some are drawn to her spiritual awareness, while others call her delirious.

In church and at the International House of Prayer of Kansas City (IHOPKC), we have come to believe that prayer and worship are forms of spiritual warfare—not against other people, but against "spiritual forces of evil in the heavenly realms" (Eph. 6:12). Now I keep thinking of a battle described in Exodus 17. Pam is like Joshua and the army of Israel, down in the plain with sword and spear, contending hand-to-hand against the foe. But her victory, even her survival, aren't determined by her own skill or strength, but by Moses and other intercessors up on a hill—at a distance, but holding her up.

That's our situation. My email progress reports, at first sent to nine, now go to twenty-three addresses, and are forwarded to at least thirty more. We are on at least one church's prayer chain. There have been prayer vigils; some have fasted and prayed. One friend rises nightly at 3:00 to pray for Pam before going back to sleep. My nephew emails me an MP3 copy of the David Crowder Band rendition of "O For a Thousand Tongues." Pam's daughter sends me a prayer adapted from fourth-century Gregory Nazianzen:

> Christ, give her strength; Your servant is not well.
> The tongue that praised You is made silent,
> Struck dumb by the pain of sickness.
> She cannot bear not to sing Your praises.
> O make her well again, O make her whole,
> That she may again proclaim Your greatness.
> Do not forsake her, we beseech You.
> Let her return now to Your service.[21]

In all these ways we are being upheld, and more. We are carried along on eagles' wings of rising prayer.

Another weekend arrives, and loyal family members come to visit—come willingly, selflessly, though they know Pam can't really visit back. She is accepting clothes now, so I am glad to see all comers, male and female. Pam is, too: she smiles, squeezes hands, says "Wow!" One woman tells me that it was Pam who led her to Christ, years ago: "It's thanks to Pam that I am saved."

Will Pam ever again use the gifts of an evangelist? If the gifts of God are "irrevocable" (Rom. 11:29), she will. Perhaps it is happening

---

[21] This prayer may be found in George W. Grube, comp., *More—What the Church Fathers Say About . . .* , *Volume 3* (Minneapolis: Light & Life, 2007), 146; available at *YUMPU*, accessed December 19, 2021, https://www.yumpu.com/en/document/read/12254013/church-fathers-v3-fr-george-grube-saint-mina-coptic-orthodox-. In the original, "her" and "she" are "me" and "I."

already. My brother has said, "God uses our vulnerabilities rather than our sufficiencies." The apostle Paul describes a time when he was unable to speak, and then goes on: "But thanks be to God, who in Christ always leads us in triumphal procession, and through us spreads [literally "manifests"] in every place the fragrance that comes from knowing him" (2 Cor. 2:14, NRSV). Is grace already triumphing here, beyond anything my eyes can see?

Just as everyone is arriving, my boss, Jim, calls and leaves a long voicemail. He is on a family road trip, and they caught part of a poem on the radio, and he gave it as his considered opinion that the author was Walt Whitman. His wife, whom I adore, snorted, and said, "Ha! Like YOU would know poetry." So they agreed to call me, quoting the fragmentary lines they could remember, to settle the bet. When I get a chance, I shoot him an email:

> Although my desperately ill wife lies unattended while I am called into the waiting room by yet another yammering phone call;

> Although my in-laws have just arrived, and I am unable to greet them, because my attention has been commandeered by a madman who insists on seizing his wife's phone even while he's driving;

> Although I am sleep-deprived and need to think calming thoughts;

> Never mind! For Jim has a trivia question.

> The answer to which is Robert W. Service . . .

> By the way, Walt Whitman was a good guess—NOT! It's like suggesting that Shakespeare probably wrote *Hey Diddle Diddle*.

> Feel free to bother me any time with USELESS TWADDLE like this. I mean, it's not as if I have ANYTHING ELSE to do.

This banter does me the same sort of good as the visitors: it's a chance to shift gears, to reconnect with life outside a hospital, to feel "normal." So, outside of visiting hours, we wander Baltimore's Inner Harbor; we eat a nice meal. Still, I feel guilty: When does Pam get a break, or a change of scene?

Browsing in a bookstore, I purchase *My Stroke of Insight: A Brain Scientist's Personal Journey* by Jill Bolte Taylor. The hospital staff still speak more of a "seizure" than a "stroke" in Pam's case, and I am not clear on the distinction, but I'm ready to learn more, and I can't quickly find a book on seizures. Taylor proves to be a good guide, as she lays out her own successful recovery plan, while explaining some of the neuroanatomy of brain functions and their disruptions. I am especially helped by her description of her "energy reservoirs" during the first weeks. Some people drain energy and must be kept away. Challenges and stimulation are vital, but pacing is important—and sleep can be the brain's way of taking a "time-out," resting while processing and preparing for the next step, though there may also be a sleeping that is simply surrender to depression.[22] *Neuroplasticity*—the brain cells' ability to adapt and learn—means recovery is possible, though the process may extend over years. Patience, kindness, and touch are essential gifts.[23] "Trust that I am trying—just not with your skill level or on your schedule."[24]

Taylor—who, like Pam, suffered a left-brain hemorrhagic stroke—also articulates in a helpful way what she was able to understand:

> With this shift into my right hemisphere, I became empathic to what others felt. Although I could not understand the

[22] Jill Bolte Taylor, *My Stroke of Insight: A Brain Scientist's Personal Journey* (2006; New York: Plume-Penguin, 2009), 93-94, 98-102, 118, 126, 193. See also Taylor's February 2008 TED talk, "My Stroke of Insight," at *TED*, accessed December 19, 2021, https://www.ted.com/talks/jill_bolte_taylor_my_stroke_of_insight. Compare Douglas James Miller's distinction between healthy *tiredness* after effort and resigned *weariness*, which must be resisted though it may be ever-present. *Stroke: The View from Within* (San Bernardino, CA: Xlibris, 2016), 25-26.
[23] Taylor, 116-26, 193-96.
[24] Taylor, 194.

words they spoke, I could read volumes from their facial expression and body language. I paid very close attention to how energy dynamics affected me. I realized that some people brought me energy while others took it away.[25]

Roaming the halls at Hopkins, I see posters raising awareness about strokes, announcing TIME IS BRAIN. I soon learn the acronym F.A.S.T., shorthand for three main signs that a stroke is occurring:

Face Drooping

Arm Weakness

Speech Difficulty

Time to Call 9-1-1[26]

I marvel that this is all new to me, but quickly discover I am not alone. A harrowing British memoir of a 1992 stroke recounts critical disinterest and delays, seemingly built into the National Health Service; a 2006 postscript notes only partial reforms.[27]

The crucial time window that is frequently mentioned is three to four and a half hours. This figure comes from *ischemic* strokes, which occur when a clot blocks the flow of blood to the brain. This is by far the most common type of stroke—87 percent of all strokes, according

---

[25] Taylor, 76-77.

[26] See the *American Heart Association / American Stroke Association* website, accessed December 19, 2021, https://www.stroke.org/. M. Shazam Hussain of the Cleveland Clinic suggests amending the acronym to BEFAST, adding Balance Difficulties and Eyes (Vision). See, e.g., Gabrielle DeGroot Redford, "Get Smart about Stroke," *AARP The Magazine* (December 2016 – January 2017), 28; available at *AARP*, accessed December 19, 2021, http://www.aarp.org/health/conditions-treatments/info-2016/stroke-symptoms-prevention-treatment.html.

[27] Sheila Hale, *The Man Who Lost His Language: A Case of Aphasia* (2002), revised edition (London and Philadelphia: Jessica Kingsley, 2007), 36, 39, 238-47.

to the National Stroke Association.[28] A blood thinner called tissue plasminogen activator (tPA) can often dissolve the clot, but it must be administered within a few hours, and the sooner the better.

Pam's case is different. She suffered a less common *hemorrhagic* stroke, which in a way represents the opposite problem: not too little blood in the brain, but too much. A blood vessel bursts or leaks; the veins can't carry the blood away quickly enough; trapped inside the solid casing of the skull, blood builds up and exerts *intracranial pressure*— pushes on the soft tissues of the brain. Precisely where it presses, how hard, and how long are all factors determining the damage wrought by a hemorrhagic stroke. And again, time is of the essence in relieving the pressure, draining the blood.

Pam has experienced both an *intracerebral hemorrhage (ICH)*, bleeding inside the brain, and a *subarachnoid hemorrhage (SAH)*, bleeding into the space surrounding the brain. This resulted in a massive left-side stroke, which counterintuitively hammered the entire right side of her body, and also struck the brain's two language centers, *Broca's Area* (expression) and *Wernicke's Area* (reception, understanding).

It felt, I said, like a cross between a brutal barroom beating and a spiritual awakening. — David Talbot[29]

To relieve the congestion in her right lung, the nurses give her occasional "chest physical therapy": rolling her onto her side and pounding her back. It's good to have family members present to help me keep her company through a couple of these sessions, stroking her arm and smiling.

The weekend passes. Time slows again. In the evening, I see that her neck is sore. I gently lift her head, and insert the stuffed dog Jim

[28] See *American Stroke Association*, accessed December 19, 2021, https://www.stroke.org/en/about-stroke.
[29] Talbot, *Between Heaven and Hell*, "Introduction."

left her; it's plump and soft, and should provide support. Two minutes later, her hand scrabbles up and retrieves it; she peers at it, glares, and hurls it across the room. So much for Plan A. (I should have known that anything from Jim could only be a pain in the neck.) With the help of a nurse, I get her a heat pack; she loves it, and settles down for the night. Making my exit, I kiss her hand, and get a great response: no words, but a big, mischievous grin and a backhand, dismissive wave of the hand, as if to say, "Aw, g'wan with ya!"

At last her chest tube is taken out. She still has a tendency to tug at the feeding tube; I gently restrain her, explaining in useless words why it has to stay in place. After one of these episodes, I release her wrist, only to see her immediately move toward the tube again. I take her wrist. She glares at me and says emphatically, "I'm not!" Surprised, I let go—and, sure enough, she only raises her hand and scratches her nose.

Later, I hold up Vaseline, offering through gestures to put some on her cracked lips. She holds out her hand in a STOP gesture and says, "No!" Only one word, but again it's on task, and the sign language is also meaningful and appropriate.

During the night she becomes agitated, and tries to get out of bed. She quiets down after thirty minutes.

I hear from the lab: the tumor was benign, after all. Good news, but anticlimactic. I haven't actually thought about the tumor in a week.

Then, on a Wednesday—precisely two weeks after Pam's surgery—good things happen in quick succession. Her staples are removed. Originally, we thought this procedure would mark the end of our stay in Baltimore: she'd have the surgery, recover for a day or two, we'd sightsee and sleep at the hotel, and finally this. It turns out to be surprisingly rapid and easy.

Next, she is released from the Neurosciences Critical Care Unit and moved to a private room on the ninth floor. When this happens, it's quite sudden; I scramble to gather up her things. Ken, the nurse who sang with us, assists us to the elevator. I am grateful, and tongue-tied. "I wish," I say, "you could have known Pam before all this."

He keeps moving, but his answer is assured, uplifting: "I feel that I do know her."

SEPTEMBER 8, 2010

The nurse who welcomes us to the ninth floor announces that we are entering a different sphere: "We get really aggressive about therapy here."

She is half right: Pam now receives small doses of physical, occupational, and speech therapy—but only on weekdays. Mostly we are left alone, for long afternoons of hand-holding and songs.

Is this my fault? The nurse also tells me the rules are much looser—they can arrange for me to sleep on a cot in Pam's room. A week ago I would have jumped at this; now, after running myself down and catching a cold, and after reading Taylor on the importance of pacing in recovery, I decide to keep coming and going on a more-or-less regular schedule.

Perhaps, then, they misread my rhythm and dial back on services, or perhaps the initial statement was exaggerated. Either way, I have few regrets. Pam is still quite weak, and even more disoriented. "Rest is a weapon," says the Christian teacher Graham Cooke.[30] She needs rest as well as stimulation.

One feature that surprises and annoys me is the television in her room. Each day when I arrive, it is switched on, with the volume turned up. Each day I switch it off, and ask that it be left off, but there is never any change. Once or twice I try watching it with Pam, and directing her attention to images, but it seems to be wholly incomprehensible to

---

[30] See the chapter with this title in Graham Cooke, *When the Lights Go Out: Surprising Growth When God Is Hidden* (Grand Rapids, MI: Chosen-Baker, 2003, 2005), 41-44. Also published as *Hiddenness and Manifestation*.

her. Not stimulation, but flickering and noise. Taylor found it "a pain-ful suction of my energy."[31]

A social worker informs me that release from the hospital usually follows quickly after this point, within several days. This also turns out not to be true for us. But I do learn that the recommendation is for the doctors to release her, not to go directly home, but to a live-in rehab facility. I will have to explore the options for that during the next few days.

There are some additional milestones on this first day. A speech-language pathologist starts singing "Happy Birthday," and Pam chimes in, fluently, with words, even completing the song on her own. (As if sensing that she's been reborn, she fills in ". . . to me.") Apparently we all learn this song at such an early age that it's deeply encoded in memory.[32]

The nurses coax Pam to ask for things, to work at communication. For the first time, she follows some simple directions, even saying "Bye" to a doctor.

These efforts tire her, and she dozes awhile. Then, when she's taken for a new MRI, she isn't very good about holding still for it. Nothing I can say, no gentle touch, will settle her.

From Pam's point of view, the high point of the day is food. For two weeks, she has lived on beige sludge delivered through a tube. Today, in her new room, she is given real (though soft) food, which she receives with great enthusiasm. She does so well that the nurses remove her feeding tube and draw up a meal plan.

I learn that strokes often disrupt swallowing, a condition called *dysphagia*. Muscles in the mouth and throat, and even the tongue,

---

[31] Taylor, *My Stroke of Insight*, 89; compare 193.

[32] But not quite all of us. Scott Bolzan, for one, had no recollection of this song after he suffered a brain injury at age forty-six. See Scott Bolzan, Joan Bolzan, and Caitlin Rother, *My Life, Deleted: A Memoir* (New York: HarperOne-HarperCollins, 2011), 56.

may be damaged, and need to relearn how to work in sync. Speech-language pathologists work on swallowing skills as well as communication skills.

On the National Dysphagia Diet scale,[33] where Level 4 represents regular and unrestricted eating, Pam is at Level 1, with everything puréed. It doesn't look like a huge advance over the beige sludge, except that she can ingest it by mouth. She must also be given thickened liquids, which are easier to swallow than thin ones; even her water and milk are sludgy and a bit lumpy. I try to think of them as milkshakes with slight personality quirks, but the consistency puts me in mind of Garrison Keillor's radio songs about Mournful Oatmeal.

Pam, though, is thrilled to be given anything to eat and drink. This evening I am able to feed her supper, which she enjoys.

Shortly thereafter, she becomes angry and delivers a stern lecture—all in gibberish. She's upset, either at me or at her inability to communicate.

Her outburst goes on for some time. I listen, but can't find a way to mollify her. Lynn, one of our new nurses, is able to calm her down. Lynn turns out to be a Christian, and stays to pray with us. Something about the very postures of prayer—drawing together, heads bowed, eyes lowered, a hand on the shoulder, a murmur of voices; and then the Spirit of Jesus rising up in us, creating and completing the circle— proves soothing to Pam. Like a frightened sheep, she allows herself to be gentled.

SEPTEMBER 9 – 21, 2010

With the help of a hospital social worker, I begin to examine our possibilities following release. I'd like to find a rehabilitation hospital

---

[33] See the four levels table at the U. S. National Institutes of Health's National Library of Medicine *PubMed Central* website, accessed December 19, 2021, https://www.ncbi.nlm.nih.gov/pmc/articles/PMC3426263/table/t4-cia-7-287/.

close to home, but travel looms as a huge hurdle, given how little Pam comprehends and how easily she becomes agitated. It might be possible to sedate her for a plane ride, but I have flown about ten times this year, and exactly ONE flight departed on time. Plus she'd be subjected to the gawking of strangers, forced confinement without actual restraints, pressure and altitude changes, and sensory bombardment.

I call an air ambulance company; also a medical escort service that would put her on a commercial flight, in a stretcher or a special reclining chair, with a nurse or paramedic alongside. The costs are high. I think of renting a car, but the medical staff all seem to agree that an ambulance is the only truly safe option for a patient unable to follow commands. In an ambulance Pam will be comfortable and shielded from bright sunlight; I'll be free to keep her company, and we'll have medical aid available.

I wonder about an eighteen-hour (or so) ambulance ride. Would we stop periodically to sleep, and stretch, and eat? A nurse tells me no, they usually drive straight through. Would we become road-weary? And what about the siren? My delusions of grandeur like the idea of a thousand miles of telling everyone to get out of our way, but surely the noise would get old.

At this point we get caught in red tape. Our insurance provider first says they'll cover the cost of transportation. A couple of days later, they tell us they don't normally pay for ambulance rides from one state to another—but, since they've already granted approval, they'll make good on their promise. The doctors authorize a mild sedative for Pam. We're all set—until the ambulance company backs out: the long trip would require two crews, and they don't have them. The next day, a higher-ranking supervisor at our insurance provider calls to rescind the payment, stating that they don't cover state-to-state trips, never would, and never said they would! Wow. This guy will go further on bluster than the disabled will ever travel on his company's dime.

I also have a great, crazy nephew who offers to drive from Kansas and ferry us home in exchange for gas money and two cases of root beer. I tell him I'd need to undergo brain surgery myself before I'd put our lives in his hands. But I'm moved.

Fortunately, I remember that I promised Pam to consult her daughter and her sister before making major decisions. Granted, this is no life-threatening emergency, but the selection of the right rehab facility might give a tremendous boost to her recovery. And while I incline toward the air ambulance, Pam's daughter and sister feel strongly that the experience of flying might be pretty scary for her, and that, with her frugal nature, she'll be aghast at the expense. Against this, all I have is a gut feeling that it might be "better" for her to have friends and family nearby—even though visiting hours might be severely limited, and more people might prove to be a distraction. One day she might even be upset if "everyone" saw her "like this."

The upshot is that they win me over and, after a week spent vainly casting about for a way to get home, I start visiting rehab hospitals in the Baltimore area. This turns into an odd dance. There are four suitable facilities in the region that are part of our insurance provider's network. I decide to visit them all, but they're also supposed to send representatives to Hopkins to assess Pam, and, if at all possible, I'd like to be present during those sessions. I spend quite a few days deferring travel, waiting for reps who don't show up.

In my mind, there is one burning question throughout this process. The facilities fall into two categories. *Acute* rehab means that, over the course of an eight-hour day (at least on weekdays), the patient receives three hours of therapy: one hour each of physical, occupational, and speech therapy, mostly one-on-one. Is Pam up to this, even if the therapy is doled out in half-hour sessions, with breaks in-between? I have no idea. At Hopkins she isn't receiving anything close to this level of attention. We are in a new world, conditions keep changing, and I simply don't know what she's capable of.

If Pam can't handle three hours, the alternative is *subacute* rehab, providing approximately half as much therapy each day. These facilities seem to be few and far between. Of the four Baltimore-area hospitals on my list, one serves subacute patients.

In an ideal world, I would think, any rehab hospital worth its salt would offer both subacute and acute programs, as one of the Kansas facilities does. When a patient turns out not to be ready for aggressive rehab, he or she is transferred to the subacute program, literally by going down the hall. But this is rare; most hospitals specialize. This is why they will have nurses come in to assess Pam: they will try to determine whether she's ready for their facility's regimen.

We may also face time constraints. A social worker warns me that as soon as *any* rehab facility completes its assessment, has a bed ready, and expresses a willingness to accept Pam, our insurance company will begin pressuring Hopkins to make the transfer—whether or not I've completed my review of the other options.

Over four days, I tour five hospitals—the last a subacute facility affiliated with one of the acute places. I schedule the longest trip—a train ride to Washington, DC—for a Saturday so that a kind and loving family member can come to Baltimore and stay with Pam, since I feel guilty leaving her alone—and have no way to give her the simple message, "I'll be in late tomorrow." Of course the hospitals all have websites, but they seem to have been written by marketing people. There are photos of smiling therapists and ravaged, determined patients; buzzwords like *aphasia* and *dysphagia* appear with reassuring frequency; but I find no answers to my questions. Eventually, a video provides me with helpful criteria for assessing staff, facilities, and program elements during my site visits.[34] A friend who is a physical therapist also writes, giving me a few more recommendations: "I would

[34] "Three Steps to Finding the Right Rehabilitation Center," *BrainandSpinalCord.org*, accessed December 19, 2021, http://www.brainandspinalcord.org/three-steps-to-finding-the-right-rehabilitation-center/.

imagine the therapy in all of these facilities is good. The larger question would be the quality of physiatrist[35] support and nursing care. Also check, which facility looks cleanest, and has call lights answered in a timely manner."

I'm armed with questions, but I'm not fully prepared for the tours. In my comings and goings at Hopkins, I've had plenty of glimpses of neurosurgery patients; I've seen surgical scars, and behavioral expressions all along the continuum from dazed to distressed. But every one of these folks is still in the very first days of recovery. All this, I have told myself, will pass and improve. This frail hope is shaken as I walk through rehab hospital corridors and see people in street clothes, looking lost and abandoned. The buildings are old and faded; it's hard not to feel that the patients, too, have been there forever. They don't appear to be in process, progressing, healing. Almost always, they are seated, doing nothing, alone even when they're adjacent. They look . . . parked.

The nurses and administrators are pleasant, welcoming. They hold their heads up as they show me around. They are proud of the services they provide. And still there is a sad air of shabbiness, no less shabby because it is called "efficiency." I come away grieving, shaking my head, wanting to advocate, thinking we have to do better. In memory I am back on a childhood trip to New Delhi, an out-of-place tourist surrounded by need and pain. Only now I can't close my eyes, walk away. I must choose. [36]

Pam has become a member of a vast community. To my surprise, I see that it's not just a population of stroke survivors, most of them

---

[35] A *physiatrist* is a Physical Medicine & Rehabilitation (PM&R) physician. See "What Is a Physiatrist?" at the *American Academy of Physical Medicine and Rehabilitation (AAPM&R)* website, accessed December 19, 2021, http://www.aapmr.org/about-physiatry/about-physical-medicine-rehabilitation/what-is-physiatry.

[36] A summary of our lives pre-stroke is the first of the blog posts associated with this book ("The Backstory," at https://irrevocablebook.wordpress.com/), but allusions will creep into the main narrative.

twenty years older than Pam. At these hospitals, the wards I am sent to are usually designated as "TBI" floors. Stroke patients are housed alongside people of all ages who have suffered *traumatic brain injuries* from falls, car and skateboard accidents, playing sports, even gunshot wounds. At first this makes no sense to me. I think of a stroke as an internal brain catastrophe, almost a massive plumbing problem, whereas a brain injury is some sort of violent blow from without. But a social worker tells me to think of "TBI" as describing behaviors, not events. The damage to brain and body is similar in stroke and TBI, and the rehab recovery process is the same.

Of the institutions I visit, one is tiny and seems to provide only minimal care. Another is in a remote location, with no hospital attached—no quick recourse in case of emergency, and no easy way to run CT scans or MRIs. The literature for this facility includes a 2008 survey in which fully 23 percent of patients and family members declared themselves *Not Satisfied* with the services received.

In one respect, the subacute facility surpasses the rest. They have animals—dogs and cats—to roam among the patients. Amazing how much this warms and softens an institution.

Somewhat compulsively, I draw up tables comparing the facilities, and try to decide which distinctions matter most. More helpful than all my analysis are the reflections of Pam's daughter and sister as they sift through my impressions and conduct their own research online. This collaboration makes me feel, not only that I have honored Pam's wishes, but that she was wise to direct me to consult them.

In the end, we choose National Rehabilitation Hospital (NRH) in Washington, DC It has an excellent reputation. Its building is the newest—although it is twenty-four years old, and looks it. It has a pool—Pam loves to swim—and a pleasant garden with a wheelchair path. In case of emergency, Washington Hospital is next door. On the Saturday afternoon when I visit, there are five RNs present, and five techs; the staff also includes psychologists and neuropsychologists. Also, programs and services extend beyond the basic therapies: they offer *therapeutic recreation* (relearning fun things) and driving instruction, as well as Activities of Daily Living (ADLs) or relearning self-care and household skills. There's also the old shell of a car, set in a basement room, so that patients can practice the complex and coordinated movements involved in getting into a car, and getting out again.

I'm a bit put off by the noisy construction project going on outside, but *every* facility is in the midst of renovations. I'm told to request a quiet room. My other misgivings I suppress—as I did during that first phone call with the Hopkins neurosurgeon. How can I trust my first impressions when the territory I'm in is wholly unfamiliar? And when a decision has been made deliberately, and bathed in many people's prayers, shouldn't one be hopeful?

SEPTEMBER 9 – 15, 2010

> He put a new song in my mouth,
> a hymn of praise to our God.
> Many will see and fear
> and put their trust in the LORD. — Ps. 40:3, NIV84

The drama of deciding next steps was largely a distraction. We return to the main narrative: the story of Pam's recovery.

Once we are out of intensive care, it is tempting to believe that Pam is out of danger. Indeed, her latest MRI is encouraging: no sign of brain swelling, bleeding, or seizures. But she tires quickly, even from eating—the effort of focusing, light chewing, and swallowing wears her out; and she goes to sleep soon after each meal.

When she is wakeful, she often seems to be in discomfort, and expresses pain whenever anyone moves her right arm. A nurse suggests that muscles have atrophied; this theory leads to more manipulation and more pain. Eventually, after an X-ray and a CT scan, the physical therapists tentatively conclude that there is some shoulder *subluxation*. This is a partial dislocation, apparently common following a stroke; due to prolonged muscle weakness, the arm basically drops out of its socket. They will give her a sling to support the arm. This is one more indication of just how much damage a stroke can do throughout the body.

The physical therapists also figure out that some areas of Pam's skin have become super-sensitive; this is one reason why she keeps trying to wriggle out of clothes and throw off sheets. Acting on their advice, I go shopping for a fleece and find a soft bathrobe. Just rubbing her skin with this fabric soothes and desensitizes the nerve endings.

Every day now, I am trying to show Pam family photos, pointing to each face and coaxing her to say the name. She seems interested, but on most days refuses to keep her glasses on for more than a minute. It's entirely possible that her vision has changed, either because the tumor is gone or because of new damage from the stroke, but everyone agrees that, as yet, there is no way to give her an eye exam. I imagine her having to answer questions like, "Which is better, number one or number two?"

Communication is getting a little better. Some days she's very conversational, though we don't understand each other. She is beginning to respond to simple commands, such as "Look at me." When I'm in the room, she often waves her arm, I think as a signal to me to hop to it—start her computer and get her songs playing. She enjoys flowers, which, now that we're out of intensive care, I can bring over for her to touch and smell.

Each day, I pray over her, and remind her of God's promises. I tell her that the surgery went well, the tumor is gone, and she is healing. I explain that she had a seizure that has temporarily affected her abilities to understand and speak, as well as her freedom to move her right arm and leg. But these are not permanent problems, and she's getting stronger every day. She nods at me, but I don't know how much she takes in.

We hold hands, and sing, and listen to songs. Once she initiates a tune, which I recognize. I sing the words for her:

Everybody ought to know, everybody ought to know,
Everybody ought to know who Jesus is.
He's the lily of the valley, He's the bright and morning star,
He's the fairest of ten thousand—everybody ought to know.[37]

This song isn't on the computer, so, again, her memory is at work.

And once, as I feed her, she picks up a napkin and wipes her lip—another unprompted memory of what to do.

But discouragement has become the elephant in the room. Pam's not making lots of visible progress. It's been a while since we've seen any breakthroughs. A different nurse now acknowledges to me that the rehab here is minimal, that the focus is on getting patients stable.

The physical therapists sometimes get her into a chair, but it's scary for her—they lift and drag her—and she doesn't seem to enjoy the result any more than the process. There's no progress at all with walking. Everyone agrees that she's in some discomfort, even apart from the shoulder, but no one knows how to pinpoint the problem.

The catheter comes and goes. Sometimes they switch to a temporary catheter. But Pam isn't able to let us know when she needs to go.

She cooperates with eating, but can't feed herself, and isn't eating enough. Sometimes she will say a firm "No!" to a food she doesn't like. She isn't crazy about puréed meat and veggies—I can't say as I blame her—but she is marvelously enthusiastic about fruit, juice, yogurt, and cottage cheese. Since these are all cool soothing foods, I wonder whether her throat is irritated.

Save me, O God,
for the waters have come up to my neck.
I sink in the miry depths,

---

[37] Harry Dixon Loes, "Everybody Ought to Know Who Jesus Is" (New Spring Publishing, 1940).

where there is no foothold.
I have come into the deep waters;
the floods engulf me.
I am worn out calling for help;
my throat is parched.
My eyes fail,
looking for my God. — Ps. 69:1-3

Sometimes these little mealtimes call forth some words. She bumps my spoon hand by mistake, and says, "Sorry"—an appropriate response, even if it's automatic. Later, I offer her some fruit cocktail. She turns her head away; taking this as a "no," I lower the spoon. A moment later, she's indignant: "Aw, come on!" "What?" I ask, startled. "I want some fruit!"

A four-word sentence may not seem like much, but it's music to my ears. I speculate that I've hit upon a formula: Pam succeeds best at finding language when I annoy her—which, fortunately, I'm very good at; it seems to come naturally to me. Thankfully, she doesn't hold a grudge—at least, not when she gets her fruit.

Still, in some respects we are losing ground. The nurses are counting her calories and warning that, if she doesn't take in enough nutrition, they may need to put in an abdominal feeding tube.

When I look ahead, I am shaken. What if her comprehension doesn't improve? How will we manage when we somehow do get home? One morning in particular, I awaken to a flood of anxieties. Right on cue, a friend feels moved to email me a couple of Bible promises:

You will keep in perfect peace
him whose mind is steadfast,
because he trusts in you. — Isa. 26:3, NIV84

> The angel of the LORD encamps around those who fear him,
> and he delivers them. — Ps. 34:7

Some of the songs stored on Pam's laptop also steady me. They still apply, still articulate the hopes and life priorities set in her heart:

> Lord, You have my heart and I will search for Yours;
> Jesus, take my life and lead me on.
> Lord, You have my heart and I will search for Yours;
> Let me be to You a sacrifice.
> And I will praise You, Lord, and I will sing of love come
> down;
> And as You show Your face, we'll see Your glory here.[38]

Because of her, I have unimaginable conversations. To get to and from the hospital each day, I ride in taxis. (Pam resourcefully negotiated a hotel rate that provides vouchers covering the cost.) Many of the drivers are from Pakistan and a variety of African countries; I assume they are Muslim. But as soon as I mention her surgery, they are intrigued; suddenly, I am not an infidel Christian but a fellow human being who has known suffering. Some face similar situations; one in particular, Khashtar, has a nineteen-year-old son with a brain tumor. We talk about prayer and trusting God.

Pam continues to defy every constraint: the leg compression sleeves that could save her life, tight socks, hospital wristbands, and more. One day as I sit by, she cocks her left index finger at me. No words, but she might just as well have said, "Don't mess with me."

I sit on my hands. "Okay," I say aloud.

There ensues an epic Godzilla-versus-Megalon battle between Pam's left hand and her diaper. After much thrashing and grunting, the tape

---

[38] Martin Smith, "Lord, You Have My Heart" (Thankyou Music, 1992).

expires and a victorious Pam unceremoniously deposits the carcass of her adversary on the floor.

The thought *The nurses will kill me!* flashes through my mind, but I continue mentally rehearsing one of my new mottoes: *Choose your battles.*

Pam's eye falls on me. "Very good!" she says.

I get a hearty laugh out of this. It's a bright burst of the old Pam in all of her sarcasm, feistiness, and sheer orneriness. Seeing me crack up, she gives me a mischievous grin. Yeah, she's proud of herself.

Another morning, when I arrive in her room, she says something that sounds an awful lot like "Finally!" (I am early—but not by her clock, set to Pamela Mean Time.)

Later, she pushes away one of her pillows, and it falls off the bed. "Man!" she exclaims.

I get up, walk around the bed, and pick up the pillow. "Man!" I echo, rolling my eyes and waving the pillow.

She doesn't say anything, but her smile has a sardonic twist at the end, as if to say, "Oh yeah, you've really got it tough."

Occasionally I try to buoy both our spirits. In her luggage at the hotel, I find a small stuffed rabbit, and take it with me to the hospital. During one of the livelier songs on her computer, I frame my face with the two stuffed animals, dog and rabbit, and lip-sync at the foot of her bed. Pam rewards me with her best I-married-an-idiot laugh.

One day, we suddenly receive a series of therapy visits. A team of three physical therapists support Pam in standing, put shoes on her, and get her to follow simple instructions. At moments, it looks as if she will have some choice words for them, but the most she comes out with is "Oh, my goodness!"

The speech-language pathologist coaxes her into singing "Happy Birthday" and "Amazing Grace." With repetition, her enunciation becomes clearer.

Then she begins initiating tunes of her own: "DOO-doo-doo-DOO-doo-doo-DOOdoodoo-DOO . . .".

At last I recognize it, and start laughing. "Who goes from 'Amazing Grace' to 'Ninety-Nine Bottles of Beer on the Wall'?" The answer, of course, is Pam. She also starts "Pop Goes the Weasel" and "This Land Is Your Land."

I am a bit dumbfounded that *this* is what the brain holds on to, but the episode motivates me to email her family, asking which songs she knew as a child, and which ones she sang to her own kids when they were little.

When the speech therapist shifts from singing to conversation, Pam responds with some gibberish, but also says, "I don't even remember, though"—her longest sentence so far—and "Well, I don't know." These strike me as poignant indications that she's well aware some of her memories have been scrambled.

SEPTEMBER 16, 2010

> The human spirit can endure in sickness,
> but a crushed spirit who can bear? — Prov. 18:14

The roots of our English words are intriguing. *Grief* is heaviness, a burdened spirit. *Sorrow* means being sick with sadness—and *sad*, linked with *sated*, points back to heaviness. *Pain* is a penalty or payment. The words themselves express our fear that nothing we suffer is simply random. We reap what we have sown; our consequences catch up with us, demand a reckoning, and drag us down.

The Bible never minimizes pain. Even though, from an eternal perspective, our afflictions are "light and momentary" (2 Cor. 4:17), and even though we're advised to embrace them with joy because of the fruit that grows out of them (James 1:2-3; Rom. 5:3-4), still, when the Bible speaks of pain, it uses strong words—like the Hebrew *daka*, "crushed." Hebrew is often a visual language, and this word calls to mind an old-fashioned pharmacist, working away with a mortar and pestle, pulverizing, grinding up, reducing to powder or to dust. "Crushed" describes an extreme form of suffering that continues over time; it's never limited to the body, but always also includes the spirit, the emotions, and the mind.

The psalmist cries out that an enemy "has crushed my life to the ground" (Ps. 143:3, RSV). "I am feeble and utterly crushed; I groan in anguish of heart" (Ps. 38:8). In the New Testament, Paul writes that during one period of trial he was "so utterly, unbearably crushed" that he "despaired of life itself" (2 Cor. 1:8, NRSV).

The word *daka* is used twice in Isaiah 53, in describing the suffering Servant of the Lord. Verse 5 says, "[H]e was pierced for our transgressions, he was crushed for our iniquities." But it's the second occurrence that takes my breath away: "Yet it was the LORD's will to crush him and cause him to suffer" (v. 10). Over and over, the New Testament writers interpret this passage as a prophecy about Jesus.

Believers know that God is anything but cruel. The book of Lamentations, written right in the midst of the worst divine judgment in the Old Testament, still affirms, "he does not willingly afflict or grieve anyone" (Lam. 3:33, NRSV). Isaiah goes further; speaking of God's faithfulness to Israel, he says, "In all their affliction he was afflicted" (63:9, RSV). The pain we feel is as nothing compared to the pain that fills His heart (see Gen. 6:6).

How then could this loving, sensitive God bear to crush His own Son? How can He crush, even now, the body of Christ, and the creation He is calling to join that body, and Israel the long-tended firstfruits?

This is the mystery of affliction. We humans are not very patient when it comes to keeping company with mystery. Set on the wheel of suffering, we use the strength that is in us to become hard. We rebel and rage.

And often, our rage is not only incoherent but blind. In John Steinbeck's great Dust Bowl novel *The Grapes of Wrath*, tenant farmers lose home and livelihood to a combination of worked-out soil and relentless weather. As tractors arrive to raze his house, the home he built with his own hands, one farmer recognizes a driver—and threatens to shoot him with a rifle. The driver persuades the farmer that he's the wrong target: he's hired by the bank, and they're acting under orders from the East.

"But where does it stop?" asks the farmer. "Who can we shoot?" And the driver answers, "I don't know. Maybe there's nobody to shoot. Maybe the thing isn't men at all."[39]

This sunny Thursday abounds in sorrow. Late in the morning, hearing a noise, I look down from Pam's window and see that the street below is jammed with police cars. For once I turn on the TV, and soon learn that an armed man has entered a different building in the hospital complex, shot a doctor, and taken someone hostage. The facts served up are liberally spiced with rumor and speculation; at one point a reporter, standing in the street outside, announces to the camera that the hospital has been evacuated. In reality, there is no effort to empty all the buildings, and no need. This is not one of those incidents where someone roams the halls, shooting indiscriminately. Our area goes into a "lockdown" mode, meaning that no one is allowed to enter or leave the floor for some hours, but we aren't in any danger. We simply forfeit a day's errands: I can't get out to tour rehab hospitals, and their reps can't get in to assess Pam.

Gradually we learn that the situation began when an eighty-four-year-old woman had back surgery. The operation didn't go well, and she was left paralyzed. Her son, upset at this outcome and overwhelmed at the prospect of caring for her, smuggled in a small firearm and shot her doctor, an orthopedic surgeon. Eventually, he then shot both his mother and himself. The doctor will live, but the mother and son are gone.

The man with the gun is referred to as a "gunman" and a "shooter." But he was also a son, a man sandbagged by sorrow and pain, wondering in what direction he might discharge his fear and grief and rage. He was crushed.

The good news of Christianity begins with the declaration that Jesus knows this feeling, that He understands and shares our pain. His spirit has been crushed, particularly in the "oil-press" Gethsemane. In the garden Jesus is under intense pressure; we see this in His "agony" or

---

[39] John Steinbeck, *The Grapes of Wrath* (1939), John Steinbeck Centennial Edition (New York: Penguin, 2002), 38.

"anguish" (Greek *agonia*), His sweat like drops of blood (Luke 22:44), and His "loud cries and tears" (Heb. 5:7, NRSV). The paraphrases use the word *crushed*: in the *Living Bible*, Jesus says to the three disciples, "My soul is crushed by sorrow" (Mark 14:34; "crushed with horror and sadness," Matt. 26:38); in *The Message* He says, "This sorrow is crushing my life out" (Matt. 26:38).

We have a myth today in popular Christianity: it says that Jesus suffered and I can go scot-free. The "abundant life" He brings us (John 10:10) is life in a bubble, happy and carefree. This finds scant basis in the New Testament. Paul summons us to "the fellowship of sharing in" Jesus's sufferings (Phil. 3:10, NIV84); Peter says that we are called to suffer "in his steps" (1 Peter 2:21). Our afflictions will often seem pointless and unbearable; they will crush us. But we are assured that there is a gracious purpose behind them, that they are transformative and even redemptive.

We need the grace of God to help us stand in our pain, and keep us from becoming hard, bitter, angry, or rebellious.

This man was upset that his mother's surgery didn't turn out as hoped, maybe even as promised. All who love Pam feel that way right now—including Pam herself. There is much to grieve.

If we let ourselves believe the lie that doctors are gods, able to dispense life, we will often be disgruntled and outraged. And if we let ourselves believe the lie that a disabled life is not worth living, we rob ourselves and others of great and surprising gifts, of all that Paul learned when Jesus stood near and told him, "My grace is sufficient for you, for my power is made perfect in weakness" (2 Cor. 12:9).

The man's mother was paralyzed. Pam cannot move freely, either. She can't read, can't converse, can't sing or see very well. Her world has shrunk to one room, and mostly to a bed. I miss our walks and drives, our banter and wisecracks, our evening prayers. She must miss these and much more.

And yet . . . while she has lost so many things, so much of what makes life rich and pleasant, SHE is not diminished. Not a bit. She is still here. Still herself. Still good company. Her spirit shines as brightly as ever. In a way, it's remarkable to get to see this, to glimpse the all-sufficiency of grace. Strip everything away, and people (or at least some people) are still beautiful, still "fearfully and wonderfully made" (Ps. 139:14). Still showing forth the image of God.

> A stroke can't make you less than the person you are.
> — Cher Stephenson[40]

Pam has been grievously injured; some of it may be irreparable. But she is alive, and she can hold my hand. She has lost her language, but she can look me in the eyes and smile. And she is in recovery: tomorrow holds new gifts.

There is nobody to shoot. On the contrary, there is Somebody to thank, and trust.

Each of us, at every moment, makes these decisions: what has value, what is important, how to regard our circumstances.

And we are all so greatly blessed. The mercies of the LORD, and His steadfast love, are "new every morning" (Lam. 3:22-23).

SEPTEMBER 17 – 22, 2010

> When my spirit grows faint within me,
> it is you who know my way. — Ps. 142:3, NIV84

Understandably, following the shooting, the hospital tries to get back to normal. What can we do after such tragedies except try to put them behind us?

I am thinking that we must somehow learn to stop, and grieve. Examine our own attitudes. But I don't. We resume our uneasy routine.

I renew my efforts to finalize our next destination, but the process takes another six days.

---

[40] Qtd. in Jon Kerstetter, *Crossings: A Doctor-Soldier's Story* (New York: Crown, 2017), 242.

Pam is eating better, and has progressed from Level 1 on the National Dysphagia Diet scale to Level 3, which at least looks like real food. Mealtimes still exhaust her, and she usually naps afterward.

Perhaps because of her ongoing war with clothing and medical technology, she is now assigned a series of "companions" or clinical aides, who sit with her during those daylight hours when I'm not there. One is a Christian, and sings with us.

Some of the Christian nurses also make time to pray and sing with us. I have the impression that Pam's presence and her need are challenging these believers to be bolder in their faith. One evening, one of them brings a friend, who doesn't join our prayers but observes attentively. Pam smiles and glows.

Though her progress seems infinitesimal, she is slowly becoming more verbal. In the course of a couple of hours, she tells one nurse to shut up and another to stop staring at her, and comes out with, "Oh, give me a break!" It's painful to see her frustrated and upset, but under the circumstances it is nothing less than glorious to hear her speak meaningful and (syntactically if not socially) appropriate sentences.

Another morning, I arrive to find a companion feeding her. Pam eats her biggest breakfast in weeks, smiles sweetly at the aide, and tells her, "You're so nice." A moment later, as I busy myself setting up her computer, she shifts into annoyance: "John has absolutely nothing to do!" I would have preferred "John is a prince among men"; still, this is a great sentence, if technically incorrect. Two minutes later, in comes a nurse, who perhaps recently drew blood or performed another vital service. Pam glares at her, cocks her left hand, and pronounces, "You suck!"

Embarrassed, I look at the others. "Now we all know where we stand," I say. "You're so nice, I have absolutely nothing to do, and you suck!" And we all laugh, while Pam eyes us fiercely.

She is making short statements. "Hi!" when I enter, and sometimes my name. "That would be great" when I suggest music, and "That was great!" after we sing. "I would like to try something else" when I offer food. And angry ejaculations: "This is so stupid!" "Don't even—!" "You don't think we're children?" Don't hold back, Pam.

How much does she know, understand, remember? I can't judge. But one book I've loved for years is *The Story of My Life* by Helen Keller. An illness left her blind and deaf when she was very young, and she was largely unable to communicate until her teacher, Annie Sullivan, helped her to a breakthrough. Keller writes:

> Gradually I got used to the silence and darkness that surrounded me and forgot that it had ever been different, . . . But during the first nineteen months of my life I had caught glimpses of broad, green fields, a luminous sky, trees and flowers which the darkness that followed could not wholly blot out. If we have once seen, "The day is ours, and what the day has shown."[41]

God has given Pam a rich and capable life. Many aspects of that life are missing now, but they are not wholly blotted out. I pray that God keeps the memory of them and the hope of them alive in her. "*I would have despaired* unless I had believed that I would see the goodness of the LORD in the land of the living" (Ps. 27:13, NASB). She sees it now, and will see it more clearly, day by day.

I succeed in getting her to look at family photos stored on the computer. She won't wear her glasses, or look through the magnifier given her by a thoughtful friend, but I hold the screen up close and she squints a little. She is intensely interested in each image, and keeps saying, "Very nice!" or, seeing one of her grandsons, "That's cute!" I name

---

[41] Helen Keller, *The Story of My Life* (1903; New York: Doubleday, Page, 1905), chap. 1; available at Mary Mark Ockerbloom, ed., *A Celebration of Women Writers*, accessed December 19, 2021, http://digital.library.upenn.edu/women/keller/life/life.html. The closing quotation is from the poem "Love and Death" by Richard Watson Gilder (published in *The Celestial Passion*, 1887).

each person, but the only name she volunteers is "John"—and that for a picture I'm not in.

The physical therapy team comes back and puts her through a thirty-minute session, but she's angry and resistant, and it leaves her exhausted. Will she be able to handle six sessions a day?

Sometimes, when nurses or therapists are in the room, she has taken to humming "O For a Thousand Tongues"—not just because she loves the song, but seemingly in an effort to shut out other things.

National accepts Pam, but makes us wait one more day, till they have a bed free. As a result, Pam's stay at Hopkins extends to exactly four weeks—two in intensive care and two on a regular ward.

On the morning of our trip, there is still some question as to whether the ambulance will have room for me and for our luggage. Eventually, this gets resolved.

Shortly before we set out, the computer crashes. I've had to depend on unsecured "guest" access to hotel and hospital wireless networks. Perhaps it was inevitable that we'd get hit by a virus; perhaps it's a miracle we lasted this long. Still, it rattles me to lose this fragile connection just as we venture into the unknown.

We finally depart, later than planned, at 3:15 p.m. The seventy-five-minute ride is uneventful. Pam keeps her eyes shut through most of it, sleeping a little, not acting disoriented. I sit beside her, holding her hand, peering out a small window.

Hunched in this rolling metal shell, I feel anxious, lost. This is no victory lap. We had hoped for a miracle of healing; failing that, we trusted we were in for a smooth medical procedure. Now we are scrambling to recoup losses. We shot for the triumphal entry, and have been given the flight to Egypt.

Will this path of humiliation lead to healing? Will it bring us closer to God?

3

RELEARNING

But soul-rejoicing health again returns,
The blood meanders gentle in each vein,
The lamp of life renewed with vigor burns,
And exiled reason takes her seat again—
Brisk leaps the heart, the mind's at large once more,
To love, to praise, to bless, to wonder and adore.

— Christopher Smart[42]

SEPTEMBER 22, 2010

Restore us, O God;
make your face shine upon us,
that we may be saved.
O LORD God Almighty,
how long will your anger smolder
against the prayers of your people?
You have fed them with the bread of tears;
you have made them drink tears by the bowlful.
You have made us a source of contention [NIV "derision"]

---

[42] Christopher Smart, "Hymn to the Supreme Being" (1756), in *Chapters into Verse*, 1:254; also available at *Poetry Nook*, accessed December 19, 2021, https://www.poetrynook.com/poem/hymn-supreme-being.

> to our neighbors,
> and our enemies mock us.
> Restore us, O God Almighty;
> make your face shine upon us,
> that we may be saved. — Ps. 80:3-7, NIV84

We are greeted at National by a very pleasant and patient young doctor. But the nurses seem harried, distracted. We get off to a bad start: the Hopkins staff, noticing some constipation, choose today to give Pam a laxative suppository. It begins working during the ambulance ride, where I have no means of cleaning her or disposing of waste, and so she arrives at NRH with a soiled diaper and a slight case of diarrhea. This elicits an immediate, indignant response from a nurse who must clean her.

Pam will share a room with another patient, an older African American woman who is also not yet able to speak. A curtain separates us.

> Broken brains and broken hopes filled the place with a palpable heaviness and an aroma of sorrow. . . .
>
> A compounded, collective sense of loss lingers like a heavy fog over everything. We were not recovering in a vacuum, alone; this recovery would be entangled, communal. But as unfair as that seemed, perhaps if the pain is shared, some hope may be also. — Jay Wolf[43]

Some critical details seem not to have been thought through very well. Pam's bed comes with a call button, but, as I point out, she has no idea how to use it; if she succeeds in pressing it, she has few words to express her need. The nurses' station is far down at the end of the floor, and,

---

[43] Wolf and Wolf, *Hope Heals*, 140-41.

while it was well staffed on the Saturday afternoon when I visited, in the evenings they seem to have just one nurse and maybe a couple of techs. Getting to the bathroom on time is a huge problem for patients. Pam's roommate, who knows how to press the call button, will use it to summon help, since she can't walk unassisted. But no helper comes. Instead, invariably, the nurse at the nurses' station responds over the intercom: "Can I help you? What do you need? Hello? Hello?" Sometimes I run down the hall to remind the nurse, "She can't talk!" (The roommate's brother does the same on Pam's behalf when I'm not there.) Do they really not know this? Must they be so understaffed that every nonambulatory patient must be catheterized and diapered, at least from 5:00 p.m. to 8:00 a.m. every day?

Pam's bed is next to a window. Immediately I notice the blinds are broken; they will not shut. An office building stands a short distance away, and people will be able to see Pam when she undresses. I point this out, and am told they will submit a work order.

Noise is everywhere: patients and visitors and staff and televisions, call buttons and intercoms; from outside, construction and traffic. It no longer feels as if we're in a protective bubble.

The NRH rep who came to Hopkins to assess Pam warned me that rehab represents a dramatic shift in focus. A general hospital like Hopkins tries to calm patients when they are agitated, but a rehab facility like National tries to make the most of agitation, to use it as energy and as a motivator. At times they may deliberately provoke patients to get them agitated. Family members are sometimes "invited out" of these proceedings, because our instinct is to be protective and comforting.

Does agitation help the healing process? Can disorganized, unfiltered noise qualify as stimulation for a damaged brain? I work as an instructional writer and designer; for years I've tried to find creative ways to challenge and engage both kids and adult learners. But we don't throw them in at the deep end without any help. My every instinct is to coax rather than provoke, to invite rather than annoy. (Then again, I try to catch mice with a glue trap.) I am filled with misgivings as I leave Pam for the night.

At 8:30, I check in across the street, at the unpromisingly named Physicians Office Building (for which I make up a slogan: "Sleep Here, and Wake Up on an Operating Table"). The upper floor offers accommodations for patient families; they turn out to be very nice.

Skipping supper, I set up the laptop. The virus has done its work; I am unable to connect to the internet, or to send or receive email. I phone Pam's sister, and she kindly sends out a group email.

I find it intensely frustrating to be locked out. And then it occurs to me that this is a small taste of what Pam must feel every day right now—trying to listen and speak, but finding that words aren't working properly for her. I must say, she handles it with a better grace than I do.

SEPTEMBER 23, 2010

> I cry out to you, O God, but you do not answer;
> I stand up, but you merely look at me. — Job 30:20, NIV84

Visiting hours at National are from noon to 9:00. We quickly establish a rhythm. I rise, eat breakfast in a hospital cafeteria, and do some work for my company in my room. Then I spend nine hours with Pam, feeding her two meals, skipping lunch myself. Most days, I miss her occupational therapy, which takes place early in the morning, helping her to get up, washed, and dressed; but I observe her physical and speech therapy. By 9:00 p.m., she is ready for sleep, and I exit. The cafeteria is closed, but I can get supper at a Blimpie. I come to know their menu very well, but I'm grateful they're open. Then I return calls, and read a little.

Today at noon I find Pam wide awake and very chatty, full of words, most of them pretty clear. "John, I love you!" she exclaims when I walk in. Then she turns to a nurse, points at me, and says excitedly, "I love my wife! I love my wife!" Now there's a backhanded compliment. Just like old times: she has managed to validate me and emasculate me in the same breath.

I meet our case manager. She explains that the therapists will spend a week evaluating Pam, and then develop a treatment plan that contains both long- and short-range goals. This sounds like just what we need, although the initial goals don't strike me as very encouraging: Pam will identify pictures with 60 percent accuracy, stand and use a walker, take seated showers, and submit to hospital restraints. These targets are measurable, and therefore good science, but they are expressed in language that is dehumanizing, even chilling. And the picture they paint falls far short of a resumption of normal life.

Today she has four half-hour sessions; I observe three.

The speech therapist assesses her ability to swallow. Pam is improving; she is now allowed thin liquids, but is still one step shy of dense solid foods.

She is attentive and engaged as the therapist poses questions, and affirms that a hammer will pound nails and a stone will sink, but is less sure of other words. Asked whether a hammer is good for cutting wood, she says, "Oh, definitely!" She also guesses that a cork will sink. What is she missing here—the object names, the verbs, some broader concept?

I notice that the speech therapist, in addressing Pam, often points to her own mouth, calling attention to the movements of lips and tongue that shape the words. So Pam is mimicking, perhaps as much as she is thinking and remembering, or even more.

The physical therapist gets her up and into a wheelchair that will be hers for the duration of her stay, or until she can safely walk without it. It's a MacGyver device that even reclines! It carries her into a gym, where she practices standing.

She is a good sport through all this, but by the end of the day she is exhausted. She doesn't eat much, and she manages to make it clear that she wants to go home.

A memory helps her, or memories from many bygone nights. Sad, sore, empty, comfortless, she thinks of closeness, and invites me to be near. Cautiously, I let down the guardrail and climb into bed with her. She can't really turn or nestle, but we lie side by side, holding hands. She relaxes. This, too, will become part of each day's routine.

I have trouble explaining why we need to be here, but she agrees to give it another day.

SEPTEMBER 24, 2010

> When Israel was a child, I loved him, . . .
> It was I who taught Ephraim to walk,
> taking them by the arms;
> but they did not realize
> it was I who healed them. — Hos. 11:1, 3

At noon today I find Pam dressed in her own clothes (rather than a hospital gown), sitting up in her wheelchair, spilling over with words. She manages to call me her "husband" this time, but I still get no respect—over and over, she tells everyone that "John is much older."

One of the therapists alerts me to a phenomenon called *perseveration*: Pam will get stuck on one particular word and apply it in all sorts of situations. Today she keeps saying "Jerusalem" and "license" whenever she's at a loss. Often, the whole sentence is coherent except for the key word. The effect is rather like walking into an Abbott and Costello routine: "John, where's the Jerusalem?" "What do you mean, 'Jerusalem'?" "You know, the license." Third base!

Discussing this with a doctor, I mention that the word of the day seems to be "Jerusalem." Pam pipes up: "Yeah, I wanted to ask you about that!"

The physical therapist gets her up and using a walker! She takes quite a series of steps, covering maybe twenty-five feet, and then rests and walks back. She uses her right leg and foot, and even, to some extent, her right arm. She also swallows medications in pill form, safely and cooperatively. And she's able to let me know when she needs a bathroom. This is thrilling progress.

Her appetite is better, and she likes one of her nurses (a Christian) and her physical therapist.

During free time, I get her outdoors into the Healing Garden. It's not that healing, considering the mosquitoes, but we both enjoy the trees and flowers, shade and sunshine, fountain, and fresh air. Except for a few moments during her ambulance transfer Wednesday, Pam hasn't been outside since the morning of August 25.

We share a cup of coffee, and I tell her that her sister can't come this weekend because their mother fell and broke her collarbone. I don't think she follows the details, but she begins sobbing, remembering her mother and thinking of her in pain. The tears come again when I show her a card from her daughter.

SEPTEMBER 25, 2010

> Save me from all my transgressions;
> do not make me the scorn of fools.
> I was silent; I would not open my mouth,
> for you are the one who has done this.
> Remove your scourge from me;
> I am overcome by the blow of your hand. — Ps. 39:8-10

Today marks one month since Pam's surgery—and what a month!

Weekends are supposed to see a slower schedule at National, but Pam still has four therapy sessions. In physical therapy, using the walker, she travels twice as far as yesterday.

Yet overall she appears to lose ground, thanks to a different speech therapist, new to us, who insists on completing a battery of tests. She shows Pam a series of common objects—cup, hammer, pencil—and asks her to name them. Pam cannot, but we have to go through all five items. Then she has to try to read written words, and then to write them. I can see the need for evaluation, but Pam is growing more and more discouraged. She recognizes that there is one right answer to each question, and she doesn't know it; this is a test, and she's failing. Afterward she complains that we spent three hours on the session; it was one hour, but it must have felt like three.

The therapist can't see this, or won't acknowledge it, because, hey, she has a *list* to complete. I am reminded of Jill Bolte Taylor's account of a similar run-in:

> I awoke early the next morning to a medical student who came rushing in to take a medical history. I thought it curious that she had not been informed that I was a stroke survivor who could not speak or understand language. I realized that morning that a hospital's number one responsibility should be protecting its patients' energy levels. This young girl was an energy vampire. . . . She might have gotten something more from me had she come to me gently with patience and kindness, but because she insisted that I come to her in her time and at her pace, it was not satisfying for either of us. . . .
>
> The biggest lesson I learned that morning was that when it came to my rehabilitation, I was ultimately the one in control of the success or failure of those caring for me. It was my decision to show up or not. I chose to show up for those professionals who brought me energy by connecting with me, touching me gently and appropriately, making direct eye contact with me, and speaking to me calmly. I responded positively to positive treatment. The professionals who did not connect with me sapped my energy, so I protected myself by ignoring their requests.[44]

---

[44] Taylor, *My Stroke of Insight*, 83-84.

I will waste considerable time and energy, both at National and later, trying to decide whether these encounters are so frequent simply because of insensitive individuals working in healthcare, or whether there is something more systemic at fault: tight timeframes, the hallowing of procedures, and the valuation of measurement and data-gathering over care and treatment. Good people having a whole lot of bad days.

I point out to the therapist that, in practical contexts when Pam wants something, she finds more words. A week or so ago, when I fed her, she managed, "I want some fruit"; just today, she couldn't come up with the word "ice," but was able to ask me for "something frozen." Why not start with an activity, and introduce objects in the context of that activity?

I have seen a similar stripping away of contexts in K-12 education. When kids are challenged to solve real-world problems, they are motivated and engaged, able to integrate and apply classroom learning and life experiences. But because the system has been skewed toward passing quantifiable standardized tests, schooling has become a mind-numbing succession of worksheets and drills.

For Pam, the damage is done. It goes far beyond Taylor's decision not to "show up" for certain professionals. After this session, Pam wants to leave; with or without me, she is determined to go home, go anywhere. I can't really blame her, and I don't succeed in convincing her otherwise, but eventually her feelings subside—until the next therapist or nurse or administrator does something to upset her. It is very hard for her to commit to this process and (some of) these people.

Emotionally, she is very fragile. Again today, I buy her coffee as a treat. I hand it to her to hold while I bend to adjust her wheelchair brakes. Her left-hand grip somehow falters, and she spills the drink—fortunately on the floor, not herself—and sobs and sobs.

We have a few good moments. We get out into the Healing Garden—which I am going to rename the Mealing Garden, in honor of the flesh-eating mosquitoes. She watches me slap at the bugs, smiles happily, and says, "Poor John!"

Then she observes two crazed squirrels chasing each other, and comments, "We better stay away from those guys." This is fascinating to me. She doesn't hang on to the simple noun "squirrel," even when I repeat it for her. But, all on her own, she can come up with "stay away," which conceptually seems pretty complex.

Her sister calls and, on impulse, I put Pam on the phone. She doesn't follow everything, but it's a loving connection.

SEPTEMBER 26, 2010

I will give you thanks in the great assembly;
among throngs of people I will praise you. — Ps. 35:18,
NIV84

I start my visit early on this Sunday. For the second time, Pam makes it clear that she was scared overnight.

We stumble upon a church service down in the basement. It's a small circle of nine people, six of us in wheelchairs because of diabetes, MS, and other conditions. And it is Christ's "power . . . made perfect in weakness" (2 Cor. 12:9). One joyful, nearly toothless older man has trouble speaking, but this only adds weight to his words of faith and encouragement. Through it all, Pam beams.

Morning rain drives the mosquitoes away, and we spend much of the afternoon outdoors. Pam says again that she wants to go home now. Somehow she remembers a physical therapist in Lawrence; she worked with him following foot surgery, and could go back to him now. I have the cruel task of insisting that it isn't safe, she isn't ready yet. At last—miserable success!—she seems to grasp it: "I guess I'm more sick than I thought." Even so, she agrees only to stay two or three more days.

This evening, lying in her bed, she wants to watch TV together. I assume she can't follow most of the words, and keep searching for animal shows and travel documentaries. But she prefers known programs with familiar faces, even if they have lots of dialogue. *Grey's Anatomy* and *Bones*, though not *Sherlock Holmes*. She wants to find a way back to the life we had. Mostly, so do I.

There are no therapies on Sundays. I feared a dull and empty day. But it was bright and full, as well as piercing.

SEPTEMBER 27, 2010

> You number *and* record my wanderings;
> put my tears into Your bottle—
> are they not in Your book? — Ps. 56:8, Ampl

What a day! Pam has a great speech therapy session; the therapist gets her talking about family. She jumbles the names, but when she thinks clearly of her grandchildren, she exclaims, "I love those guys! Love them love them love them!"

Ten minutes later she somehow becomes convinced that I am working against her, scheming to keep her here instead of helping her go home. She shuts down and won't converse with her physical therapist, although she cooperates with the exercises—walking a long distance using a walker, and then practicing climbing stairs. (Lead with the strong foot going up, and with the weak foot going down.)

Then, in her free time, she lets me tell her the story of the days immediately after her surgery. We both weep as I describe her unresponsive period, and how she began to show alertness, and then how she sang praise. I'm not sure she understands it all, but she is moved, and I think it helps confirm for her that she has been very sick.

And then she is in fine spirits, and wants to try talking on the phone. We reach her younger son, and he's a great sport about getting past the garbled words. As he comments, "This is the longest I've ever gone without talking with my mom." Pam is delighted with the experience. God is good.

Jenny calls from my work to say that she has taken up a collection to help defray my expenses for room and board and whatever. She raised $4,000—a huge sum, given that our company has only forty employees and I work remotely. They have granted me paid leave, and now this! I keep being surprised by people's kindness.

SEPTEMBER 28, 2010

> Be merciful to me, O LORD, for I am in distress;
> my eyes grow weak with sorrow,
> my soul and my body with grief. — Ps. 31:9, NIV84

Homonymous hemianopsia. It sounds like the scientific name for a rare and ugly species of fruit fly, but it's a visual condition. It means that half the visual field, for both eyes, has been lost. Pam's physical therapist gives me this term, after observing that Pam isn't seeing obstacles. It appears that her left-brain stroke has knocked out her right-side vision. The problem isn't really in the eyes themselves, but in the neural pathways connecting eye and brain. Still, to be safe, Pam must be trained to go slowly and turn her head, scanning left to right.

We can't be sure of this diagnosis yet; it's possible that she might have a right-side inattention problem instead. Either way, learning about this, just as she is starting to walk again, seems like a cruel trick. I think again of one of Pam's old prophetic words: she's on roller skates, having fun, going really fast, and suddenly something stops her and she has to go back, start over. Does it truly glorify God to rein in her joy and enthusiasm? We see the woman in Solomon's song "coming up from the wilderness leaning on her beloved" (Song 8:5), but what then? Is she to be hobbled forever? Will she never again run after Him (1:4), never leap and cavort like an unpenned calf (Mal. 4:2)?

At least her tongue is loosening. Laughing, today she tells me, "You're a loser!" Seems like old times.

Today, for the first time, she has all six half-hour therapy sessions. She handles them like a champ. Language is still slow and spotty, but she speaks by phone with her daughter and a friend from work. And when she stops this evening to encourage her roommate, her words come fluently.

SEPTEMBER 29, 2010

> What will he do to you,
> and what more besides,
> you deceitful tongue? — Ps. 120:3

Again, Pam navigates a full day of six sessions, and tonight she speaks with her son. Her appetite is better, and her sweet tooth is certainly coming back.

The doctor says that, if all goes well, Pam should be ready to go home around October 13—in two weeks. The date "magically" matches the three-week limit set by our insurance provider, but whether we'll really be prepared to cope at home is another issue.

Her main speech therapist tells me the team agrees that Pam is right on top of any topic that's in the present; she's alert, and she finds ways to get her meaning across. As one moves away from the here and now, though, she falls behind. Fairly quickly, she stops communicating. Either things become too abstract, or she simply can't find the vocabulary yet.

Comfortless alternative! What remains of relationship when our words are gone?

Most of our culture's professions of undying love stop short of this. When Shakespeare writes,

> Let me not to the marriage of true minds
> Admit impediments. Love is not love
> Which alters when it alteration finds,
> Or bends with the remover to remove:

> O, no! it is an ever-fixed mark,
> That looks on tempests and is never shaken; . . .
> Love's not Time's fool, though rosy lips and cheeks
> Within his bending sickle's compass come;
> Love alters not with his brief hours and weeks,
> But bears it out even to the edge of doom.[45]

—when Bill writes this, he considers only the bodily decay of "rosy lips and cheeks." There's no impediment because the two "true minds" still stand, both unimpaired. We pride ourselves on intellect, identify ourselves with it; and in severe accordance with this principle, we devalue people whose brains have been injured. When "alteration" strikes here, the injury becomes the "ever-fixed mark," and our poor love trips over an "impediment," and falls.

But I am starting to believe that conceptual reasoning is overrated. Much as I prize Pam's words, I'm relearning what I first mastered in our courtship: to read her expressive face and posture. Most of all, I draw strength from her singing spirit.

In therapy today, I watch her struggle with the numbers one to ten, the days of the week, the months of the year. She cannot rattle them off—but then, Pam never was one to color within the lines. She would rather subvert a test, and thereby share a laugh, than achieve a lonely distinction. I see flashes of this spirit still—as when, asked to sort objects, she supplies her own sweeping category: "Cheap crap."

Nouns and proper names are tough for her. Just now she calls most people, male and female, "Jeff." But she doesn't seem to hear what she herself is saying. A typical conversation goes like this: I show Pam a picture of her son Brian, and she says, "Jeff." I say, "No, this is Brian. THIS"—producing a photo of her brother Jeff—"is Jeff." Pam: "What

---

[45] William Shakespeare, "Sonnet 116" (1593?-1601?, published 1609); available at *The Folger Shakespeare*, accessed December 19, 2021, https://shakespeare.folger.edu/shakespeares-works/shakespeares-sonnets/sonnet-116/.

do you mean?" Me (alternating the photos): "Brian, Jeff. Brian, Jeff."
Pam (pointing to the picture of Jeff): "Why do you keep showing me
this?" Her language is good, and I think even her logic, but the names
are mixed up.

Similarly, most nouns are missing. She continues to perseverate,
calling many objects "ovens," "movies," "the salvation," "the Jerusalem,"
"the license." The fill-in words keep changing, and I have no clue where
she's plucking them.

She pleased me by calling me "a teacher." Then, during therapy,
shown a picture of a toilet, she says that it "teaches." Does she perceive
some sort of equivalence here? Or am I only sensitive because my name
is John?

At Hopkins I was led to believe that her recovery of language will
be more episodic than incremental, coming back in sudden bursts:
plateau, breakthrough, plateau, breakthrough. I have clutched this as
a fervent hope, and at last, today . . . her potty mouth returns. Off
and on throughout the day, she takes great delight in swearing at me,
exuberant, savoring every word: "Bite me!" she says; "piece of s—!"—
laughing so hard in her bathroom stall that, as soon as she emerges, she
must rush back in and pee some more.

This wasn't quite the way I had imagined a speech-language
breakthrough would look.

But I welcome it gratefully. "She's BAA-ACK!" I tell her sister,
summing up the cusswords. Indeed, she is still coming back. Let me
admit no impediments to the marriage of spirits, nor to the power of
the living God.

SEPTEMBER 30, 2010

> How lovely is your dwelling place,
> Lord Almighty! . . .
> Blessed are those who dwell in your house;
> they are ever praising you.

> Blessed are those whose strength is in you,
> whose hearts are set on pilgrimage. — Ps. 84:1, 4-5

A day of visitors. I find Pam chatting happily with a young man named Charles. He is a hospital volunteer, one of the unsung heroes who put a caring face on every hospital. Pam was such a volunteer at the hospital in Lawrence.

Charles's job is to go from room to room with a book cart, and normally this might tick Pam off—"I can't read!" I've heard her declare with annoyance. But the books are incidental to Charles, a mere foot in the door; his mission is to encourage people in recovery and doing rehab. He is eminently qualified, because in 2005 a stroke left him paralyzed (in all four limbs) and without much speech. Refusing a wheelchair, he insisted that he would walk out of the hospital—and did so, four weeks later. His insurance wouldn't cover much therapy, and he couldn't afford to pay out-of-pocket, so he learned to speak again by watching television. (Better than radio, he reasoned, because you can watch the mouth movements that produce the various letter sounds.) I ask whether he chose educational programs like *Sesame Street*. He scoffs: "Nah! I watched the shows I liked! Cop shows."

His story is also something of a cautionary tale. When his stroke hit, out of the blue, he was a dynamic sales rep with a territory to cover. He sensed that something serious was happening, and was at least dimly aware that TIME IS BRAIN, but he made a snap decision to drive himself to the hospital instead of calling 911. He steered through traffic, getting worse by the minute. He made it to the hospital, but passed out, in his car, in the parking lot. Fortunately, someone found him fairly quickly.

This is more common than I would have supposed. Kevin Sorbo, who played Hercules in a 1990s TV show, suffered an aneurysm and three strokes. As his brain "went haywire," he insisted on driving himself home, going through with a talk show appearance, and then going to bed at home.[46] Independence is our rocket fuel, but, when it runs out, we are too intoxicated by its fumes to make a course correction.

Today Charles speaks well and moves smoothly, leaning a little on the book cart. He serves as vice president of a local brain injury support group. He is a great model for Pam, and promises to stop by again.

This afternoon, a wonderful Lawrence couple comes to see us. They are on the East Coast to attend a conference, but have made a big detour to visit Washington.

For days, I have been trying to tell Pam just who is coming: "Cheri and Pat will be here to see you." But this is what is so frustrating, for both of us—names mean nothing to her. I don't have photos of them on my phone; even if I did, there's no guarantee that she could see them well enough, on a tiny screen, to make out distinguishing features. We never prepared for challenges like this, or for a condition in which everything, absolutely everything, becomes a challenge.

When our friends arrive, I arrange to meet them privately in a gift shop. I feel the need to warn them that she may not recognize them at all. I'm not sure just who I am protecting—them? Pam? myself?— but I am terribly anxious. A lot is riding on this, in my mind. These are dear friends; what if she doesn't know them? What if her external connections, like so many internal ones, are now irretrievably lost?

I haven't quite told them, told anyone, how bad things are. I don't say, even now, how I found Pam yesterday, sitting up with her hand jammed into a shoe. She didn't remember that a shoe goes on a foot. Each day, many times a day, we are at a level almost too basic to describe, accept, acknowledge.

---

[46] Kevin Sorbo, *True Strength: My Journey from Hercules to Mere Mortal and How Nearly Dying Saved My Life* (Cambridge, MA: Da Capo-Perseus, 2011), 46-52.

I don't know what to expect. But as soon as we walk into Pam's room, she lights up: "Hey! You guys!" She is thrilled, and everything is fine. The names don't matter. She knows them.

They sit with us, listening past the garbled words (Pam's and mine). They pray with us. Pam lets Cheri brush her hair.

Since our computer is still out of commission, Cheri agrees to send out an email update to family and friends. She writes:

> Much to our surprise and delight, we found Pam sitting up in a wheelchair beside her hospital bed waiting for our arrival. She looked up to see us, and a spark of life animated her body as she immediately recognized both of us and stood up on wobbly legs to embrace us in the type of hug reserved for dear friends not seen in a long, long time. Oh, what a welcome relief we felt as we all embraced and felt the goodness of God in the warmth in our little circle of love!

> During our hospital visit, Pam continued to amaze us at all she was able to do. One nurse entered the room during our conversation and she commented on how talkative Pam was. We explained that this is the Pam we knew, and that this is normal for her. Pam spoke fluently, although at times the words were not the appropriate words to use. For example, when she spoke of anything challenging, she used the word "oven" to describe the situation. It took us a while to catch on to this. In fact it wasn't completely clear until we reflected on our conversations with her later. We are not really sure why this word was selected out of her memory bank to use. We are guessing that the heat of an oven is perhaps her best ability to describe having to work so hard at the skills she is having to relearn.

> And learning she is doing!! We could see the determination in her spirit when she explained the "oven" of breathing

into a portable device that measures her lung capacity. She proudly showed me how far she could raise the red ball inside the device by blowing hard into the mouthpiece. It was obviously a difficult thing to do, but she repeatedly blew hard into the mouthpiece in triumph, even though it was exhausting for her.

She also proudly showed us her ability to move her right hand back and forth in a grasping motion and to raise her right arm to shoulder height. She has obviously been working hard on the "ovens"! She asked for a Coke, but did not recall the name of it, but instead pointed to an empty Coke bottle on the bedside table. She was able to hold the small cupful of Coke in her right hand and bring it to her own mouth. Her hand was shaky, but she was able to do it on her own.

She could walk to the bathroom with very little assistance. She noticed her hair in the bathroom mirror and mentioned how messy it was, so she patiently allowed me to brush out the tangles and seemed thankful for the assistance. She was concerned at her appearance, and with her hair pulled back into a ponytail, asked for approval from everyone as to how her final hairdo looked to us. . . .

John also reports that Pam is ministering to her roommate. When Pam has been up walking around, she remembers to stop by the bedside of her roommate to give her a hug and pray for her. Pam is continually full of the joy of the Lord. I could see the love her young doctor and her nurses had for her as they ministered to her needs. Others are naturally drawn to Pam in love because she has joy in all circumstances that comes from her intimate relationship with Jesus.

During our conversations with Pam, she mentioned that some things were "lost" in her memory. In her own words as she was describing it, she said, "I was hidden," and "I was in a dark place." Do we dare to hope for complete recovery for Pam? Do we dare to hope there is a God that loves us and is able to hear us when we place our hope in him? Yes! "The eyes of the LORD are on those who fear him, on those whose hope is in his unfailing love." — Ps. 33:18

As Pam's hair is being brushed, a great peace envelops us. Pat says simply, "The Spirit of God is in this room." He is. He is.

OCTOBER 1, 2010

If it had not been the LORD who was on our side
—let Israel now say—
if it had not been the LORD who was on our side . . .
then the flood would have swept us away,
the torrent would have gone over us;
then over us would have gone the raging waters. . . .
Our help is in the name of the LORD,
who made heaven and earth. — Ps. 124:1-2, 4-5, 8,
NRSV; compare Jonah 2:3-6

Of the couple that came to see us yesterday, Pat is a church worship leader, while Cheri is an intercessor who rises during the night to pray for others, including Pam. She told us of a vision she received, of flood waters rising, rising up to her chin. Then a huge pair of feet came down and stamped, and the waters stopped.

The imagery is biblical:

Waters flowed over my head;
I said, "I am cut off!" — Lam. 3:54, NASB

[The LORD] stills the roaring of the seas, . . . — Ps. 65:7,
NASB; compare Luke 8:22-25

[The LORD said to the waters,]
"Thus far shall you come, and no farther,
and here shall your proud waves be stayed." — Job 38:11,
RSV; compare Ps. 104:5-9

Your path led through the sea,
your way through the mighty waters,
though your footprints were not seen. — Ps. 77:19

The picture of an overpowering flood, and of a God who is there to
deliver, seems to me very apt for Pam's experience. When I ask her now
what she remembers, and what the early days at Hopkins were like, it's
hard for her to find words, except to say that she was "hidden" or "lost."
But the Good Shepherd never lost sight of her, and never left her side:

Do not fear, for I have redeemed you;
I have called you by name, you are mine.
When you pass through the waters, I will be with you;
and through the rivers, they shall not overwhelm you;
when you walk through fire you shall not be burned,
and the flame shall not consume you.
For I am the LORD your God,
the Holy One of Israel, your Savior. — Isa. 43:1-3, NRSV

. . . we went through fire and water,
but you brought us to a place of abundance. — Ps. 66:12

OCTOBER 2, 2010

My tears have been my food day and night,
while people say to me continually, "Where is your God?"
— Ps. 42:3, NRSV

I've always found keeping company with young children both a marvelous and a frustrating experience. A child is so focused on the concrete, the present moment, here and now. And so, babysitting, I look at a butterfly or a blade of grass with new eyes; but, ten minutes later, there is a huge tantrum over strained beets, and I find myself growing impatient and thinking, *It's only lunch. Can't we rise above this? Why does every little thing have to be such a big deal?*

Mealtimes are becoming a tussle with Pam. More often than not, when her tray comes, she announces, "Probably won't like any of it." I lift the lid, and she inspects the food and says with great disdain, "Nope. No good. Won't eat any of it." Or today, surveying her repast with wild scorn: "So there's nothing!" Excellent language, but my heart sinks. Now I will have to coax her to try at least a bite. Then I'll help her eat the bits she likes. Then I'll chase down an alternative, rushing so she won't be late for the next therapy.

The staff kindly put her on a list to receive an evening snack, perhaps a cup of yogurt. A last opportunity, each day, for a little nutrition.

Feeding her, when she actually eats, is peaceful and deeply satisfying. It's the motivational ground-laying that I could do without. And I grumble and think, *It's just food. Why does it have to turn into a battle?*

But Pam's life, right now, is all about the very particular. Her job is to take the next step, and to come up with the names of everyday objects. If that also means the taste or appearance of food is important, well, maybe that comes with the territory. I have to admit, my habitual approach—*It's only food; there are more important and more urgent things; rise above it and move on*—causes me to miss a lot in life. Plus, in Christian theology, the central fact isn't "rising above"; it's the incarnation, God coming down, entering into. In Jesus, the Eternal God took on human flesh, human pain and circumstances, embracing and shouldering and caring about all our messy particularities. Even what's for lunch.

OCTOBER 3, 2010

> He has taken me to the banquet hall,
> and his banner over me is love. — Song 2:4, NIV84

We have more great visitors this weekend. They help to coax Pam off *food* or *the nurses* and onto positive topics.

Yesterday it was Pam's ex-brother-in-law, making his fourth visit since her surgery. A strong, kind man, he is ever a steadying presence. You instinctively feel that nothing bad will happen on his watch. If it does, he will bear witness, in stalwart prayers, not to be denied.

Today Pam's sister returns, with her husband. We find Pam sobbing, convinced that a nurse is angry at her. She calms down, and eventually we get her out of the hospital entirely, over to the Physicians Office Building. The change of scene, and the badass criminal mischief feeling of going AWOL, brighten Pam's mood enormously. We order a pizza; as we discuss toppings, Pam causes general hilarity by volunteering, "I want to try something man-flavored." I joke that the Lorena Bobbitt Meat Lovers Special isn't available on Sundays.

It's great to see her feeling normal, interacting with loved ones, enjoying a simple treat. Though I'm at the hospital every day, I lose touch with what it's like for her, simply because I get to leave at night. Most of the time she either feels imprisoned or works frantically, gripping and stepping and speaking, trying to earn her release.

Back on Pam's floor, we solve one mystery. An older nurse, who perhaps doesn't hear perfectly, comes into her room, talking loudly. She is smiling and speaking with evident affection, but Pam asks me, "Why is she angry at me? Why is she so mean?" Apparently, just now, *loud* comes across to her as *angry*. This is receptive aphasia, not only of words but of tones and mannerisms. A garbling even of emotions and body language.

OCTOBER 4, 2010

> Why do you complain, Jacob?
> Why do you say, Israel,
> "My way is hidden from the LORD;
> my cause is disregarded by my God"?
> Do you not know?
> Have you not heard?
> The LORD is the everlasting God,
> the Creator of the ends of the earth.
> He will not grow tired or weary,
> and his understanding no one can fathom.
> He gives strength to the weary
> and increases the power of the weak.
> Even youths grow tired and weary,
> and young men stumble and fall;
> but those who hope in the LORD
> will renew their strength.
> They will soar on wings like eagles;
> they will run and not grow weary,
> they will walk and not be faint. — Isa. 40:27-31

Today the physical therapist gets Pam up and walking without the walker, and without any assistance or support. She goes farther and farther, and asks, "Why is this so easy?"

I don't dare try this when a physical therapist isn't present. Pam and I practice using her walker, with a special "grabbable" belt around her waist; I watch for right-side obstacles she may not see, and am wary lest her right foot drag and catch. But today's performance points to a day when she'll again walk easily, fluently.

Triumph makes her cocky. "You're pathetical," she teases, smiling. And tenderly, when I leave for the night: "See you later, alligator."

OCTOBER 5, 2010

I heard, but I did not understand. — Dan. 12:8

I don't know or understand what you're talking about.
— Mark 14:68

Anomia (or *anomic aphasia*). That's the speech therapist's word for Pam's type of language difficulty, the inability to come up with names of people and things. I remember reading that the eloquent Ralph Waldo Emerson struggled with this in his later years. He wouldn't be able to find the word *umbrella*, and so he would deliver a long and elegant circumlocution: "I can't tell its name, but I can tell its history. Strangers take it away."[47]

Pam's descriptions just now are less helpful. Today she asks for "more of the green stuff"; by trial and error, I am eventually able to figure out that she means milk. Apart from the occasional Dr. Seuss book or Saint Patrick's Day novelty, I haven't seen green milk since my bachelor days; still, Pam somehow tags it as "green."

She has also taken to asking for "something man-flavored" or "woman-flavored" or even "wisdom-flavored." It may be a while before she's ready to order for herself in a family restaurant.

On the other hand, when she couldn't come up with my boss's name, she referred to him as "the guy who owns you"—which pretty much matches Jim's view of the situation.

For some reason, her favorite television show just now is *House*, Hugh Laurie playing a brilliant but caustic doctor. Pam can't come up with the name, but the other night she asked whether it was on by pointing to the TV and saying, "That old guy. Mean to everyone. Nobody likes him." I asked, "You mean Jim?"

----

[47] Robert D. Richardson, Jr., *Emerson: The Mind on Fire* (Berkeley and Los Angeles: University of California, 1995), 569.

Pam has an old friend who has struggled with aphasia, and she shares with me a positive spirit and some helpful pointers:

- The way some wrong names just get stuck in the brain. She had the hardest time relearning the word *refrigerator*, and instead would call it "the TV": "Why don't you go to the TV and get something to eat?" Her family still teases her about this.

- A tendency to swap letters between words. Once, when her son wanted to stay at a friend's house, she said firmly, "No. You cannot steep at Sleeve's."

- A worsening of symptoms, including perseveration, when she's tired. On those days, every object becomes *the thing*: "I took the thing out of the thing and put it on the thing." And indeed, today Pam is in a small speech therapy group, and one man, at a loss for words, says, "The thing that is thinking a thing," which sounds like a philosopher's definition of the mind.

Many of the slips are amusing, and Pam often enjoys the consternation she causes. But the path from startled merriment to scowling frustration is shorter than one might expect. When she's thirsty, the fact that she's asking for "green stuff" isn't funny to her. The sooner we solve her problem, the better. She may laugh about it later.

I make some progress with our other communication failure, visiting the hospital's IT department and finding a technician who will fix our infected laptop in his spare time for fifty dollars. This is an achievement, but, when I finally make it to Pam's floor, I find her crying: she's lonely, and she missed breakfast because of an early occupational therapy session. She cheers up after eating lunch, and later rediscovers Cheerios.

Charles, the volunteer, recommends that we find a stroke or aphasia or brain injury support group when we get home. It has made all the difference to him to gather with people who understand, who share his struggles.

I tell myself that Pam continues to improve, and what is difficult today may be a distant memory in a week or two. We'll look back on all this and laugh . . . won't we?

OCTOBER 6, 2010

> I will make your tongue stick to the roof of your mouth so that you will be silent and unable to rebuke them, though they are a rebellious house. But when I speak to you, I will open your mouth and you shall say to them, "This is what the Sovereign LORD says." — Ezek. 3:26-27, NIV84

What is it like to lose your language?

Besides being "hidden" and "lost," Pam says of the first days following her surgery that "everything went black." (A couple of times she has also said that all was "blonde," which may be a profound poetic image or the dim memory of a category of joke.)

Darkness is a primal terror, dreaded by every child. Psalm 23 pictures suffering as a dark valley; the traveler descends further and further out of the sunlit peaks and meadows into a threatening shadow-realm. One feels abandoned, and expects to be attacked:

> For the enemy has pursued me,
> crushing my life to the ground,
> making me sit in darkness like those long dead.
> Therefore my spirit faints within me;
> my heart within me is appalled. — Ps. 143:3-4, NRSV

Confusion and silence make matters worse, much worse; it seems as if one is entirely alone. When proud King Nebuchadnezzar is overtaken by the judgment of God, he loses his reason (Dan. 4:34) and it's as if his mind has been changed to the mind of an animal (4:16; 5:21). Until God restores him, he is driven away from human community. As Job says, this is one of the most awful of God's visitations:

> He deprives of speech those who are trusted,
> and takes away the discernment of the elders. . . .
> He strips understanding from the leaders of the earth,
> and makes them wander in a pathless waste.
> They grope in the dark without light;
> he makes them stagger like a drunkard. — Job 12:20,
> 24-25, NRSV

Job himself still has the power of speech, but the very depth of his suffering separates him from others. "If I speak, my pain is not lessened," he says (Job 16:6, NASB). His "plans are shattered" (17:11): "my eyes will never see happiness again" (7:7). Yet he remembers when he could speak powerful, effective words (29:21-25), and cries out, "Oh, that I had someone to hear me!" (31:35). His friends don't, perhaps because the person who's at ease tends to despise the one who is hurting (12:5). One "friend" describes Job as lacking understanding and hunting in vain for words (18:2); another implies that Job is an idiot (11:12); Elihu, the youngest, is preoccupied by his own need to speak and find relief in venting (32:17-20). It may be that the central content of God's "answer" to Job is simply that He shows up, indicating that Job has been heard.

In silence, sorrow grows worse (Ps. 39:2). Yet there is a time to be silent (Eccl. 3:7). The author of the book of Lamentations says it is good to wait silently, in faith, believing that God will save (3:26, 28), because He is the One who pleads our cause (3:58-59)—and yet this writer still cries to Him for help (3:55-57). How can one be both silent and not silent? Perhaps because God hears even a sigh, even a groan.[48]

> O LORD, you have searched me
> and you know me. . . .

---

[48] Ps. 38:9; Ex. 2:23-24; 6:5; Acts 7:34; Rom. 8:26.

Before a word is on my tongue
you know it completely, O LORD. . . .
[E]ven the darkness will not be dark to you.
— Ps. 139:1, 4, 12, NIV84

In the dark valley, there is an intimacy deeper than words; in the silent place, we develop a longing to worship: "Set me free from my prison, that I may praise your name" (Ps. 142:7; compare 51:15). Mysteriously, when everything is stripped away, faith grows.

The Lord turns silence into praise (Ps. 30:11-12). The father of John the Baptist was struck dumb for a time; when his mouth was opened, "he began to speak, praising God" (Luke 1:64). Nebuchadnezzar, his reason restored, testified that everything God does is right and just (Dan. 4:37). Perhaps closest to Pam is the prophet Ezekiel, who was made mute for a time; both his silence and the opening of his mouth were signs to the people around him, to call forth their faith (Ezek. 3:26-27; 24:27; 33:22).

So we pray, "I am Your servant; give me understanding" (Ps. 119:125, 169, Ampl); "Let my soul live that it may praise You" (119:175, NASB). And we affirm, "Hope in God; for I shall again praise him" (42:5, 11; 43:5, NRSV).

OCTOBER 7, 2010

All my enemies whisper together against me;
they imagine the worst for me, saying,
"A vile disease has afflicted him;
he will never get up from the place where he lies." — Ps. 41:7-8

Our case manager at National is putting together a plan that will have us returning home on or around October 13. But not fully: the suggestion is that Pam first spend some time, as an inpatient, at a facility in or near Lawrence. From one perspective, I like this idea; it gives me time to safety-proof our home, installing grip bars in the bathrooms and railings on the front steps.

But I'm not thrilled that the strategy is insurance-driven. National will use up the days our provider offers for acute rehab. To get the maximum amount of covered rehab, the idea is that we should next check into a subacute facility, where Pam will receive one and a half hours per day of therapy rather than three hours. When we've exhausted that provision, probably in thirty days, we'll move on to the final category, outpatient rehab.

This is a most illogical progression. If we had known we would do all three, it would have made much more sense to begin with subacute rehab and work up to acute. At Hopkins, though, the strategy wasn't about maxing out our coverage; the goal was to move Pam directly into the most aggressive program she could handle.

Moreover, there are strings attached. Pam has asked if she can go home first and rest for a few days. This sounds reasonable to me, but the case manager warns that the insurance provider might consider this a "discharge" and refuse to pay for the subsequent admission. For the same reason, she won't be able to go home on weekends (when no therapy is offered) to get a good night's sleep; the best they can offer is a day pass to get out for a few hours. We won't know exactly how long she'll be in the new facility until they complete their own evaluation.

Pam isn't on board with this plan at all. I can't find the right words to explain that insurance is calling the shots. (Today I finally did manage to convey the word *insurance*, but only because she used to sell home and auto policies. She didn't make a connection to what's happening next week.) She seems to believe that I'm being mean, or that I don't want her at home.

Our case manager isn't much help. She's always in a hurry to make the next round of calls, and has no time for explaining anything to Pam. In fact, she pointedly ignores her, and speaks only to me. Taylor would call her an "energy vampire," but the effect is even worse. Her visits always leave Pam angry, and anxious.

Pam has a lot of wisdom, even after brain damage. She may not understand insurance, but she knows what she needs most. I am beginning to think that she is right—that we should get her home sooner rather than later, even if it means giving up some "covered" rehab.

But I also suspect that this case manager will release us only to another facility. Our best course may be to go there, and then leave after a few days, "against medical advice" if need be.

OCTOBER 8, 2010

> LORD, you are the God who saves me;
> day and night I cry out to you. . . .
> Why, LORD, do you reject me
> and hide your face from me?
> From my youth I have suffered and been close to death;
> I have borne your terrors and am in despair.
> Your wrath has swept over me;
> your terrors have destroyed me. — Ps. 88:1, 14-16

Pam is clearly tired of hospitals, but is she ready to live at home? I cannot tell. Every day seems to bring new complications.

She has finally been able to communicate that she is experiencing headaches, and will ask for pain medication, maybe two days out of every three. She has some swelling in her right shin and ankle, and today we go for an ultrasound exam; it shows no sign of a blood clot, so we are hoping the problem is just muscle pain.

She still hasn't recovered the full range of motion in her right arm, and she is apt to bump into anything on her right.

Again today, she gets angry as the case manager breezes in and out, ignoring her. At least I spirit her out again, over to the adjacent buildings. Her mood improves as we share a pizza. She laughs, remembering a time, shortly before her surgery, when I experienced a charley horse or muscle spasm in my leg. "I'm SO glad you enjoy my pain," I tell her; "I live for your amusement."

When I take her back to her floor, the nurse on duty scolds me. I am speechless. The hospital orientation never mentioned a sign-out procedure, and I have been taking Pam off the floor whenever I could, every day for two weeks. This is a broken system.

As always, I stay till visiting hours end at 9:00. I lie beside her in her bed, we say our prayers, and then put on TV while she dozes. Tonight we catch part of *Titanic*, and she loves it.

I stroke her leg, and all at once she says, "You are making me sexual." I freeze. I am encouraged that she feels the stirring, and impressed that she knows the word. But the statement also strikes me as an accusation. Do I have the right? Does she still know me in that way? So much has changed. Since she woke up, altered, we have kissed a few times, but gently, as one cups a baby bird. I well remember our last kiss of passion: it was on August 25, after I took her wedding ring and before she was wheeled away.

Where are we now? Who are we to each other? I move my hand aside. On screen, the ship sinks down; catastrophe divides the lovers.

Curfew sounds.

Earlier in the day, I retrieved the repaired computer. Now, back in my room, I fire it up. Like one awakened, I am online for the first time in two weeks. I have 306 emails waiting in my inbox, and don't know where to start.

Disinfected, rebooted, but still not connected.

OCTOBER 9, 2010

> Hear, O Lord, and answer me,
> for I am poor and needy.
> Guard my life, for I am devoted to you.
> You are my God; save your servant who trusts in you.
> Have mercy on me, O Lord,
> for I call to you all day long.
> Bring joy to your servant,
> for to you, O Lord, I lift up my soul. — Ps. 86:1-4, NIV84

Unfortunately, deception requires few words. This morning, when I arrive in Pam's room, she holds out a cup containing what looks like orange soda. She is also prepared with a polished speech, which she must have plotted and practiced all night: "Here, John," she says. "Try this. It's really good!"

Of course, it is horrible—so bad that I drink all her water and devour half her breakfast tray, just trying to obliterate the aftertaste. She cackles the whole time, proud to have slipped me a mickey. Later, she brags of her success to the coffee stand attendant, as well as every nurse who will listen, explaining that it was "Nasty stuff. Makes you poop." The first time or two, I exclaim, "Makes you poop? You mean, besides the bad taste, I'm gonna be running to the bathroom all day?" which only adds luster to her sociopathic triumph.

We have found our way back to our assigned parts: she, the devious deviser of schemes, Lizzie Borden with a soupçon of subtlety, crafty Odysseus crossed with the Lucy who toys with Charlie Brown's dream of place-kicking a football; and I, the eternal victim, the comic butt of every prank, the man whose middle name is Gullible.

This sad story, inexplicably amusing to some, illustrates Pam's progress with language. She is still missing most nouns and names, but she's getting better and better at using other words to convey her meaning. Vexed over a chin hair, she can't find the words *tweezers*, *hair*, or *chin*, but makes gestures and says, "It's embarrassing; it's hugely embarrassing"—and a doctor and I understand.

On the other hand, today I try to explain why *taste* isn't the best word to use when she wants lotion or a tissue—she seems to be calling every sensation a *taste*—and my efforts only confuse her; worse, she thinks I'm angry with her. For now, it may be best to let her communicate using the words she has.

On this quiet Saturday, we again go AWOL. We eat pizza, and I show her my room. It's her first real experience of privacy in more than six weeks. We doze in my bed.

I book our trip home. A commercial flight—no air ambulance, no medical escort. Depending on tests, depending on Pam's further progress, we may have to pay a fee to alter these arrangements; even so, it seems remarkably inexpensive compared to our options just a couple of weeks ago.

Pam can walk, but not far. We'll use an airport wheelchair, and try to board early.

We live by hope (Rom. 8:24, Syriac MSS); indeed, we are "prisoners of hope" (Zech. 9:12). Today this life of camping out in provisional spaces appears to be passing away, and "home" is on our tongues. Even though we dimly know that there can be no simple going back to our life that was.

OCTOBER 10, 2010

> Comfort, comfort my people,
> says your God.
> Speak tenderly . . .
> You who bring good news to Jerusalem,
> lift up your voice with a shout,
> lift it up, do not be afraid;
> say to the towns of Judah,
> "Here is your God!"
> See, the Sovereign LORD comes with power,
> and he rules with a mighty arm.
> See, his reward is with him,
> and his recompense accompanies him.
> He tends his flock like a shepherd:
> He gathers the lambs in his arms
> and carries them close to his heart;
> he gently leads those that have young. — Isa. 40:1-2, 9-11

We need to be reminded, not informed. One of the great truths that is always slipping away from us is the value Jesus sets on us, His little ones. The "spoils" of His service and suffering aren't glory and power, for He had those already, even before the world began (John 17:5). Rather, *we* are His recompense, His reward.[49] His request is, "Father, I desire that they also whom You have entrusted to Me [as Your gift to Me] may be with Me where I am, so that they may see My glory, which You have given Me [Your love gift to Me] . . ." (John 17:24, Ampl). He gathers us and brings us to Himself.

This morning we attend the church service at National, as we did two weeks ago. We are ten people, including six in wheelchairs and Pam with her walker. Half of the congregation has changed, what with departures and new arrivals. One of the newcomers is a woman whose life is different following a fall from a stepladder. She weeps during a song, and Pam goes to comfort her, mostly without words, and does admirably.

There is a crease in Pam's Bible; it easily falls open to Isaiah 61, which begins:

> The Spirit of the Lord God is upon me,
> because the Lord has anointed me
> to bring good news to the afflicted;
> He has sent me to bind up the brokenhearted,
> to proclaim liberty to captives
> and freedom to prisoners;
> to proclaim the favorable year of the Lord
> and the day of vengeance of our God;
> to comfort all who mourn, . . .
> giving them a garland instead of ashes,
> the oil of gladness instead of mourning,
> the mantle of praise instead of a spirit of fainting.
> So they will be called oaks of righteousness,
> the planting of the Lord, that He may be glorified.
> — Isa. 61:1-3, NASB

---

[49] He will be "satisfied" when He justifies many (Isa. 53:11: NABRE "content"; Msg "he'll see that it's worth it and be glad he did it").

Pam has circled these verses, writing above them *Pam's Calling*. One can hardly doubt this. She bears good news, wrapped in whatever words she has; laces wounds with her own fingers; lends her strength to shoulder others' sorrow; spills tears, and laughter. Where she walks, God scatters seeds.

Once more we escape the ward, and treat ourselves to pizza. Then she asks to go to my room, to take a bath. Shy and scared, I join her, and am rewarded by her crooked grin. "Naked boy," she says, and welcomes me.

Pre-stroke, throughout our marriage, Pam had the unfortunate habit of talking during sex. At last I shared with her the opening of a wonderfully odd eighteenth-century novel, *Tristram Shandy*. The hero recounts that, at the very moment of his conception, his parents had this conversation:

> "Pray, my Dear," quoth my mother, "have you not forgot to wind up the clock?" — "Good G—!" cried my father, making an exclamation, but taking care to moderate his voice at the same time, — "Did ever woman, since the creation of the world, interrupt a man with such a silly question?"

Tristram explains that this circumstance determined "the very cast of his mind," which is nervous and disturbed.[50] After that, when Pam continued to discourse on matters great and small during intimate maneuvers, I had only to put a finger on her lips, and one of us would say, "Pray, Mr. Shandy, have you forgotten to wind up the clock?"

This afternoon, Mr. Shandy winds the clock the whole way up.

OCTOBER 11, 2010

When the LORD brought back the captives to Zion,
we were like men who dreamed.

---

[50] Laurence Sterne, *The Life and Opinions of Tristram Shandy, Gentleman* (1759-67), Oxford World's Classics (Oxford and New York: Oxford, 1983, 2000), 1; available at *Project Gutenberg*, accessed December 19, 2021, http://www.gutenberg.org/ebooks/1079.

> Our mouths were filled with laughter,
> our tongues with songs of joy.
> Then it was said among the nations,
> "The LORD has done great things for them."
> The LORD has done great things for us,
> and we are filled with joy. . . .
> Those who sow in tears
> will reap with songs of joy.
> He who goes out weeping,
> carrying seed to sow,
> will return with songs of joy,
> carrying sheaves with him. — Ps. 126:1-3, 5-6, NIV84

Today we confirm our travel plans. I am firm with the case manager, refusing to consider another hospital stay. Abruptly she turns helpful, and arranges outpatient rehab in Lawrence.

Pam is cheerful. In physical therapy, she walks backward, then sideways, and climbs stairs.

I take her into the garden, and out for pizza. She wants to take a bath, but today the water in my room is tepid at best; the other guest rooms have used up the hot water. I explain this to Pam as best I can. She is incredulous, and then, in an instant, turns roguish. "No sex for you!" she announces.

OCTOBER 12, 2010

> [Elijah] ate and drank and then lay down again. The angel
> of the LORD came back a second time and touched him and
> said, "Get up and eat, for the journey is too much for you."
> So he got up and ate and drank. — 1 Kings 19:6-8

A day of waiting, disrupted by a fire alarm.

Pam is tired all day, and grumpy about food, but she does good work in therapy. "J-O-H-N, John," she says during her speech lesson.

The words of an old hymn, a song still in Pam's memory somewhere, run through my mind:

'Tis grace hath brought me safe thus far,
And grace will lead me home.[51]

OCTOBER 13, 2010

But as for you, the LORD took you and brought you out of the iron-smelting furnace, out of Egypt, to be the people of his inheritance, as you now are. — Deut. 4:20

I pack up everything, including Pam's walker and two big bags of medications.

For three weeks I have observed most of her therapy sessions, apart from morning occupational therapy. But we were also promised family/caregiver education, and it hasn't happened. I ask again, but everyone is busy with a staff training event. An occupational therapist steps out and gives me five minutes. She advises me to accompany Pam to the bathroom, to continue using adult diapers, and to keep a change of clothes in the car at all times. That's about it.

The case manager sours Pam's mood one last time, simply by failing to acknowledge her. She is sullen during the taxi ride to the airport, refusing to look as I point out national monuments.

It's odd. Pam suffered a catastrophe at Hopkins, but we look back and feel that we mostly received great care. National gave us aggressive therapy, and yet we are largely disappointed.

---

[51] John Newton, "Amazing Grace," #1.41, in John Newton and William Cowper, *Olney Hymns* (1779), 93; available at *Christian Classics Ethereal Library*, accessed December 19, 2021, https://ccel.org/ccel/newton/olneyhymns.

Someone suggested to me that everyone hates their rehab hospital. Maybe so.[52] But my own list of complaints is pretty specific:

- Pam received no therapeutic recreation. She never once visited the swimming pool. There is a "home-like" room set up, and patients are supposed to get one practice overnight stay in this environment; it never happened. Perhaps she wasn't ready for some of these tools—but if not, neither were the others on her floor. Features that are mainly withheld shouldn't figure prominently in marketing brochures and websites.

- When I asked the neuropsychologist whether it was too soon to make an assessment of Pam's cognitive abilities, she said, "Oh, no." Yet this was never done, or the results never shared with me.

- A good nurse observed that Pam is "very social," and tried to move her out into the hall during the long periods of downtime. But she seemed to be in the way there, and the nurse really had little time for her. There was no natural gathering place for patients who wanted one.

- Once, on a weekend, a brass band played. Otherwise there were no attempts at music or art therapy.

- I have not been prepared, at all, to take care of her at home.

Months later, I'll field a phone call asking Pam to answer questions about her satisfaction with the services she received at National. I reply that Pam has severe aphasia, and isn't up to the task, but add that I

---

[52] In the same vein, Julia Fox Garrison calls the rehab hospital a "torture chamber." *Don't Leave Me This Way: Or When I Get Back on My Feet You'll Be Sorry* (2005; New York: HarperCollins, 2006), 41. David Talbot describes it mechanically, as a "stroke patient 'assembly line.'" *Between Heaven and Hell*, chap. 4. Alison Bonds Shapiro says that a *good* rehab hospital brings you "face-to-face, no-holds-barred, with just how profoundly disabled you are." *Healing into Possibility: The Transformational Lessons of a Stroke* (Novato, CA: New World Library, 2009), 23.

was with her every day, and would be happy to offer feedback. The rep declines, explaining that he is authorized only to talk with patients.

So I never share with them my mixed impressions, my conflicting emotions: She received great therapy here, but not very good care. She absolutely hated it, and yet made tremendous progress.

Shortly before it's time to leave, I make a last check of the window blinds beside Pam's bed. It's been three weeks to the day, and they still won't close.

This is a broken system.

4

ADJUSTING

An Unfamiliar Home

When they arrived in Bethlehem, the whole town was stirred because of them, and the women exclaimed, "Can this be Naomi?"

"Don't call me Naomi [*Pleasant*]," she told them. "Call me Mara [*Bitter*], because the Almighty has made my life very bitter. I went away full, but the LORD has brought me back empty. Why call me Naomi? The LORD has afflicted me; the Almighty has brought misfortune upon me." — Ruth 1:19-21

I'm still not getting dressed without assistance. I need help with brushing my teeth and showering. . . . I can't even release the spoon I'm holding in my left hand without professional coaching. I want the insurance analyst who determined my length of stay to come over here right now and look me in the eye while I point my spoon at his head and threaten, "Do I look rehabilitated to you?" . . .

I imagined leaving on much different terms. According to the scene that I've been directing in my head for weeks, my exodus always went something like this: With joyful tears in everyone's eyes, I would hug and thank each member of my medical team for their role in my full recovery and promise to keep in touch. Then, accompanied by the theme song to *Chariots of Fire* and while waving farewell with my left hand, I would walk with confidence and without a cane through the lobby, which would be packed with applauding therapists, physicians, and patients. The staff would be overwhelmed with pride, the patients would be filled with hope, and I'd be an inspiration to everyone. At the end of the lobby, the automatic doors would peel open, and I'd step through into a clear, sunny day. Into freedom and my old life. — Lisa Genova[53]

Searching for an image to describe his conversion to Christianity, G. K. Chesterton compared himself to "an English yachtsman who slightly miscalculated his course and discovered England under the impression that it was a new island in the South Seas." Once the mistake was cleared up, others expected him to feel rather foolish, but Chesterton insisted that his dominant emotion would be joy:

> What could be more delightful than to have in the same few minutes all the fascinating terrors of going abroad combined with all the humane security of coming home again? . . . How can we contrive to be at once astonished at the world and yet at home in it?[54]

But for the person who has had a stroke, the voyage is reversed. You journey home, and find that you are in a foreign country. Your familiar comforts aren't sprinkled with the glitter of adventure; they are almost entirely withdrawn. The names are not exotic but tantalizing; they dance out of reach. The terrors are too numerous to fascinate, as you

[53] Lisa Genova, *Left Neglected: A Novel* (New York: Gallery-Simon & Schuster, 2011), 149, 152.
[54] G. K. Chesterton, *Orthodoxy* (1908; Garden City, NY: Image-Doubleday, 1959), 9-10; available at *Christian Classics Ethereal Library*, accessed December 19, 2021, https://ccel.org/ccel/chesterton/orthodoxy.

spin wildly from one strange apparition to the next. You are disoriented, unmoored.

For us, the trip itself is stressful. Airport security is an awful scramble: I wheel Pam to the next station, then move our bags, then return to her. Checkpoints designed to prevent smuggling present all sorts of obstacles to someone who is visually impaired and learning again to walk.

Once we are close to our gate, she needs a bathroom. I assist her, taking care not to let the carry-on bags out of my sight. Then she gets mad because I have parked her, and myself, in an out-of-the-way corner; she wants to be closer to people. I move us, but now I am frustrated and angry, throwing the bags down. Hearing a noise, I look up, to find her convulsed with laughter. Oh yeah, I forgot: she thinks it's hilarious when I lose my temper.

She laughs and laughs, and it breaks the ice. I relax too. We share a sandwich. We are okay—at least till the next situation arises.

I have asked the gate attendant to grant us the privilege of early boarding on our flight. They are short-staffed, so I offer to wheel Pam and juggle our carry-on bags, as I have through the terminal. We get to the bottom of the ramp, and I'm helping Pam out of the airport wheelchair when an airline rep appears and says he needs to take our walker and check it as luggage.

I gaze at him blankly. "She needs it," I say.

"You can't carry that on the plane. It's metal."

"This isn't a weapon. She's had a stroke; she literally needs it to walk safely."

At this point, out of sight, the gate attendant begins general boarding—releases the hounds, the herd. Rushing to find their seats and wait. The stampede thunders down the ramp. The first couple of passengers push past us, and trample our bags. I turn on them, snarling, loud: "So much for early boarding!"

A woman clutches her husband's arm: "Let's wait a minute."

I surrender the walker, hoist the bags, and direct Pam to keep a firm grip on my arm. We shuffle aboard the plane, take our seats. Pam sits calmly; I am shaking.

The flight itself goes well—marvelously, considering all the fears and frustrations of a month ago. Pam is calm and cooperative. Cabin pressure, noise, turbulence don't upset her or elicit any visible symptoms.

But all the while I keep wondering, *Have I become the person who "loses it" in public? Was I always that guy, even when I despised and judged him, and does it only take stress and responsibility to reveal it—as a car accident and an X-ray brought to light a mass near Pam's brain? What is our future, if I continue to give way?*

We are home by 9:00, back in our own house—and ready to turn in, but suddenly I must take charge of all her meds. Shouldn't we have practiced this, under supervision, before we left the hospital?

Three times in the night, Pam is up to use the bathroom. I rise with her, walk beside her, steady her. We both sleep poorly.

> The Scarecrow listened carefully, and said, "I cannot understand why you should wish to leave this beautiful country and go back to the dry, gray place you call Kansas."
>
> "That is because you have no brains," answered the girl. "No matter how dreary and gray our homes are, we people of flesh and blood would rather live there than in any other country, be it ever so beautiful. There is no place like home."
> — L. Frank Baum[55]

The next days are filled with good moments, but much busier than I would like. We shop for groceries, and pick up seven weeks' worth of

[55] L. Frank Baum, *The Wonderful Wizard of Oz* (Chicago: George M. Hill, 1900), chap. 4; available at *Project Gutenberg*, accessed December 19, 2021, https://www.gutenberg.org/files /55/55-h/55-h.htm.

mail at the post office. We return overdue library books, including *Mad Cow Nightmare*, and pay fines. I stay up late paying bills.

We get reacquainted with neighbors, and Pam's daughter visits with the grandkids. They are great, entirely natural with Pam. (Sample question, from the three-year-old, addressed to his mom out of an innocent upturned face: "Can I poop in these pants?"—after which he is rapidly whisked away into a bathroom.) Pam delights in the kids, and manages to find presents for them.

Following this visit, at my request, Pam's daughter writes an email update:

> Mom seemed to be getting around a lot better than I imagined. She was walking and even going up and down the stairs on her own, albeit slowly and using different techniques similar to my toddlers. I was also impressed with the way she managed to get ideas across even though specific words often elude her. She uses a lot of gestures and some of what she would say reminded me of a game of Taboo. I left feeling relieved with how much she's improved from the first couple of weeks post-surgery and was reassured that she is indeed still in there. Watching her interact with the grandkids and tease John just like old times brought tears to my eyes. Anyway, the three of us had a really good "talk."

Friends and family bring food, which is very welcome. Pam can now eat anything except very dense foods like nuts. A bigger problem is that many dishes taste or look strange to her, and she won't eat them. I have little success in predicting her changing tastes, and mealtimes remain a daily challenge.

A wonderful handyman postpones other jobs to come and safety-proof the house, installing grab bars by the toilets and in the shower stall, a sloping railing beside the front steps, and a horizontal railing all along the second-floor hallway, for Pam to grip as she heads to the bathroom at night.

These tasks had to wait till now simply because we didn't leave a house key with any of our great friends. We were so confident that everything would go swimmingly, and that we'd be home in two weeks.

Neighbors have mowed our lawn and watered our few flowers. But there's been quite a drought, and a row of young trees, planted just this year, are all dead. Eventually I make time to replace them, but for some days they stand like stark sentinels, gaunt, brown-leafed, accusing. Stricken.

I take Pam to a physical therapist, the one she's worked with before, and we schedule three appointments per week. His homework assignment is that we should walk fifteen minutes a day. We no longer need a walker or a special belt. She is stable enough just to grasp my arm.

Pam's primary care physician helps with referrals, overall planning, and a handicapped tag for the car. But the first appointment is mostly taken up with me filling him in; despite all my requests and authorizations, the hospitals haven't sent him any records.

We attend church, and Pam loves the twenty minutes or so of singing. The rest is impossible for her to follow. I am aware, as never before, that our church services are mainly a series of monologues: announcements, sermons, many of our prayers—even though the apostle Paul says that "the kingdom of God is not a matter of talk but of power" (1 Cor. 4:20). How I wish I could take her to messy, uproarious renewal or revival services, filled with the presence and power of God. Failing that, I wish some local church would bring back that old standard, the children's sermon: a short narrative with visual aids.

Our friends Cheri and Pat come to our rescue, for some months hosting an evening service in their home, just the four of us. And our pastor and his wife come often to our house to pray with us.

I drive Pam to each appointment. Almost every day, I am on the phone with our insurance provider—as I tell Pam, "fighting with idiots." Because her tumor was discovered following a car accident, some of the initial medical expenses are chargeable to our auto insurance. Naturally, our medical insurance provider is trying to make out that *everything* stems from the accident. It should rank as a great medical anomaly that driving your car into a concrete barrier can give you a fifteen-year-old brain tumor.

It often takes me half an hour to sort out meds, and longer to make meals. After a couple of weeks, I ask all our kind meal preparers to stop; I am hopeful that we can cook together, further spurring her recovery. But it's a bumpy process, and we eat out a lot. Once, on impulse, I buy the ingredients for cranberry bread. They sit awhile. One day Pam opens the bag of cranberries, announces, "This looks really good, John!" and pops one into her mouth. A moment later, "Haa-ack!" and a lot of spitting as she tastes the bitter fruit.

I am finding, too, that it falls to me to serve as a gatekeeper—to keep an eye on Pam's stress and energy levels, and to say no to people and occasions that may overwhelm her. Well-meaning folks want to include her in large gatherings, but these are the worst settings because there's too much stimulation. On a good day, during her high-energy hours, she can follow a conversation and perhaps contribute to it. But place her in a noisy atmosphere with three conversations going at once, and she lacks the ability to select one and ignore the others. She simply drowns in a sea of noise.

I have to get back to work, but my days are eaten up by planned appointments and endless interruptions. I begin staying up till 3:00 a.m. each night, just to get work done, and then till 4:00.

I come down with another cold.

*   *   *

The phone rings again as I'm in my office, typing. Carelessly, I pick up without checking call waiting. Curses! It's Jim, passing along a problem: "One of the websites we branch to has a picture of naked men dancing."

Ever the consummate professional, I investigate: "Okay, and what were you searching for when you found it?"

"No, no," he stresses; "a teacher reported it."

"Uh-huh. Sure, Jim. A *teacher*." And we are off to the races. Truth be told, a big part of this job involves the deft and diplomatic handling of complaints. As I've often mentioned to Jim (who needs rather to be reminded than informed), when users call me to complain, I like to express my sympathy and then encourage them to pursue the proper channels. "I tell them, 'You need to let my boss know. He won't listen to me, but he'll hear it from you.' Then I give them your name and your home number. 'He's a night owl,' I say, 'so the best time to call is around 2:00 in the morning. And he's really hard of hearing, so be sure to shout.'"

Today, I am just getting warmed up about the nude dancers when Pam bursts in. She announces that TV is talking about tomato warnings, and says she's called for help. On her heels is a small army of friendly firemen, kindly checking our smoke alarms. Waylaid by a homophone!—a pair of like-sounding words. Jim enjoys the commotion at my end, and from the memory vault of his misspent youth dredges up the movie *Attack of the Killer Tomatoes*.

Our lives are back to normal.

Everywhere we go in Lawrence, Pam knows people, even if she can't come up with their names. In the grocery store, she recognizes fruits and vegetables. I can almost see her brain making connections.

She is talking more, and her language is improving, but sometimes we both stop and howl at the funny terms she comes out with: "making meestick," "another deeter amount," "half a doat." We put up post-it notes, everywhere, labeling common objects—*table, plate, cupboard*— to try to restock her vocabulary.

She still perseverates, but no longer talks of "ovens" and "licenses." Now everything is "the dollar amount"—a mouthful, but maybe appropriate now that we're out of hospitals and back to a world of purchases. Sometimes, she will even exclaim, "Oh, a dollar AMOUNT!"

as if she is having a private "Eureka!" moment that she can't quite share with the rest of the class.

Many of our conversations still seem to have been scripted for the Theater of the Absurd: "John, where are the dollar amounts?" Me: "WHAT dollar amounts?" Pam: "You know, those dollars." Me: "Do you mean food? Pills?" Pam: "Yes." Me: "Which one?" Pam: "The dollar amount."

> Our conversations don't always make sense but they are wonderful. — Abigail Thomas[56]

Names are difficult. Pam calls Walmart "Vomit"—which seems oddly appropriate, but causes a certain amount of confusion: "John, can we go to Vomit?" When we finally start outpatient speech therapy, Pam works with a woman named Katie, but persists in referring to her as "Weevil." On many days, I am "Jeff" or "Michael," and once "John Never."

We pray together. "God," she says solemnly one night, "please bless John." Pause. She opens her eyes, looks at me. "Are you John?"

Another night, I burst out laughing as she prays, "God, please bless John's face." I'm tempted to ask what's wrong with my face, but am relieved to think that it's nothing a good blessing won't fix.

She starts writing. One day it's her name—just that, but she isn't tracing or copying. Three weeks later, she spontaneously writes all the days of the week—spelling even "Wednesday" correctly—and then wonders aloud, "Where did that come from?" But I have been cautioned that this type of performance, reciting the sequence of months or days without being able to pick out the current member, is the signal characteristic of *automatic language*.[57]

---

[56] Abigail Thomas, *A Three Dog Life* (Orlando, FL: Harcourt, 2006), 62.

[57] The English neurologist John Hughlings Jackson drew the distinction between (parroted) *automatic* speech and (conscious, meaningful) *propositional* speech. See, e.g., Oliver Sacks, *Musicophilia: Tales of Music and the Brain* (New York and Toronto: Alfred A. Knopf, 2007), 217-18.

She journals voluminously. I joke that she is writing, over and over, *Kill John! John must die!* but in fact these are rich and varied musings, often chasing after some memory. Some words and sentences are garbled, but the gist is usually clear. Oddly, she can't read what she has just written.[58]

I try to hire caregivers to keep her company from 10:00 to 6:00 on weekdays, so that I can work. We don't need nurses, but I hope that these companions can drive her to appointments, practice conversation, and work with her as she relearns cooking and daily living activities. One in particular seems perfect: a young woman whom Pam has hired several times in the past, for everything from yard work to sorting through old clothes. They've always had a good, playful rapport.

Fairly quickly, we discover that Pam finds these helpers mostly irksome. She is private, and doesn't enjoy the pressure of having to entertain someone; she is independent, and reacts sharply against any perceived attempt to "manage" her; she tires quickly and unpredictably, and needs rest. As social as she is, and as good as they are, she doesn't want them. One by one, abruptly, she fires everyone I find.

And so we are left mostly alone. She appears to prefer it that way, and to enjoy much of our life together. Chatting with her doctor's receptionist, she confides happily, "It's so nice not to be normal again!"

She also gives me perhaps the greatest backhanded compliment of all time: "I love hanging out with you. When I'm with you, I don't feel so messed up."

THREE CITIES

> For none of us lives to himself alone and none of us dies to himself alone. — Rom. 14:7, NIV84

And now a word about Lawrence, Kansas.

---

[58] Taylor (*My Stroke of Insight*, 110) reports a similar inability to read what she'd just written, although she was typing, and Pam was writing longhand.

We are not as individual and solitary as we fancy. Not only do believers become the body of Christ, but the whole groaning creation coheres in Him. Small as we are, we take this in by way of little microcosms, and so place is important: we cannot live in a community without in some measure sharing its spirit, and gathering up into our own stories something of its hopes and fears.

Pam's stroke and recovery have been lived out mainly in three cities. First came **Baltimore**, where she nearly died. Like most cities, its beauty is deeply shadowed. A cab driver told me of high crime rates and wrenching poverty. The hospital resembles a fortress, not just on the day when police kept siege outside.

> The truth is that we neither live nor die as self-contained units. — Rom. 14:7, Phillips

While Pam was still at Hopkins, I thought of Fort McHenry. During the War of 1812, the sight of this Baltimore landmark inspired Francis Scott Key to write "The Star-Spangled Banner." Push past its familiarity and think of the author's central image: the rockets' red glare lights up the dark sky and shows that, despite heavy bombardment, the fort hasn't fallen to the enemy. The flag is still standing, still waving—just as Pam emerged from the night of coma still singing, circling her one good hand in praise. Like the landmark, she was unvanquished; as Baltimore must, she modeled endurance, persevering unto victory.

Washington, DC is different. Laid out on a rational plan, designed to be a grand and stately capital, it became a repository for the nation's pains, especially the agonizing and persistent ones.

There is a peculiar phrase in Scripture. Though God is "the Father of compassion and the God of all comfort, who comforts us in all our troubles" (2 Cor. 1:3-4), though the Holy Spirit is given as our Comforter or Counselor (John 14:16-17; Jer. 8:18), still some believers "refuse to be comforted": Jacob when he believes his son Joseph has died; David when his son is deathly ill; all Israel, north and south, personified as weeping Rachel, when her posterity is carried away into exile. Though surrounded by loving comforters, these bereaved parents—and Hannah when she cannot bear children, and the Shunammite woman whose son dies—all dig in their heels and will not be consoled.[59] This can happen in any affliction, any severe anguish:

> When I was in distress, I sought the Lord;
> at night I stretched out untiring hands
> and my soul refused to be comforted. — Ps. 77:2, NIV84

The Lord Jesus enters the world against just such a backdrop of inconsolable sorrow, Herod's "slaughter of the innocents" in Bethlehem:

> Then what was said through the prophet Jeremiah was fulfilled:
> "A voice is heard in Ramah,
> weeping and great mourning,
> Rachel weeping for her children
> and refusing to be comforted,
> because they are no more." — Matt. 2:17-18, quoting Jer. 31:15

The pain of the world rises to a crescendo, daring the gift of God even to try to assuage it. As the prophet says, "My wound is incurable!"[60]

Yet God does not rebuke the sufferers who cry to Him. He doesn't call them stubborn; He seems to accept their unwillingness to settle for easy comfort, "light" healing, as a divine restlessness, a spark of faith. He promises real comfort that will put an end to grief: the healing of the incurable wound, the restoration of the dead to full and vibrant life:

> This is what the LORD says:
> "Your wound is incurable,

---

[59] Gen. 37:35; 2 Sam. 12:17; compare 18:32-19:8; Jer. 31:15; 1 Sam. 1:7-8; 2 Kings 4:27-30.
[60] Jer. 10:19; compare 8:22; 14:19; 15:18; Lam. 2:13.

your injury beyond healing. . . .
But I will restore you to health
and heal your wounds,"
declares the LORD. — Jer. 30:12, 17

This is what the LORD says:
"Restrain your voice from weeping
and your eyes from tears,
for your work will be rewarded,"
declares the LORD.
"They will return from the land of the enemy.
So there is hope for your future,"
declares the LORD.
"Your children will return to their own land."
— Jer. 31:16-17, NIV84

Our nation's capital seems ever to be a place where "They have healed
the wound of my people lightly" (Jer. 6:14; 8:11, RSV). But "her sickness and wounds are ever before me" (6:7); the pain finds expression,
and the afflicted continue to hope for complete deliverance.

During the Civil War, the poet Walt Whitman served in Washington as a hospital volunteer, bearing witness to sheltered and half-
hidden pain and death:

Bearing the bandages, water and sponge,
Straight and swift to my wounded I go . . .
The crush'd head I dress, (poor crazed hand, tear not the
bandage away;) . . .
Thus in silence, in dream's projections,
Returning, resuming, I thread my way through the hospitals;
The hurt and wounded I pacify with soothing hand,
I sit by the restless all the dark night—some are so young;

Some suffer so much—I recall the experience sweet
and sad.[61]

More than twenty years later, asked whether he ever went back in
memory to those days at sickbeds, Whitman replied, "I do not need to.
I have never left them."[62]

One hundred years later, on the steps of the Lincoln Memorial,
Martin Luther King, Jr. declared to Washington and the nation that his
people refused to be comforted by anything less than fullness:

> There are those who are asking the devotees of civil rights,
> "When will you be satisfied?" We can never be satisfied as
> long as the Negro is the victim of the unspeakable horrors
> of police brutality. . . . We cannot be satisfied as long as the
> Negro's basic mobility is from a smaller ghetto to a larger one.
> . . . No, no, we are not satisfied and we will not be satisfied
> until justice rolls down like waters and righteousness like a
> mighty stream.[63]

Years ago I went to Washington on business. I flew on Sunday, and
chose an early flight so I'd have time to look around. I was drawn
to the Vietnam Veterans Memorial. It happened to be Father's Day,
and the area was crowded, though remarkably hushed and still. The
war had been over twenty-five years, the dead long buried; yet here
the families were, some traveling long distances to trace a name with

---

[61] Walt Whitman, "The Dresser," *Drum-Taps* (New York, 1865), 32-34; available at *The Walt Whitman Archive*, accessed December 19, 2021, http://whitmanarchive.org/published/other/DrumTaps.html.

[62] Qtd. in Angel Price, "Whitman's *Drum Taps* and Washington's Civil War Hospitals," at *American Studies at the University of Virginia*, accessed December 19, 2021, http://xroads.virginia.edu/~cap/hospital/whitman.htm.

[63] Martin Luther King, Jr., "I Have a Dream," August 28, 1963, qtg. Amos 5:24; available at *American Rhetoric*, accessed December 19, 2021, https://www.americanrhetoric.com/speeches/mlkihaveadream.htm.

fingers. I cannot say that anyone I saw was refusing to be comforted, much less that they had gotten stuck somewhere in sorrow; but, clearly, inside them, grief still tore, and hope still camped alongside pain and loss.

As I lingered, with evening coming on, park rangers quietly began to gather up the objects left beside the wall that day: letters, cards, drawings, photographs, uniforms, medals, flags. Everything is carefully taken away and stored in a museum, added to a national deposit of pain and yearning.[64]

Something like this happens, sometimes, following a stroke or traumatic brain injury, as numerous accounts attest:

> Some patients become extremely agitated and cannot be comforted.[65]

> He said, "I want to be consoled for my pains and losses, yet don't come too close to console me. I want to be alone in my sullen misery. Which you can't understand, because I can't understand. It is a grief that is too big."

> Hearing this, we both became aware that he often took the stance of "rejecting consolation" and that it contributed to the "remoteness" of his character. He was working through a defense mechanism that had been in place since childhood and that helped him block off the immensity of his loss.[66]

It was while we were at National Rehabilitation Hospital, in Washington, that Pam began to recognize that some parts of her wound are

---

[64] See a virtual collection at the *Vietnam Veterans Memorial Fund* website, accessed December 19, 2021, https://www.vvmf.org/items/.

[65] Richard Senelick and Karla Dougherty, *Living with Brain Injury: A Guide for Families*, 2nd edition (Birmingham, AL: HealthSouth, 2001), 55.

[66] Norman Doidge, *The Brain That Changes Itself: Stories of Personal Triumph from the Frontiers of Brain Science* (New York: Penguin, 2007), 234-35.

incurable. For much of our three-week stay, she was grieving—which, at the time, frustrated me to no end. She spurned my consolations and encouragements. She wanted fullness.

When you adopt an "all or nothing" attitude, it's easy to let a few failures convince you that "all" is impossible, that you'd better settle for "nothing." I watched my dad, at a very different stage in life, stop trying, and give up. His wife had died, he'd suffered a heart attack; nurses kept urging him to get up and walk, but he couldn't find the will to care.

> Nothing could console me. What I wanted one minute, I
> did not want in the next. — Christine Hyung-Oak Lee[67]

Pam didn't do this. She exerted herself, diligently, to achieve even incremental success. Over and over, people would tell me that they were inspired by her hard work.

But it was never simply determination; she had an intemperate, tameless faith. Determination asserts, with the *Rocky* theme blaring, that I will walk again; faith stirs the foot, but also calls loudly to the passing Christ. Determination pushes past the pain; faith stores up every sorrow, and is enlarged by groaning. Determination heals lightly, visualizing success and imagining it taking shape, consoling oneself right up to the brink of despair; faith refuses lesser comforts and clings to a hope that cannot be seen. Determination clutches a wish; faith, the promises and character of God. Determination boasts that nothing can ever keep me down; faith bows down, to the dust, crying, "Lord, my children and my hopes are taken from me, and yet I know they are safe in Your hand."

Lastly, we come to **Lawrence**, where Pam had lived for some thirty years at the time of her stroke. Lawrence was founded in 1854

---

[67] Christine Hyung-Oak Lee, *Tell Me Everything You Don't Remember: The Stroke That Changed My Life* (New York: Ecco-HarperCollins, 2017), 49.

by emigrants from the Northeast determined to ensure that Kansas became a "free" (nonslavery) state. The city was sacked by proslavery forces in 1856, and devastated by Quantrill's Raid in 1863. Following the latter event, one minister wrote:

> So many had been killed that every man we met on the street seemed to come from the dead. The first salutation was: "Why, are you alive?"[68]

After the initial shock faded, succeeding generations papered over the scars and horrors, even using the raid as the basis for a proud, we-can-survive-anything optimism. Today the city seal shows a newborn phoenix rising out of flames; the motto is "From Ashes to Immortality."

This is hardly a biblical conclusion to draw. The holy God uses the fire of affliction to purge our hearts from evil; if we go through one flame but are still filled with impurities, He must raise the temperature:

> See, I will refine and test them,
> for what else can I do
> because of the sin of my people? — Jer. 9:7[69]

Those who lived through the tragedy took a different view. Here is a passage from a later sermon by survivor Richard Cordley:

> Many years ago we were reading out of the Gospels in the course of our morning worship. We had come to the account

---

[68] Richard Cordley, *Pioneer Days in Kansas* (New York, Pilgrim, 1903), 218; available at *The Kansas Collection*, accessed December 19, 2021, http://www.kancoll.org/books/cordley_pioneer/cordley.00.html. See also Cordley, *A History of Lawrence, Kansas from the First Settlement to the Close of the Rebellion* (Lawrence: Lawrence Journal, 1895; reproduced by Douglas County Genealogical Society, Walsworth Publishing, 1976), 240; available at *The Kansas Collection*, accessed December 19, 2021, http://www.kancoll.org/books/cordley_history/.

[69] Compare Jer. 6:29-30; Isa. 48:10.

of the Crucifixion. As we read, the story seemed unusually vivid. We read how Jesus went in silence from Pilate's judgment hall to Calvary, bearing his cross till he could bear it no longer and then another must bear it for him. We read how the soldiers took him and nailed him to the cruel cross, casting lots for his clothes; how the multitude gathered about him as he hung on the cross, and mocked him. One said: "Let the King of Israel come down from the cross, and we will believe him. Thou that destroyest the temple and in three days buildest it again, save thyself" [Matt. 27:42, 40, KJV, modified]. Another replied: "He saved others, himself he cannot save" [27:42]. And another said: "He trusted in God, let God deliver him now, if he wants him" [27:43]. Another, more bold still, shouted to the sufferer: "If thou be the Son of God, come down from the cross" [27:40]. Just before me sat our daughter, then a child, following the story with intense interest and growing indignation. I could see she was mightily moved. As I came to these words, "If thou be the Son of God, come down from the cross," she could contain herself no longer, and spoke out in her impulsive way, "Why didn't he come down?" Yes, why didn't he come down? I presume we have all asked that question many and many a time. Why didn't he come down and confront his foes then and there? Why didn't he come down and end all controversy as to his divine authority and power? Why didn't he come down? No answer. Christ never comes down from the cross, either in his own person or in the person of his disciples. They are all made to bear until "It is finished" [John 19:30]. They see not the promise though they witness a good report [Heb. 11:39]. "Not accepting deliverance" [Heb. 11:35] is the testimony of them all, and it is the testimony of common life as well. Again and again there is no lightening of the lot, no lifting of the load, no turning away of the blow. The blow comes—and comes hard, too. "Made perfect through suffering" was not the truth alone of the Captain of our Salvation [Heb. 2:10]. It is true of his followers as well. His people bear about in their own bodies the dying of the Lord [2 Cor. 4:10].[70]

For Cordley, faith is not an expectation of miracles but a willingness to endure sufferings. This is admirable submission, and it can lead to a deep identification with Jesus's sufferings. Taken too far, though, it becomes resignation and unbelief.

In the early twentieth century, the African American writer Langston Hughes spent much of his childhood in Lawrence, encountering segregation and racism. During a revival service, he felt pressured to convert, and complied—privately feeling it was all a lie: "I didn't believe there was a Jesus any more, since he didn't come to help me."[71]

Note how Hughes's language echoes Cordley's: Why didn't Jesus come down? Part of the spiritual history of Lawrence, which Pam would have to contend with, was an entrenched belief that miracles are rare, that usually God calls us to soldier on through suffering.

Another prominent early resident of Lawrence went further. James Henry Lane, later a U.S. senator from Kansas, told an antislavery militia group in 1857, "Jayhawks remember, 'Vengeance is mine, sayeth the Lord' [Rom. 12:19, KJV, modified], but we are His agents!"[72] Lacking a miracle, we are apt to try to become our own saviors, and others' judges.

----

[70] Richard Cordley, "'Hold Fast the Profession of Your Faith' (Hebrews 10:23)," *Sermons* (Boston: Pilgrim, 1912), 89-91; available at *Internet Archive*, accessed December 19, 2021, https://archive.org/details/sermonsbyrichard00cord.

[71] Arnold Rampersad, *The Life of Langston Hughes*, Vol. 1: *1902-1941: I, Too, Sing America* (New York: Oxford, 1986), 21.

[72] Qtd. in Sara Shepherd, "New Plaque Notes Little-Known History of KU's Oldest Building," *Lawrence Journal-World* (December 5, 2016), A1-2; available at *Lawrence Journal-World*, accessed December 19, 2021, http://www2.ljworld.com/news/2016/dec/05/plaque-completed-mark-little-known-history-kus-old/. Lane omits God's words, "I will repay."

Unvanquished (though severely injured). Inconsolable (but filled with hope). Unhealed (yet trusting, praising). These values shaped the frame of Pam's recovery.

CARE

> For I will restore health to you,
> and your wounds I will heal, says the LORD,
> because they have called you an outcast:
> "It is Zion; no one cares for her!" — Jer. 30:17, NRSV

Care is a very strange word. Consider *caregiving* and *caretaking*: although there are nuances (we are a bit more likely to say that we *give* care to persons and *take* care of property), they are virtual synonyms. Of how many things can it be said that to give it means the same as to take it?

The root meaning of *care* is a lament—an emotional state, often expressed first of all in speech.[73] It's a deep concern, allied with empathy: I am so identified with the other's deepest needs that giving and taking begin to merge. But, with our distrust of feeling ("mere sentimentality") and penchant for doing, we have developed a linguistic spectrum. At one end, *care* becomes a paralyzing state of feeling ("the cares and anxieties of life"); at the other, it is a brisk and impassive efficiency ("Our hospital cares for two thousand patients").

The biblical writers mostly marvel at the care—the affectionate interest and thoughtful tending—extended by God to His creation:

> When I consider your heavens,
> the work of your fingers . . .
> what is mankind that you are mindful of them,
> human beings that you care for them? — Ps. 8:3-4; Heb. 2:6

---

[73] *Webster's Seventh New College Dictionary* (Springfield, MA: G. & C. Merriam, 1971), 126. (Hereafter *Webster's*.)

We all doubt this sometimes—as the disciples reproachfully ask Jesus, "Teacher, do you not care that we are perishing?" (Mark 4:38, NRSV), and as the religious leaders try to kindle unbelief in Jesus Himself, taunting Him as He dies: "He trusts in God; let God deliver Him now if He cares for Him *and* will have Him" (Matt. 27:43, Ampl). Still, when "no man cares for my life *or* my welfare" (Ps. 142:4, Ampl), the psalmist turns to the good and bountiful God. When Jesus works miracles, the people erupt in wonder and praise:

> A great Prophet has appeared among us! And God has visited His people [in order to help and care for and provide for them]! — Luke 7:16, Ampl

Peter invites us to lean with our full weight upon our mighty God: "Cast all your anxieties on him, for he cares about you" (1 Peter 5:7, RSV).[74]

More problematic is our care for one another. In Jesus's parable, the good Samaritan takes care of the beaten man—up to a point; then he hires another to take care of him (Luke 10:34-35). Within the body of Christ, there is a corporate responsibility: "the members all alike should have a mutual interest in *and* care for one another" (1 Cor. 12:25, Ampl). Yet, ultimately, it still comes round to each one of us. In His simplest scenario of Judgment Day, the one that always startles us to silence, Jesus Himself stands before us, before me; and though He now shines in all His glory, He says, in part, "I was sick and you visited Me with help *and* ministering care" (Matt. 25:36, Ampl). Or He says—and the terrible accusation drops echoing; this is all that matters; it pierces at once my every excuse—He says,

---

[74] Many of our English versions, going back to KJV, use "cares" twice in this verse: we may cast our cares on God because He cares. But the Greek uses different words, distinguishing our worrying from His life-altering solicitude.

> I was hungry and you gave Me no food, I was thirsty and you
> gave Me nothing to drink, I was a stranger and you did not
> welcome Me *and* entertain Me, I was naked and you did not
> clothe Me, I was sick and in prison and you did not visit Me
> with help *and* ministering care. — Matt. 25:42-43, Ampl

Then our dazzled eyes, just beginning to grow accustomed to glory, will be darkened again; and our minds will be staggered, no matter how often we have sought to remind ourselves of the great and elusive truths. For on that day even the righteous, betraying themselves, will answer a gasping, "Lord, when—?"

And at last—too late for most of us, as we depart still uncomprehending—at last will come the revelation: not of His glory (that is the easy part, though it be overwhelming), but of the strength of His love for "the least of these," the ones He calls brother and sister. He has chosen the least esteemed in all the earth to be His reward; He sees them as lambs and gathers them up, and carries them close to His chest (Isa. 40:10-11). No mature sheep—able and self-sufficient, fruitful and wool-producing—can ever come between these little ones and His heart. So pure is His humility that, even as Judge and King, He stands in the lowest place of all; and if I have not followed Him there—if I have clung to the tatters of my imagined dignity, and fashioned for myself a middle ground, a modest stronghold of deflecting, deferential pride—if I live a thousand daily self-serving lies, I will lose Him, eternally.

On that day, when I stand before Him, He will not ask me whether I drove Pam to appointments or paid some bills. It won't buy me much if I can think of a rare day when she got angry and chewed me out, and I bit my tongue and didn't lash back. The single question will be, *Did I love and serve her with devotion, getting down low to wash her feet, honoring her as I would the King of Glory?*

And not her only. In that instant, I believe, He will appear to me arrayed in many faces, His persistent, suitor's visitations throughout my life. Can I hope that He will accept me if I despised all but one of His outstretched appeals? I have already averted my gaze, closed my heart, turned my steps from the beggars of Hong Kong and New Delhi. How many more can I fail? Pam is only the most patient of His manifestations to me, offering me the most chances.

And yet . . . He does not wish me to fail. He sends Pam, and others, as church bells that call me to prayer. My heart is selfish and bent. I do not lament with others for more than an hour; I cannot care adequately for even an uncomplicated plant; I need the compassion and kindness of God, His steadfast love, His heart of mercy. I am, at my very best, the man with a barren cupboard who goes at midnight to rouse a resourceful friend, begging bread on behalf of another in need (Luke 11:5-10). On Judgment Day, if I am welcomed, it will not be because I discovered in myself some strength to love. Rather, all creation will witness the enactment of a holy mystery: Jesus Himself in His humiliation, incarnate as pain and need, encountering Jesus Himself in His gracious, outpouring love.

> Again Jesus said, "Simon son of John, do you love me?"
> He answered, "Yes, Lord, you know that I love you."
> Jesus said, "Take care of my sheep." — John 21:16

Jesus comes—still, always, till that day—"to seek out and to save the lost" (Luke 19:10, NRSV). In Pam and the others, He knocks at the door of my bolted heart, begging to save me from myself. She is God's gift to me, far more than I can be to her.

I need every reminder, every sticky note; I always forget. On that day, it will come to me as a complete surprise that Jesus was there, all along, in the Pam who teased me as "pathetical" and asked God to bless my face. Still, here and now, day to day, I can hope for this much: that I learn to see her as He does. He has showed it to me in a fleeting story:

> The kingdom of heaven is like treasure hidden in a
> field, which a man found and covered up; then in his

joy he goes and sells all that he has and buys that field.
— Matt. 13:44, RSV

We have an inclination to read this parable backward, with Jesus as the buried prize and ourselves as the seeker who possesses the wisdom to recognize Him and the brave faith to give up all we have. In fact, we are the ones trapped in dirt. Jesus has journeyed far, and dug down very low, to find us. He sees in us, in Pam, a rare and beautiful jewel; a true collector, He is not moved by avarice, but His heart leaps with a lover's joy. Initially, He hides her again, not to suppress but to safeguard, covering her with His wings. He goes and pays a great price, which all think exorbitant, because none but Jesus can fully, properly see Pam's value. He lays down His life for her, and this changes everything. Before, she was simply entombed; now she is buried with Him (Rom. 6:4; Col. 2:12)—since He, too, has gone to ground; and when He rises from the dead, her "life is now hidden with Christ in God" (Col. 3:3).

The prize securely in His possession, He draws it forth gradually. Her heart is not a treasure like oil, that gushes out at once; it is like ore, to be mined and broken and sifted and refined over time, slowly. He alone has the patience and skill to attempt this process, and He does it with delight. Passersby marvel, because He's not stripping off mere rocks and dirt; rather, He seems to be destroying a *field*—a productive, fruitful outer life. "What a waste," comments one; "I coulda got two thousand bushels of wheat outta that land." But He sees a hidden treasure worth far more; and so He guards, and digs, and sifts.

And waits. And so must I.

*   *   *

One of Pam's chief concerns before her surgery was that, if things went badly, she'd have to depend on me to take care of her. She had stout reasons: I am a lousy cook. I get overwhelmed, which in turn kindles her anxieties. I don't multitask. I am not forceful in shushing her and countermanding her impulses, nor in mounting siege against doctors and insurance providers until she gets the help she needs. I am not technically savvy. I am busy with work, and distracted by its demands. I make inappropriate jokes.

Plus, as our pastor points out, it's difficult to change well-established roles, particularly in our closest relationships. "John's your husband; he can't suddenly become your teacher," he tells Pam.

Worst of all, probably, our moods become enmeshed. She often complains that I make her anxious, or that our separate anxieties ping-pong and escalate. Just before we flew to Baltimore, she wrote to a friend:

> *Both of us were filled w/ anxiety today as we began packing—My doc had prescribed an anti-anxiety med 4 me but John was white-knuckling it. The poor guy kept snapping @ me 2nite and that was so against his nature that God gave me the grace to see it for what it was—stress—and I was able to just ignore it until he finally calmed down. . . . I'd been thinking I'd like to just move in w/ you after surgery irregardless as 2 whether he had 2 travel 4 business. I'm over that now cuz I gently confronted him + learned he simply felt helpless.*

I don't disagree—heck, if I had a stroke, I wouldn't want someone like me as my caregiver. I keep marveling at the ways of God. I am one of those people who can do only a few things well—in my case, these mostly involve getting off by myself to think and write. One might suppose that God was shaping me to do exactly that, to use what strengths I have . . . and then Pam's stroke yanks me out of my comfort zone and saddles me with endless tasks, all of which I perform badly.

I can glimpse, at times, how this stretching is good for *me*—how weighty responsibilities cause me to despair of my own strength and cry out to the God who sustains and saves. But how is this beneficial for Pam? I cast about for biblical analogies. I recognize that Job's afflictions and losses prepare him for a deeper revelation of God, but is it an essential part of the process that he should be "supported" by friends who are "worthless physicians" (Job 13:4) and "miserable comforters" (16:2)? Balaam's eyes must be opened to see the living God, but, out of all the possible methods for accomplishing this, is the best one really to frustrate him with a talking jackass (Num. 22:21-31)?

Pam certainly experiences frustration. Sometimes in anger she complains that I am a terrible caregiver, or none at all. For a little while we take to telling people that I am her helper monkey; this lightens the moment, and serves as a public acknowledgment that I'm not dominating or even guiding her recovery. But the quip ceases to be funny whenever she needs help.

Every now and then, someone suggests that Pam should have one trained professional to serve as care coordinator or case manager, overseeing all the specialists and watching for additional, unaddressed needs. But we never find anyone to fill this role. This is a major reason why the remainder of this book has to be written topically, rather than as a chronological narrative. Once she became an outpatient, we lost all coherence; we have turned into a pair of vaudeville performers, rushing madly about the stage, trying to keep an assortment of plates all spinning at once—therapies, doctors, pills, exercises, rest, meals, routines. Except in the eyes of insurance providers, nothing is ever finished, accomplished; we just continue scrambling. A good day is one on which no plates crash to the ground and shatter.

Recovery is a long road. One student of neuroscience outlines five stages of neuroplastic healing.[75] They cannot be rushed, but neither will they happen without steady and persistent effort. So we set out, each day. For me, as perhaps for most spouses, it has been "an essential article of faith that [Pam] could think as clearly as ever" and "that in

---

[75] Norman Doidge, *The Brain's Way of Healing: Remarkable Discoveries and Recoveries from the Frontiers of Neuroplasticity* (New York: Viking-Penguin, 2015), 108-13. A survivor has attempted to identify five *emotional* stages—anxiety, weariness, emptiness, isolation, anger ([Miller], *Stroke*, 17)—but it is difficult to match this progression to the experiences of others.

most cases of aphasia nothing is permanently lost."[76] It may be that this insistent optimism gets in the way at times, causing me to be impatient with the process and unappreciative of small gains.

In these early days of our return, I often look back wistfully at the long afternoons in Hopkins. At the time it all seemed an overwhelming trial because her mind and body were severely injured. Still, her spirit lived, and as we sat, sang, worshipped, prayed, held hands, the Spirit of God seemed very close. In retrospect, it was a foothill of the Mountain of Transfiguration, a place where the glory shone. Like Peter, James, and John, we loved it there, and tried to set up camp (Matt. 17:1-9), but Jesus led us downward, back into the world of busyness and conflict. At home we make time to pray, and sometimes to sing, and we resume our hand-holding walks; but now we move in shadows, warmed only by remembered glory.

With no guide, no care coordinator, and no plan, Pam has to take charge of her own recovery. Help is available, but she has to conceive goals and find motivation. My attempts to help are usually tone-deaf: when I caution, I am overprotective, and when I prompt, it generally strikes her as stress and leads to a seizure or a migraine. It is her attitude, her hope, her faith, her strength, her prayers, and, yes, her anger that not only keep her going but cause her to get up and start going again each time she crashes. Because she cares, she receives care.

ENVIRONMENT

> But those who suffer he delivers in their suffering;
> he speaks to them in their affliction.
> He is wooing you from the jaws of distress
> to a spacious place free from restriction, . . . — Job 36:15-16

After a major change in life, home can turn into a fickle friend or a depleted soil. While she was in the rehab hospital, the image of home

---

[76] Hale, *The Man Who Lost His Language*, 102, 157.

drew Pam on; it crystallized her hope for a return to normalcy. Yet once we are there, back in the house on Michigan Street, the very familiarity mocks and tantalizes. In every room of the house, in every corner of the yard, a dozen silent voices scream, *Why don't you know my name? Why don't you remember what to do with me?* It all chafes, like an outgrown shoe.

She has lived in this house, off and on, for twenty-eight years. It is filled with memories, but, at this point, they remind her of another self, of things she can no longer do and children who have moved on. There are many days when she wanders, lost in the mazes of the past— often reaching back to childhood, before she ever knew this house, this town; remembering, oppressed and angry, and, when I enter, greeting me with fear and rage. Some of her happy memories are recent, but geographically distant. She has almost no recollection of Hopkins, but tells me that she really misses the evenings at National, the hospital she hated, when we snuggled in her bed and she fell in love with me again. So we resume that custom. Although I have to stay up late to work, I'll get in bed with her after our prayers, perhaps waiting until she falls asleep.

> He gazed vaguely and mournfully about him, as if he missed
> something precious, and missed it the more drearily for not
> knowing precisely what it was. — Nathaniel Hawthorne[77]

She complains that she no longer hears from God. Weeping, she prays, asking Him why He is angry with her.

It is during our worship services with Cheri and Pat—at their home, which she calls a safe place—that she sometimes remembers more distinctly, and senses the presence of God.

---

[77] Nathaniel Hawthorne, *The House of the Seven Gables* (Boston: Ticknor and Fields, 1851), chap. 10; available at *Project Gutenberg*, accessed December 19, 2021, https://www.gutenberg.org/files/77/77-h/77-h.htm.

Then we go home, and the heaviness is waiting: clutter, chores, inaccessible familiarity and the overwhelming labor of recovery, my work, her aloneness and pain. She writes to me, brokenly:

Dear John,

I am sorry I was upset with my pain. Pour are kinder and lover. I have been wrong. You deserve love and perfect praise. I was so unkind. I kish I pnew better love towards you also. I'm not why I'm unshur with too many things. Jesus is the most favorite I have ever known so much of me in my life always. Jou are my berfect love I've ever had perfectly love. Things I don't thow any more in my life has changed for wears.

Still the memories flood her hours. One day she is again a child, on the road with her family, stopping for the night at a junkyard, picking out a wreck. Another day she weeps in terror, recalling the restraints at one of the recent hospitals. Even when we play Christian music over her all night, setting the CD on repeat, she has a nightmare in which a baby is taken from her. I wonder if the baby represents her own life.

Other changes swirl around us. My employer, the little startup in Connecticut, is acquired by a larger company in Texas. As part of the deal, our executives, including Jim, are let go. I share the news with Pam, and that evening she prays for "those guys who lost their dodge [jobs]." I tell her that Jim lost his "dodge" a long, long time ago.

I'm not impressed with the Texas firm,[78] but their city is home to a rare intensive aphasia program that might be great for Pam. And Jenny, still my supervisor, is relocating. So Pam and I talk about settling there,

---

[78] Sample mordant wisecracks from this period: "I work for a very biblical company—unfortunately, they're stuck on the passage about making bricks without straw"; "Have you heard about the new action figure based on our CEO? Wind him up and he kicks the Important Decision can down the road"; "My employer continues to sink slowly in frozen waters while the managers play 'Nearer, My Golden Parachute, to Thee.'"

perhaps for a couple of months. We make an exploratory visit, but it is disastrous—too much stimulation for Pam, plus I get called into the office. We come home chastened.

When spring 2011 arrives, Pam tackles yard work—and contracts poison ivy; she no longer recognizes plant species, or even tell-tale warning signs. The itching makes her frantic, and she quarrels with a neighbor.

I am still running madly, but she can see that plates are hitting the floor.

Those are our darkest days, worse than anything in either hospital. Pam seems to be caught up in a cycle. Often she wakes in pain, but she starts many days cheerfully—for she still knows the joy of the Lord; that pilot light has never entirely died out. Soon enough, though, she grows frustrated, what with failures of language and memory, hunger, pain, the house . . . a hundred things. She gives way to inarticulate rage, her outbursts deliberately escalating over time: taunting, testing. Eventually, the fury spent, she feels deep contrition; even then, her love for me has to battle both shame and fear. Usually, the old inner vow resurfaces—*I'll reject you before you can reject me*—and she again takes up the armor of rage.

We experiment with coping mechanisms: An overnight getaway together. Pets. Pam going off by herself to stay in a motel for a few days. These measures afford some relief, but it is so fleeting that we try each one only once. There is a desperation in all our endeavors.

It grows worse and worse. One day she starts writing on the walls of our living room, venting her anger. The next day she continues, but already the writing has morphed into prayer requests. Underneath all the storms of emotion, her spirit steadily lies facedown, crying out to God.

At times she seems to be ruled by impulsivity and randomness. Once she can drive, she buys truckloads of furniture, and then, a day or two after it is delivered, decides that our carpets have to go, because they make it hard for her to navigate when foot pain prompts her to use a wheelchair. Then again, when I am patient, I may sometimes see an underlying logic. As we move into summer, she puts more energy into yard work, hiring help, straining her back. I am moved to see that she takes great pains to replant and water one of the dead trees, eager to see it live again.

In September, she insists that we look at apartments, and soon we find one she likes. I try in vain to explain that this is not a prudent move financially. We have finally paid off the mortgage on the house, and are in a position to save money while working on renovations, and gradually sorting through belongings in preparation for an eventual move to a smaller home. To jump the gun and move now will add expenses and force us to accelerate the processes of fixing and downsizing—just when we are busy with her recovery.

As often happens, my logic is more wrong than right. I miss a lot. I resist change, whereas Pam is often its agent. When life turns scary, I'm still the kid clutching the edge of the pool, and Pam once more embraces the dare, launching herself on a bungee cord and a prayer. I have learned, over time, that her instincts are usually sure. In her boldness, faith is stretching.

As soon as we settle in at the apartment, Pam becomes calmer and more cheerful. She thrives in the simpler, smaller, quieter, less cluttered, stairless, temperature-controlled, maintenance-free environment. And she starts to live in the present. Despite the costs, I am soon kicking myself that we didn't do it earlier.

Sadly, I am also partly correct. During the ensuing months, I try to make time to go through the items left at the house; I sell off some furniture. But in August 2012, an upstairs pipe springs a leak, and, because we aren't residing there, the water gushes for at least twenty-four hours before we discover it and shut it off. It causes extensive damage to first-floor ceilings and walls, and also results in mold. Remediation and renovations cost us a small fortune.

In April 2014, two and a half years after the move, we at last sell the house. To me the sale comes as an immense relief, but Pam has misgivings—until, a few weeks later, driving past, she sees one of the new owners sitting on the front stoop, watching a toddler. She had sat just so with her own kids a quarter-century earlier. Something inside her relaxes, and something heals. The desire to hold on to the house and its memories has been shattered, as vain hopes must, but in its place God gives her something better: an opportunity to pass along a legacy.

ROOTS

> As therefore you received Christ Jesus the Lord, so live in him, rooted and built up in him and established in the faith, just as you were taught, abounding in thanksgiving. — Col. 2:6-7, RSV

In *Eve's Diary*, Mark Twain pays the ultimate courtly tribute to his late wife Olivia, less than two years dead. The book's final words are spoken at Eve's grave by a grief-stricken Adam: "Wheresoever she was, *there* was Eden."[79]

Here, we say, is a great and noble love. Beneath the veneer of the crusty, crabbed old master beats a tender, grieving heart. She was his light, transfiguring all surroundings. O to love, and be loved, like this!

Except that it is all a bald-faced lie. When we buy into it—when the lyrics, from "You Are My Sunshine" to "You Light Up My Life," get inside our heads—we are boarding an express train that leads directly to a mound of dirt. In that cemetery, only a few sunny graves are labeled DEATH; the vast majority are marked with obscure headstones, barely legible: HEARTBREAK, REJECTION, DISILLUSIONMENT.

And, often, STRICKEN. I think of the male night nurse who tended Pam during one of her hospital stays in Lawrence, an irritable

---

[79] Mark Twain, *Eve's Diary: Translated from the Original MS* (1905; London and New York: Harper & Brothers, 1906), 109; emphasis in original; available at *Internet Archive*, accessed December 19, 2021, https://archive.org/details/evesdiary01twaigoog.

man whose every gesture showed deep sadness; he told me that his wife, too, had suffered a stroke. "One thing's for d— sure," he said in savage summary: "she isn't the woman I married." I think of a sales assistant in an educational supplies store where we shopped, who at last confided to me that his wife, too, was in recovery; he wouldn't speak to Pam, or even look at her. And a missionary, a dear friend of my parents, who cared for her husband following his stroke, stated simply, "He wasn't himself anymore."

> . . . that Christ may dwell in your hearts through faith, as you are being rooted and grounded in love. — Eph. 3:17, NRSV

I know that I am one of the lucky ones. From the day she woke up worshipping, I have never doubted that Pam is still Pam. Slowly or not, she has come back to life in all her singing, cursing, zany, demanding, irrevocable complexity. It's so nice to see her not be normal again.

Yet she and I have also each stood grieving beside our graves of buried hopes and dreams. We have learned, fumblingly and after many failures, the aptness of an ancient New Testament phrase: that husband and wife are "heirs together of the grace of life" (1 Peter 3:7, KJV). *Heirs*, not benefactors: she cannot be my light, nor I hers. We are but empty vessels, hollowed out. Undeserving and astonished, we are adopted into the family of God through Jesus, the Elder Brother who has gone before; we are made co-inheritors, and showered with all that God has stored up for His own. We are given such abundance that we even become stewards, called to extend grace to all the least of these, and to share it with one another. For as long as we know that we are but heirs, kneeling together with empty hands and open faces turned to the Eternal Fount, we shall lack for nothing.

But romantic love is bent on making idols. We forsake the spring of living water and build our lives around broken cisterns that always leak and leave us perishing of thirst (Jer. 2:13). C. S. Lewis writes that "youthful love . . . must *always* be lost in some way: every merely natural love has to be crucified before it can achieve resurrection."[80] By early middle age, Emerson had buried his father, several siblings, and his beloved firstborn son. And still he mourned his sweetheart wife, dead fifteen years; still he strove to lift his eyes up higher:

> Though thou loved her as thyself,
> As a self of purer clay,
> Though her parting dims the day,
> Stealing grace from all alive;
> Heartily know,
> When half-gods go,
> The gods arrive.[81]

Only the living God can make an Eden. In Milton's telling, when sin results in banishment from the garden, Eve bravely says to Adam, "with thee to go, / Is to stay here." Yet as they set forth, "hand in hand, with wandering steps and slow," theirs is a "solitary way."[82] They enter the wide world as orphans, with the life-giving presence withdrawn.

And so in every generation. People of faith are "strangers and exiles on the earth," fixing our eyes on an unseen "better country" (Heb. 11:13-16, RSV), surpassing even Eden; we are pilgrims who march through wasteland singing, "All my springs (my sources of life and joy) are in you" (Ps. 87:7, Ampl). We receive even our beloveds as good gifts from His hand, knowing we cannot possess them, any more than we can catch and hold in its freshness the spray from a

---

[80] C. S. Lewis, letter to Sheldon Vanauken, February 10, 1955; qtd. in Vanauken, *A Severe Mercy* (1977; New York: HarperOne-HarperCollins, 1987), 184, 211; emphasis in original.

[81] Ralph Waldo Emerson, "Give All to Love" (1846), in Stephen E. Whicher, ed., *Selections from Ralph Waldo Emerson: An Organic Anthology*, Riverside Editions (1957; Boston: Houghton Mifflin, 1960), 437. Also available at *Emerson Central*, accessed December 19, 2021, https://emersoncentral.com/texts/poems/give-all-to-love/.

[82] John Milton, *Paradise Lost* (1667, 1674), 12:615-16, 648-49, available at *Christian Classics Ethereal Library*, accessed December 19, 2021, https://ccel.org/ccel/milton/paradiselost.

fountain. Together, as husband and wife, we dwell in impermanent lean-tos; betrothed, like Hosea and Gomer, waiting for God to come in His fullness, returning with trembling in search of His goodness (Hos. 3:3-5).

In this posture, we declare by faith that disease can rob us of nothing eternal nor essential. There is nothing on earth that our God cannot redeem, as He sent His prophet to learn by observation:

> This is the word that came to Jeremiah from the LORD: "Go down to the potter's house, and there I will give you my message." So I went down to the potter's house, and I saw him working at the wheel. But the pot he was shaping from the clay was marred in his hands; so the potter formed it into another pot, shaping it as seemed best to him. — Jer. 18:1-4

Marred, spoiled, ruined: the clay itself is flawed and impure.[83] Damaged goods. According to human logic (and especially our culture of efficiency), the Potter should cut His losses, recognize that this clay is junk, discard it, and start over with a fresh batch. He never does. Never One to give up easily, He still sees potential in the original material. Skillfully, wisely, He reworks it.

Even so, when the Potter's hands lie heavy upon us, at least we know that we are not abandoned. He has not failed us; He never will forsake us. He is reshaping us, stricken and caregiving all alike. To us His fingers may move slowly, may press against our own designs, may hurt, may seem to mar; but they have strength and skill to bring His good work to completion.

Nor is this all. Corporately, as the body of Christ, He makes us— stricken and caregiving alike—coworkers with Him, fingers as well as

---

[83] Ronald Youngblood, note on Jer. 18:4, in *The NIV Study Bible*, gen. ed. Kenneth Barker (Grand Rapids, MI: Zondervan, 1985), 1152.

clay, vessels already in service, exiles with one foot set firmly in a secure patrimony, lovers restored to the springtime of His grace:

> The LORD will guide you always;
> he will satisfy your needs in a sun-scorched land
> and will strengthen your frame.
> You will be like a well-watered garden,
> like a spring whose waters never fail.
> Your people will rebuild the ancient ruins
> and will raise up the age-old foundations;
> you will be called Repairer of Broken Walls,
> Restorer of Streets with Dwellings. — Isa. 58:11-12

Wheresoever He comes in His mercy and grace, *there* is a foretaste of heaven.

ALL GRACE

"All of you, clothe yourselves with humility toward one another, because, 'God opposes the proud but gives grace to the humble.' . . . I have written to you briefly, encouraging you and testifying that this is the true grace of God. Stand fast in it. . . . And the God of all grace, who called you to his eternal glory in Christ, after you have suffered a little while, will himself restore you and make you strong, firm and steadfast." — 1 Peter 5:5, 12, 10, NIV84

> The crayons inside my mind once sketched God's grace
> As a plump, smiling face;
> As gentle rain, without hail;
> As stores of grain, without fail;
> As a triumphant life of deeds;
> As growing fullness, shrinking needs;
> As arms to hold me every night;
> As darkness swallowed up by light;
> As all my wishes well supplied;

As Jesus always by my side—
Quite palpable, and constantly
His murmuring voice affirming me;
As all my enemies struck mute;
As huge results and instant fruit
Accrued like daily dividends;
As a warm family and friends;
As good repute; as wealth and fame;
As sufferings, but pretty tame,
And always noble, high, and grand,
And ones that I could understand;
As an angelic welcome home
Into God's stately pleasure-dome—
So I, with childish art,
Drew to myself the kindness of God's heart.

But God, confounding my designs, has shown
A grace I had not known:
Grace as an enemy
Given free rein with me;
Grace as mockery and blame,
Negligence, rejection, shame;
As countrymen who worship Baal;
As friends who practice sly betrayal;
As injustice, without courts;
As unflattering reports;
As an empty life of toil;
As dreams that others lightly spoil;
As dingy room and lonely bed;
As condemnation in my head;
As a long, helpless agony;
As burdens no one shares with me;
As dumbstruck floundering when accused;

As trying hard and feeling used;
As being put on sad display
With God unmoved, or far away;
As hardship like a senseless flood;
As consequences like dank mud;
As life bereft of plan or clue
Or point or joy or tune or hue—
Grace wielded like a rod—
Gripped in the hand of cruelty, and of God.

Yet this is grace
Because at times a stricken face,
Narrowed by pain and grief,
Sickened by a hard world of unbelief,
Harrowed by loneliness and fear,
Awful to look upon, draws near
And whispers, "Peace, My child. Don't be appalled
At Me or at My ways. For you were called
To follow in My footsteps, so to be
Done with sin, and able to know Me.
Stand fast in this true grace."—Then, Lord, I stand
Mute and entrusted, under and in Your hand.

5

PAIN

AGONY

> And all the unknown joys he gives
> Were bought with agonies unknown. — Isaac Watts[84]

Pain lies deeper than speech; it predates and outlasts thought. Sometimes we see that the whole creation is groaning (Rom. 8:22): we and it are all spread as a single skin, ashiver with nerve endings; we and it are all rolled as one gut, sucker-punched and gasping; we and it tear open as one wound, one mouth. The universe is a vast delivery room, birthing a single undernourished and wasted child; sickly and blind, it takes breath, and wails.

Offended reason tells us that the god of such a system can only be a monster. Yet the God of Scripture assures us that He hears even our groanings (Ex. 2:23-25; 6:5)—inarticulate cries of pain, devoid of faith—and accepts them as a prayer.

Pain finds its voice. It distracts the mind but focuses the heart. Created things in pain are intercessors, even for us, ceaselessly crying to God, giving themselves and Him no rest (Isa. 62:6-7).

> The disciples have their most powerful experience of seeing
> Jesus when he shows them the wounds in his hands and

---

[84] Isaac Watts, Hymn #3.12, in *Psalms and Hymns*, 935.

feet: the way forward will be into the heart of the wounds.
— Serene Jones[85]

Initially, following her stroke, Pam had no words to name or local-
ize her pain. It might show as restlessness or anger. The nurses and
I resorted to trial and error in making her comfortable. Often, her
distress went undetected. Even years later, it often happened that she
would abruptly realize, with a start, that she was having a headache.

When we first came home, I thought of her pain as manageable.
Weeks of bed rest in the first hospital had taken away her foot pain; the
tumor that had pressed against the optic nerves, making her eyes hurt,
was gone; the shoulder subluxation had resolved; and the incision pain
from her surgery had faded. I hoped that, though recovery lay ahead of
us, bodily pain lay all behind.

It was not to be. Within weeks, a physical therapist coaxed Pam into
performing toe raises. That act of stretching brought back all the pain
of her decades-old plantar fasciitis. From that time on, she was never
without foot pain—particularly in her left foot, which has suffered one
affliction after another.

Today I still take her for periodic cortisone shots in that foot. I
always jokingly ask the doctor to prepare two injections—one for my
hand, which Pam squeezes tightly throughout the procedure.

Her stroke left her with a temporomandibular joint (TMJ) disorder. Essentially, she wrenched so violently that she dislocated the
joint on each side of the jaw, displacing the cushioning discs, resulting
in bone grinding on bone. She could not open her mouth wide, nor
chew easily. Even yawning was painful. We consulted a TMJ specialist
who prescribed upper and lower appliances (bite plates) to coax the
discs back into position, and a treatment process; the whole would cost
$5,000, and our insurance provider kept referring us instead to oral

---

[85] Serene Jones, *Trauma and Grace: Theology in a Ruptured World* (Louisville, KY: Westminster
John Knox, 2009), 41.

surgeons. Remarkably, Pam declined all of this. Sitting at home, she worked diligently at moving her jaw, making stretching and chewing motions. She was able to fix the problem on her own.

The dentist also reported a decreased pain threshold, and at first was unable to complete a routine cleaning. Once the TMJ resolved, this went away. But we heard a lot about *peripheral neuropathy*— a generalized nerve pain, common among stroke survivors. It's as if, on top of everything else, the stroke had knocked some nerve endings out of whack, and they kept firing pain signals even when there was no immediate pain event. Some areas of skin became abnormally sensitive to touch.[86] This seemed a distinct possibility: I remembered Pam at Hopkins, casting off sheets, and the physical therapists instructing me to rub her legs with a soft fleece to desensitize the nerves. But when, at home, we followed up by trying a medication for neuropathy, it made her so dizzy and disoriented that we had to discontinue it at once. We were left chasing specific pains. And there were many; as she wrote once, *Why am I usually left in so much pain?*

Many survivors experience "so much pain" following stroke or traumatic brain injury. The blow falls suddenly, and it clobbers everything. One book helpfully provides a table summarizing "consequences": twenty-eight symptoms, organized into five categories: physical, cognitive, emotional, behavioral, and "secondary psychological."[87] Pain isn't even listed, though in some sense every deficit is felt as pain. Maddeningly, as the very idea of neuropathy suggests, much of this pain—even the distinctly bodily pangs—is rooted in the brain, difficult to treat, or

---

[86] On neuropathy, see Doidge, *The Brain That Changes Itself,* 177-95; Doidge, *The Brain's Way of Healing,* 1-32.

[87] Diane Roberts Stoler and Barbara Albers Hill, *Coping with Mild Traumatic Brain Injury* (Garden City Park, NY: Avery, 1998), 16.

even to enlist in treatment. "No other body part is both the thing that conducts healing and the object of the healing."[88]

Just before Thanksgiving, six weeks after our return to Lawrence, Pam became so dizzy that we rushed to our local emergency room. There she had a grand mal *seizure*,[89] terrifying to witness: face drooping on the right side, no responses, and then wild thrashing and convulsions. The nurses cushioned her and administered Ativan; the doctors scanned her brain, but found no new events. Eventually, we learned from our neurologist that scar tissue in the brain, a vestige of the tumor surgery, left her forever vulnerable to seizures. She must continue to take two anticonvulsant medications, and cannot afford to skip a dose.

That first seizure in our ER almost made me despondent, simply because the staff at Hopkins had tried to soften language, to say "seizure" and studiously avoid the word "stroke." Under their care, Pam experienced both, but one is far more devastating. Without a clear distinction in my mind, observing her convulsions, I thought, *One seizure took away her language and her memory, and messed up her entire right side. What will this one destroy?*

In fact, Pam would have numerous seizures, all scary to watch; each time, the experience and the Ativan would knock her out for a day, but then she would bounce back, good as new.

Even today, when a seizure is coming, Pam experiences an *aura*—a dizziness and a fearful sense of everything sliding out of control; almost a premonition. Her right hand may lose its grip, her speech slurs toward unintelligibility, and her face may sag. We take these symptoms very seriously and set out at once for the ER. To date, we have always arrived during the warning stages, so that the seizure, if it comes, occurs in

---

[88] Lee, *Tell Me Everything You Don't Remember*, 119.

[89] On seizures following stroke or brain injury, see Vani Rao and Sandeep Vaishnavi, *The Traumatized Brain: A Family Guide to Understanding Mood, Memory, and Behavior after Brain Injury*, A Johns Hopkins Press Health Book (Baltimore: Johns Hopkins University, 2015), 155-62.

a protective environment. But Pam has also learned to take extra medications immediately in an effort to halt the event. She has not had a full-blown seizure for several years.

What triggers an aura? Certainly stress—if we are arguing, and even sometimes if she is just straining to use the bathroom. But some incidents are mysterious, and lack any evident trigger.

Four to five years after her stroke, Pam began having *migraines*—or at least we came to recognize that some of her headaches were unusually severe and persistent. These too come with auras, and, when an aura descends, we don't know for sure which is coming, a seizure or a migraine.

Pam has also suffered discomfort in eating and digestion. She was lactose intolerant even before the stroke, but now foods taste odd to her, and some of her medications have a constipating effect. On many days, it becomes a major preoccupation to find food that looks appetizing to her, and to encourage her to eat enough of it. She is still underweight.

As a supplement, she relies on the nutritional drink Ensure, which she has an unfortunate tendency to call "Impure." I have visions of her inquiring for it by that name at the grocery store, and I tease her that she will have impure thoughts after drinking it.

Every day, Pam stretches and exercises, ices and elevates, manages medications and vitamins, plans nutrition. It takes an immense effort to keep pain at bay.

At one level, she is immensely fortunate. So many conditions are degenerative: think of the grim prospects of someone with dementia. In contrast, Pam is improving; barring a second stroke, she will continue to get better and better over time, particularly with practice and stimulation. But this comparatively sunny prognosis has also meant that, with fear at arm's length, pain can command the whole of her attention.

We have no single strategy or solution for Pam's pain. The dulling effects of medications help against headaches, seizures, arthritis. The discipline of exercise has restored mobility to jaws and limbs. At least once, loving care has soothed hypervigilant nerves. Prayer to the loving Father has brought occasional immediate relief and slow-ripening progress.

But she has also been willing to stand in the pain.

*   *   *

Pain unstrings the mind, and tunes the spirit and the heart only to sound a single shrill and ceaseless note. This is not the ordered serenade, the serenity, I crave. But I must go there, if I would know Jesus. He has called me into "the fellowship of sharing in his sufferings" (Phil. 3:10, NIV84). He walks in nature, reigns in heaven, dances in music, touches in church, but He became incarnate in a body of pain and death. He dwells in pain.

John Stott captures both the grace and the offense presented by a suffering God:

> In the real world of pain, how could one worship a God who was immune to it? I have entered many Buddhist temples in different Asian countries and stood respectfully before the statue of the Buddha, his legs crossed, arms folded, eyes closed, the ghost of a smile playing round his mouth, a remote look on his face, detached from the agonies of the world. But each time after a while I have had to turn away. And in imagination I have turned instead to that lonely, twisted, tortured figure on the cross, nails through hands and feet, back lacerated, limbs wrenched, brow bleeding from thorn-pricks, mouth dry and intolerably thirsty, plunged in God-forsaken darkness. That is the God for me! He laid aside his immunity to pain. He entered our world of flesh and blood, tears and death. He suffered for us. Our sufferings become more manageable in the light of his.[90]

[90] John R. W. Stott, *The Cross of Christ* (1986; Downers Grove, IL: InterVarsity, 2006), 326-27.

And, standing in the blasted aftermath of World War I, Edward Shillito invokes the "Jesus of the Scars":

> The other gods were strong; but thou wast weak;
> They rode, but thou didst stumble to a throne;
> But to our wounds only God's wounds can speak,
> And not a god has wounds, but thou alone.[91]

My proud, fearful mind would rather contemplate the bloodless expiration of Socrates, the ancient Greek philosopher, as described by Plato in the dialogue *Phaedo*.[92] Sentenced to death by the court of Athens, he calmly drinks poison and continues to discourse upon philosophy and the soul. It is a serene and noble death, rising above the body and its pain without regrets. Again, like Stott, I am drawn to the Buddha—though he tells a grieving mother to go and beg a bowl of rice from a home which has not seen death; and when she cannot find one, his final word is only, "No one can escape death."[93] In other words, *Resign yourself to pain and grief. Get over it.*

But Pam is racked by pain; her body fails her every day. All of the sensations most present to her consciousness are forms of pain. I cannot, in good conscience—or as I hope for domestic tranquility—simply tell her to resign herself or to rise above. She doesn't have those luxuries; she is in pain. To her wounds "only God's wounds can speak."

---

[91] Edward Shillito, "Jesus of the Scars" (1917); qtd. in Stott, 328. Also available at *Poetry Explorer*, accessed December 19, 2021, https://www.poetryexplorer.net/poem.php?id=10126835. Compare Dietrich Bonhoeffer: ". . . only a suffering God can help." *Letters and Papers from Prison* (Minneapolis: Fortress, 2010), 479, letter of July 16, 1944; qtd. in Philip Yancey, *The Question That Never Goes Away* (Grand Rapids, MI: Zondervan, 2013), 86.

[92] See the modern (2016) translation by George Theodoridis at *Bacchicstage*, accessed December 19, 2021, https://bacchicstage.wordpress.com/plato/.

[93] Christian Mission to Buddhists, *The Gospel in Chinese Art* (Shatin, Hong Kong: Tao Fong Shan Christian Institute, 1964, 1972), 46.

Our English word *agony* denotes "pain too intense to be borne."[94] The Greek root *agonia* derives from *agon*, an athletic contest:[95] think of a wrestling match against a powerful but unseen opponent or ant*agon*ist.

Today we contrive to keep pain private, to hide the sufferer, quarantine the hurt; to shield ourselves and others. But the *agon*, the contest, is inherently a public spectacle. I see Pam in the food court, attracting the young people to her story; I recall the nurses gathering at her bedside to pray. Despite our niceties and our best efforts, nothing is hidden. Pain is always on the main stage.

Jesus was "in an agony," an *agonia*, in the garden of Gethsemane (Luke 22:44, RSV). Not only then, it is safe to assume: the contestants who battled and bled in the lonely place, almost unobserved, continued their savage conflict before all eyes, in the outdoor court, through the streets, and on the bare hillside. Here there was no gentle resignation, no noble rising above, but agony: brutish combat, bloody sacrifice. Even the idle onlookers—even I, even we—turn our faces from One so marred, so disfigured (Isa. 53:2-3).

Yet, in this awful spectacle, "the punishment that brought us peace was on him" (Isa. 53:5). So, now, He Himself is our peace (Eph. 2:14; John 14:27).

When Pam wakes in an agony, a "pain too intense to be borne," I am of little help to her. I am the gawking looker-on. I am the disciples, "sleeping for sorrow" (Luke 22:45, RSV) while the battle rages. I toss off a flippant prayer for healing, and grow impatient when she continues to hurt. I head back to the drive-through window of popular Christianity, and scan a menu where pain has been airbrushed away, and feed my mind on a diet of quick faith and easy triumph. Demand a miracle . . . or your money back. (Some restrictions apply.)

---

[94] *Webster's*, 243, under synonyms for *distress*.
[95] *Vine's Complete Expository Dictionary of Old and New Testament Words* (Nashville: Thomas Nelson, 1984, 1996), New Testament section, 20 (*agony*). (Hereafter *Vine's*.)

But Jesus comes to me, in the still clarity of parable, resplendent in glory and formed to many faces, Pam's among them, and the common denominator of all the "least of these" is pain. Persistent pain, that I can't wish or wick or whisk away. Pain that must be fed, clothed, and given a home, visited and cared for. Pain that refuses to leave me feeling good about myself; that discomfits, demanding, not drowsy incantation, but throbbing, groaning faith.

When Pam is gripped by pain she cannot bear, her face is still turned toward me. More truly than she realized, she wrote to me, *I love you with all my hurt*. My empathy is shallow. I let her down. She is the battleground, and I am only a supply sergeant at headquarters, requisitioning gauze.

But Jesus does not fail her. He meets her precisely in her inarticulate, defenseless pain: she is the fledgling bird, peeping and fluttering; and He is the mother advancing with warm wings outspread. He gathers, enfolds, shelters, and shields; and she nestles, feeling His heartbeat, never even noticing that He is all bloodied.

As Kevin Prosch sings, "Quieter than rain, He knows all your pain."[96]

There is a holy mystery here, and I am largely shut out from it. I hear the communion within, and the door is labeled FAITH, but the only key is called AGONY.

ANGUISH

Too happy Time dissolves itself
And leaves no remnant by —
'Tis Anguish not a Feather hath
Or too much weight to fly —
— Emily Dickinson[97]

---

[96] Kevin Prosch, "Harp in My Heart" (Forerunner Worship, 2002).

[97] Emily Dickinson, #1774 (ca. 1870), in Thomas H. Johnson, ed., *The Complete Poems of Emily Dickinson* (New York and Boston: Little, Brown, 1960), 716. (Hereafter Dickinson, *Complete Poems*.) Also available at *Wikisource*, accessed December 19, 2021, https://en.wikisource.org/wiki/Too_happy_Time_dissolves_itself.

Pain invades the body, but its sights are set further on. The mind and emotions seek shelter in some inner sanctum of the self, but the barrier is only a flimsy curtain, easily penetrated. There is no immunity. The Greek *pathema*, "sufferings," signifies both afflictions and their consequent emotions.[98] English has numerous inadequate words for distress of mind; *anguish* "suggests torturing grief or dread."[99] Pushing past the body's pain, the public *agon*, this is the sword-tip that pierces in private or even dismembers the self:

> My God, my God, why have you forsaken me?
> Why are you so far from saving me,
> so far from my cries of anguish?
> My God, I cry out by day, but you do not answer,
> by night, but I find no rest. — Ps. 22:1-2

A stroke does not cut off thoughts and emotions; it bursts a dam and sets them free to cascade. Pam has walked or surged the entire valley, groping or sloshing her lightless way through every twist and turn.

There is, first, the overwhelming grief, the sense that a life has been lost, and even a person. John Hale, aphasic following a stroke, put on a brave face for his wife, until the day when she arrived early at the hospital, and found him weeping, in despair:

> He pushed me away. He opened his mouth and pulled at his tongue and lips. He grabbed a pencil and scribbled violently in the air and then threw it on the floor. He did a wordless imitation of himself trying to enunciate words. He mimed himself as an idiot, head lolling, index finger in his mouth, eyes rolling. He began to talk in his wordless voice. I listened and realized that I understood what he was saying.[100]

---

[98] *Vine's*, New Testament section, 17 (*afflict[-ed]*, *affliction*).
[99] *Webster's*, 834, under synonyms for *sorrow*.
[100] Hale, *The Man Who Lost His Language*, 60.

Spouse, family, friends grieve too: "I'd never before had to mourn for someone who was still alive."[101] Often, these manifold griefs remain separate and silent.[102]

Like so many survivors, Pam retained an inner sense of self but lost most of the abilities, relationships, and activities that clothed that identity. The heaviness of grief pressed down on her in a silent, empty place:

> *I miss people daily.*
> *I am unable to take myself place's without pain.*
> *When John drive's me places to get help I'm happy.*
> *Yet, I get so depressed once we arrive home.*
> *John offer's me anything I often turn him down.*

This journal entry is undated, but she might have written it on almost any day since her stroke. She teeters on the edge of hopelessness. Once she overheard a family member tell someone else, "If I had Pam's problems, I'd put a gun to my head." The remark was well-intentioned, even empathetic, but it left her with a renewed sense of questioning the value of her existence.

---

[101] Diane Ackerman, *One Hundred Names for Love: A Stroke, a Marriage, and the Language of Healing* (New York and London: W. W. Norton, 2011), 41. Lori Fox writes, "We have no place in our culture for this kind of grief; when someone dies, we have a funeral, and everyone comes and holds the people who are left behind and says *We are so sorry for your loss.* This was unavailable to me. I faced this grief alone. Gabrielle was still there—it just wasn't the *her* I had loved." "Not Dead but Gone: How a Concussion Changed My Girlfriend's Personality Forever," *The Guardian* (April 24, 2019); emphasis in original; available at *The Guardian*, accessed December 19, 2021, https://www.theguardian.com/lifeandstyle/2019/apr/24/grief-brain-injury-took-girlfriend-away.

[102] ". . . I grieved for him, for the lost and previous Paul. He grieved for that man, too. Both our griefs were mainly private, internal, unuttered." Ackerman, *One Hundred Names for Love*, 286.

> . . . violent pain of mind, like violent pain of body, *must* be
> severely felt. — Samuel Johnson[103]

Agony and frustration kindle anger, but after every outburst comes the cudgel, the "crippling or disabling" pain of conscience.[104] One sees this in one of Pam's earliest letters to me after we came home, in the poignant statement *I am sorry I was upset with my pain.*

In the silence of aphasia, anxiety reverberates, rising easily to panic.[105] Pam wrote to me, grasping for words (and, when she couldn't find them, drawing blank lines), after a tense evening drive to the emergency room. She was experiencing an aura, and couldn't wait; when I stopped for a red light, she jumped out of the car and speed-limped off, and I had to chase her down. Next day, she wrote:

> *I'm sorry I let my behaviour blast out on you alone. I'd learned what would happen if I'd fallen through on a seizure. . . . Now I am derified every time I begin to _____ I FREAK OUT! So, please run faster and honk the car each time I let you know somethings happening. Do Not slow down, wait till you place our _____ 2 carry me 2 our car. Please!*

---

[103] James Boswell, *The Life of Samuel Johnson LL.D.* (1791, 3rd edition 1799; Chicago: Encyclopaedia Britannica, 1952), 294; emphasis in original. Also available at *Project Gutenberg*, accessed December 19, 2021, https://www.gutenberg.org/files/1564/1564-h/1564-h.htm.

[104] See C. A. Pierce, *Conscience in the New Testament: A Study of Syneidesis in the New Testament; in the Light of Its Sources, and with Particular Reference to St. Paul: with Some Observations Regarding Its Pastoral Relevance Today,* Studies in Biblical Theology 15 (London: SCM Press, 1955).

[105] Even though he did not suffer severe aphasia, Douglas James Miller writes that, after his stroke, "Anxiety . . . was a living companion that continually writhed inside." *Stroke,* xi. "Although my pain was real and grew worse in the first few days, and needed sedation, my main problem was severe anxiety/restlessness. . . . It is very hard to describe, but the anxiety was just as much of a physical thing as it was an emotional one. My body simply would not be at rest unless sedated." This condition persisted for many weeks, in hospital and at home, before gradually leaving (5-6).

Grief was the gaps left by all that she had lost, and loneliness was the stillness into which no friend could come. Those spaces were fertile ground for fear of abandonment, and for jealousy. Pam penned this prayer to God:

> *I scream, run away and freak out all throught days. Why? He's not doing anything so why do I tell him I'll divorce him? Help me, Father. I believe that John deserves a better wife. But you places us together. I think, at time's, that I'm fine. You know that I'm not. . . .*
>
> *Help me Never, ever push John away. Why am I behaving as if I was with a stranger. . . .*
>
> *I think I'm terrified that John may realize that I'm a mess and he can easily meet a better wife.*

There are two species of shame: the utter inadequacy that is exposed and the sense of an original purity now covered or smeared with muck.[106] Pam suffered both, asking, in an abashed and grieving prayer, *Please help me become the precious woman he used to write to year's ago.*

There is no therapy for anguish. You cannot set a benchmark, follow exercises, and make incremental progress. There is only the strengthening presence of the Shepherd who knows the way.

Charles Spurgeon, in his battles with depression, found that Jesus had gone before him; he believed that a "heaviness" grew upon Jesus over the course of His ministry:

> . . . at last the Saviour Himself, though full of patience, was obliged to say, "My soul is exceeding sorrowful, even unto

---

[106] On the former, see Jer. 13:26; Nah. 3:5. On the latter, see Ps. 44:15-16; Jer. 51:51; and also W. C. van Unnik, "'With Unveiled Face': An Exegesis of 2 Corinthians iii 12-18," *Novum Testamentum* 6 (1963): 153-69.

death" [Matt. 26:38, KJV]; and one of the evangelists tells us that the Saviour "began to be very heavy" [Matt. 26:37, KJV]. What means that, but that His spirits began to sink? . . . The Saviour passed through the brook, but He "drank of the brook by the way" [Ps. 110:7]; and we who pass through the brook of suffering must drink of it too.[107]

In her way through the wilderness, Pam leans on Him.

ASKING "WHY?"

Why is my pain unending
and my wound grievous and incurable?
You are to me like a deceptive brook,
like a spring that fails. — Jer. 15:18

When you've been broken, broken to pieces,
And your heart begins to faint
'Cause you don't understand,
And when there is nothing to rake from the ashes,
And you can't even walk
Onto the fields of praise, . . .
But I bow down and kiss the Son. — Kevin Prosch[108]

If I were God, and I loved the people I'd created, and set out to write a single book to win their hearts, I rather doubt that I'd devote a large percentage of the pages to registering complaints against Myself. But the Bible often reads like one long gripe fest. The Whine List includes most of the books of Job, Ecclesiastes, and Lamentations. Cain, Moses,

---

[107] Charles Haddon Spurgeon, *The New Park Street Pulpit*, 1858; qtd. in Elizabeth Ruth Skoglund, *Bright Days, Dark Nights: With Charles Spurgeon in Triumph Over Emotional Pain* (Grand Rapids, MI: Baker, 2000), 81.

[108] Kevin Prosch, "Kiss the Son" (7th Time Publishing, 1998); available at *Song Lyrics*, accessed December 19, 2021, http://www.songlyrics.com/kevin-prosch/kiss-the-son-lyrics/.

a slew of psalmists, Elijah, Jonah, Habakkuk, and Jeremiah line up to take their shots at Him—not to mention a host of disgruntled sons, servants, and subjects in Jesus's parables.

And when voices rise to defend Him, they astonish us more than they at first illuminate our darkness. Twice we read in parting words that His ways are just and He does nothing wrong: once from the lips of Moses, condemned to relinquish his lifelong dream because of a hissy fit, and again centuries later from Nebuchadnezzar, a pagan king whom God has made bat-crazy.[109] That these men are not bitter, that they take their last bows on the stage of life with unqualified worship and praise, should make them the most credible witnesses of all; but we are baffled, and only scratch our heads.

The agony and anguish of Jesus take up all other sufferings, and put them to silence by giving them a perfect voice. He becomes the one stumbling block, the name for all our outrage; the cross doubly offends us because Jesus appears entirely innocent, utterly weak, and the Father wholly heartless. He is, moreover, our representative, our priest, though this we barely grasp.

In a remarkable passage, Leanne Payne explores how we, in our pain, can enter into the words and the priesthood of Jesus:

> Mario Bergner, beloved colleague and team member in this ministry, just ministered to a black woman whose history included such poverty that the mother had attempted to kill her at birth. After receiving much healing (actually a trauma of birth healing), she looked up to Mario in tears without the least trace of bitterness or blaming and simply asked: "Why?" Mario's heart was thoroughly wrenched within him. As he did not answer the question, she again asked, "Why?" Then, "Why did my whole family have to experience starvation?" He felt helpless to answer her and

---

[109] Deut. 32:4; Dan. 4:37.

simply continued to comfort her in Christ's name. The next day he got down on his face before the Lord with the same question, asking why she had to suffer this way. Before long he heard these words: "Blessed are those who mourn, for they shall be comforted [Matt. 5:4]. Those who mourn ask, why?"

He then reflected that Jesus on the Cross asked the Father, "Why have You forsaken me?" [Matt. 27:46]. And then he knew, deep within his spirit, that we may not get the answer, but *we shall receive the comfort.*

Continuing to think about this, Mario thought that perhaps the fact that Christ had to ask why is the source of one of the greatest blessings for those who mourn. That is because it opens the way for us to ask, and then to listen. Mario knew that "because Christ asked it of the Father, we too can ask it of the Father." Mario saw that three days after Christ asked the question, the Father replied, not with an answer to the question, but with the comfort to the pain. He did this through resurrecting His Son. After this answer to his question, Mario joyously concluded that our job is to minister resurrection power to those who ask why.[110]

Pam has also known long, pain-racked hours, feeling forsaken and asking why. Two months after we came home, I noted in my diary that she spent much of a day weeping and praying—grieving, but also asking God why He was angry with her. She struggled with unbelief, journaling:

---

[110] Leanne Payne, *The Healing Presence: Curing the Soul through Union with Christ* (1989; Grand Rapids, MI: Hamewith-Baker, 2001), 208; emphasis in original.

I think I believe in God. Do I care, kind off. He didn't save me so why should I?

Pain and confusion brought her into a perpetual condition of asking *Why?* She was haunted by the fear that she could no longer hear from God—the very heart-cry of forsakenness. To her doctor, she wrote:

> . . . *I suddenly had a STROKE and fell into a COMA. The doctor + others tried to keep me alive for 4 days and nights. Then I woke up in pain all around my right full side not moving and held down, top + bottom. I no longer realized I had a husband, not name anything, nor did I know of sisters, brothers, mothers, dad, friends or a god, Jesus, holy spirit.*

> *After 7 or 8 weeks, kept by a John and was sent back to Lawrence, KS. I had began to meet some people, especially John Espy, but no God. WHY?*

Yet we experienced signs that she was not wholly forsaken. We continued to visit churches—switching between three or four, since we seemed to fit nowhere and she would get lost in the words. One Sunday in April 2011, we returned to a little nearby church. A new youth pastor preached a very simple message, holding forth Jesus as the loving Savior. He closed by giving an altar call, inviting his hearers to come forward and meet Jesus. Pam was in a wheelchair that day because of foot pain, but she tapped me: she wanted to respond. I wheeled her to the front of the church, and she rose, and took a few steps, and fell to her knees. We were the only "takers" in the congregation that day, and the pastors took time to pray with her as she sobbed and worshipped.

How often in this life we are only wheelchair attendants—helper monkeys—pushing others to divine appointments that we witness, but cannot comprehend. We stand on the outskirts, beholding mysteries and miracles. I was there, but I am not at all sure what transpired that morning.

In Pam's telling, there were two distinct moments. First, when she cried, "Jesus!" it was as if a dark and lowering embankment of clouds was swept away. She knew His presence once more, not only in the kind pastoral hands upon her head, but in the leaping assurance of bubbling joy within.

At one level, this baffles me. Had she not "prayed the prayer" four decades earlier? Did she not wake up from her coma singing praise? Had we not prayed each night, and often with friends and pastors, calling specifically upon the name of Jesus? What then had been omitted; what still was lost? I cannot say, but I hazard the guess that this day had mostly to do with her recovering mind; her spirit already knew Him, and was known. But I welcome this experience, and every startling moment when our eyes are suddenly opened to recognize Him standing near.

Then Pam says that at once, instinctively, wholeheartedly, she cried out to her Lord with an accusing question: "Where were You?"

That is the very question, the why of whys. Job, probing with words to find his way through a dense, dark jungle of pain and rage, at last realizes that his central complaint is simply that he misses God:

> If only I knew where to find him;
> if only I could go to his dwelling! . . .
> But if I go to the east, he is not there;
> if I go to the west, I do not find him.
> When he is at work in the north, I do not see him;
> when he turns to the south, I catch no glimpse of him.
> — Job 23:3, 8-9

And so, when the Lord speaks, Job is content; though the presence overcomes him, though nothing is explained, still he is satisfied:

My ears had heard of you
but now my eyes have seen you. — 42:5

It is all there in that word from the cross: "forsaken." And now, because our obedient high priest has gone before, we have a promise that we shall never be forsaken:

> . . . for He [God] Himself has said, I will not in any way fail you *nor* give you up *nor* leave you without support. [I will] not, [I will] not, [I will] not in any degree leave you help-less *nor* forsake *nor* let [you] down (relax My hold on you)! [Assuredly not!] — Heb. 13:5, Ampl

Though we may be pursued by enemies, we will not be "left to their power: left in the lurch."[111] As Jesus says in promising the gift of the indwelling Holy Spirit,

> I will not leave you as orphans [comfortless, desolate, bereaved, forlorn, helpless]; I will come [back] to you. — John 14:18, Ampl

So we feel all the more appalled, betrayed, when it appears that our Lord has left us, that we are abandoned, handed over to ruthless tor-turers, to pain. When she called on Jesus at the front of the little church, Pam received a clearer memory or picture of what was going on during the days when she was in a coma: she was lying in a coffin, unable to move, with a demon always standing by her feet. Some-times other demons would come and move her to a cold place. (I later pointed out that, in the hospital, orderlies sometimes came to wheel her down to Radiology in the chilly basement.) She had no power to defend herself. Terrified, she tried to cry out, and couldn't.

---

[111] Marvin R. Vincent, *Word Studies in the New Testament*, 2nd edition, 1888 (Peabody, MA: Hendrickson, n.d.), 3:313, on 2 Cor. 4:9. (Hereafter Vincent.)

At times, she was even aware that there were people nearby; she could hear our voices. But the coffin was shut, and she couldn't make herself heard, and the voices died away. Only the demons remained, and those she could see; perhaps they were inside the coffin with her, or visible through its wall.

> I cry out to you, God, but you do not answer.
> — Job 30:20

Apparently this oppression, this troubled state, went on even as she was singing with me, responding to worship music.

All of this rose up in her question to God: "Where were You?" Even now, more than seven months later, it seemed to her that He had only just returned.

The answer she received, there on her knees amid prayers and tears, has been one of God's great gifts to us. He might have granted her an explanation, perhaps a vision: a wide-angle view disclosing that, though a demon attended her feet, a glorious, all-powerful Savior stood closer and shielded her heart and her head, while, in the shadow of His wings, her spirit sang. But there was no vision.

He came to comfort one who mourned, and His comfort didn't take the form of an explanation as to why or where. Instead, He spoke to her a single word:

Ask.

> He loves our importunity,
> And makes our cause his care. — John Newton[112]

Nothing makes sense to us—tumor, coma, stroke, aphasia, demons, pain. But on that Sunday morning our loving God broke through, and, instead of silencing her cry and laying matters to rest, He invited His

---

[112] Newton, #1.106, in *Olney Hymns*, 220.

child to press on and to go up higher. This corresponds to the wider meaning of the English verb *comfort*, and the Greek *parakaleo*: giving not only consolation but encouragement, filling us with the "Spirit of power and courage."[113] One scene in the eleventh-century Bayeux Tapestry, depicting the Norman Conquest of England, shows a mounted bishop "comforting the troops" (according to the caption) by urging them onward with a brandished club or mace.[114]

We have taken the invitation "Ask" in the sense in which Jesus uses it in Matthew 7:7-8:

> Keep on asking and it will be given you; keep on seeking and you will find; keep on knocking [reverently] and [the door] will be opened to you. For everyone who keeps on asking receives; and he who keeps on seeking finds; and to him who keeps on knocking, [the door] will be opened. (Ampl)

That little word has served as a stimulus, urging Pam on to seek God, encouraging her to keep bringing Him her questions, and especially spurring her to speak. God's "Ask" and her own anger / hunger have been the primary motivators in her recovery.

*   *   *

Pain as correction (but not punishment), as personal transformation, as a door to serving others: I have some reflections on all of that. But some readers will not be greatly interested, and my musings shift the focus away from Pam. So I have opted to place that section in a blog

---

[113] William Barclay, *New Testament Words* (1964; Louisville, KY: Westminster-John Knox, 1974), 216-17; Barclay, *In the Hands of God* (New York and Evanston, IL: Harper Chapel, 1966), 80.

[114] See, e.g., Alister McGrath, *"I Believe": Exploring the Apostles' Creed* (1991; Downers Grove, IL: InterVarsity, 1997), 81. The tapestry may be viewed online at *Reading Museum*, accessed December 19, 2021, https://www.readingmuseum.org.uk/collections/britains-bayeux-tapestry, but a close-up of Bishop Odo appears at the top of the *Wikipedia* article "Bayeux Tapestry," accessed December 19, 2021, https://en.wikipedia.org/wiki/Bayeux_Tapestry.

post.[115] The wider considerations of philosophy and life experience will be found there, while Pam's story continues below.

FRUITS

. . . in faithfulness you have afflicted me. — Ps. 119:75

A prophetic word she received some years earlier was, "God's going to keep you on a short leash for a time." For Pam, the leash has been pain.

I most of all dread the fearsome seizures, but much of her frustration centers round her left foot—where, over the years, she's experienced a sprained ankle, plantar fasciitis, heel spurs, a stress fracture, a neuroma, scar tissue from neuroma surgery, an ingrown toenail, arthritis, and possible neuropathy. Hobbled, almost daily. Having to ration time on her feet, even when the grandkids are around; having to pay in pain for each additional step, each extra moment standing.

And, recently, the migraines. Becoming more delicate, more sensitive than anyone would aspire to be. Feeling overwhelmed even by positive excitements. Sitting for hours in a quiet, darkened room, even on lovely days. Setting a course for calm.

There are many reasons why God may permit affliction to enter a person's life. We still are not daring to speak of great cataclysms that touch whole communities; we stay within the circle of our own pain, and draw no definite conclusions concerning other individuals. To a point, it is good and even faith-building to muse on the whys. Eventually, though, as we submit, as we trudge forward waiting for perseverance to complete its work in us (James 1:4), we start to look for fruits. We cease to ask God where He was, and start to praise Him for the visible signs that He walks with us now, and that He is working in us and through us.

What fruits do Pam and I discern, some years after her stroke? Several come to mind.

---

[115] "The 'Why' of Pain," at https://irrevocablebook.wordpress.com/.

a. She is grateful for her life.

This took a little while. Three months after her stroke, Pam and I re-watched *Forrest Gump*. She wept over Lieutenant Dan, a broken, damaged man convinced he should have died. For a long time he is furious at the idiot who rescued him. Then God shows up in a hurricane and, shouting defiance, Dan realizes he wants to live—at first, if only out of spite. Soon enough, though, he says, in calm and chastened tones, "Forrest, I never thanked you for saving my life."[116]

Pam turned to me and, echoing the film, thanked me for saving her life. I didn't, of course; I was only a witness, walking with her through "such a great salvation" (Heb. 2:3, Ampl). But she was again receiving consciousness, existence, as a gift.

Gratitude is the flag run up when humility conquers the heart. Caged in a prison, Paul opens a heart guarded by peace (Phil. 4:7); speaking to those he loves, he warbles with joy and contentment and confidence, for Jesus is with him (vv. 1, 4, 9-13). He models a rich and positive thought life:

> . . . whatever is true, whatever is worthy of reverence *and* is honorable *and* seemly, whatever is just, whatever is pure, whatever is lovely *and* lovable, whatever is kind *and* winsome *and* gracious, if there is any virtue *and* excellence, if there is anything worthy of praise, think on *and* weigh *and* take account of these things [fix your minds on them].
> — Phil. 4:8, Ampl

It was an AA sponsor who first set Pam the ongoing task of compiling a list of all the things for which she could honestly give thanks—keeping an eye out for them, and deliberately writing them down:

---

[116] *Forrest Gump*, written by Winston Groom and Eric Roth, directed by Robert Zemeckis; Paramount, 1994.

I'm glad my sponsor . . . is having me write a Grattitude card
/ list just about how I feel regarding how I've been continually
blessed by my husband. Your list continues to grow as I remem-
ber so many things about you since we first met.

Some days, her lists have been very specific: *I'm grateful for more milk,*
yogurt, oatmeal, banana's and bread. And once she thanked me for the
birds, meat, cows, and pigs in our freezer.

Take the very hardest thing in your life—*the* place of difficulty, outward or inward, and expect God to triumph glo-
riously in that very spot. Just there He can bring your soul
into blossom! — Lilias Trotter[117]

Like clouds rolling in and obscuring the view, pain recalls us to the
present. Still, when the gaze is thwarted, anxiety and resentment show
themselves. This is the opportunity for faith to rise from ambush and
rout its foes—by resolutely turning its back on them, changing perspective by practicing gratitude. I wrote to her sister:

Pam is calmer today; one virtue of the near-seizures is that
they serve as a reality check. She stops worrying about all the
things I do wrong and is grateful simply that I'm there.

One day, in our evening prayers, she took my breath away by actually thanking God for her pain. Again, five months later, she wrote:
Bless You for the pain I'm experiencing in my back and 2 feet. Now that
is faith.

---

[117] I. Lilias Trotter, *Parables of the Cross* (1890); qtd. in Miriam Huffman Rockness, *A Passion*
for the Impossible: The Life of Lilias Trotter (Grand Rapids, MI: Discovery House, 1999, 2003),
49; emphasis in original. Also available at *Project Gutenberg*, accessed December 19, 2021,
http://www.gutenberg.org/ebooks/22189.

Already in 2012, two years after the stroke, her lists and thank-you notes and prayers show a depth of faith, a theological profundity:

Thank You for breaking back the years the Locusts had eaten. I am alive and I am filled with Your Glory each day and night. You have healed me in ways I never could imagine. You are the blessing and honor and Glory. . . .

Lord I may not be able to read as well as I had before John joined me in Baullimore, but You have brought back to me more than I ever could have dreamed.

By 2015, her lists read like confessions of faith:

Gratitude List today

I know God sent his Son, Jesus

Jesus died for me. Now the Holy Spirit is here with me

God saved me from dying when I asked Jesus into my heart

I have gifts that irrevokable like singing, salvation

I can speak out loud in the Name of Jesus + demon's have to flee

I have a husband I love who love's me

God brought me out of a coma, tumor and stroke + Aphasia

I am recovering and I have a testimony to share so other's will hear and learn they can ask Jesus into their hearts

I'm grateful for Music Therapy helping me with songs + guitar

John found a good neurologist who help's me to prevent another stroke, seizures and pain. Medication works well on my Anxiety, too.

John come's with me to Alanon + AA meeting.

I have a good church. God has given me friends there . . .

*My 3 children love me and I love them, grandkids + I'm remem-
bering their names.*

At about the same time, Pam wrote:

*Thank you, Father, for sending me your only Son. My Grattitude
is for you, Lord. Thank you for sending Holy Spirit to Earth to
give us one to talk to whenever I feel sad, lonely, helpless, unim-
portant and no-longer needed by anyone. Now I do know I've
been saved. I may be weak, but You are strong. I praise You,
Lord. Thank You for introducing me to John Espy to love me. I
love him in so many ways. I stay with him because He loves You
more than he loves me. You, alone know how important that is
to me. . . . His humor is so fun and incouragable to me and others. Many are affected by us still being happily married in spite
of our ups + downs.*

This is a voice of mature and tested faith; this is one "coming up from
the wilderness leaning on her beloved" (Song 8:5). Pam almost echoes
Catherine of Siena, who wrote six centuries earlier, "All the way to
heaven is heaven, because Christ is the Way."[118]

b. She has learned the fear of the Lord, the starting point of wise living.

The fear of the Lord is the beginning of wisdom,
and the knowledge of the Holy One is insight.
— Prov. 9:10, NRSV[119]

---

[118] Qtd. in Regis Martin, *The Last Things: Death, Judgment, Hell, Heaven* (San Francisco: Igna-
tius, 1998), 39; see *Wikiquote*, accessed December 19, 2021, https://en.wikiquote.org/wiki/
Catherine_of_Siena.
[119] Compare Prov. 1:7; 3:7; 14:16; 15:33; Job 28:28; Ps. 111:10; Mic. 6:9.

We take offense at the very notion of "fearing" God; when we read this verse, we automatically gloss *fear* as *reverence*. This is a good start—my dictionary defines *reverence* as "profound adoring awed respect"[120]— but the fact remains that I can revere William Shakespeare and Rosa Parks. The "fear of God" isn't fandom; it comes closer to Rudolf Otto's creature-consciousness in the face of overwhelming majesty.[121] In the presence of the Holy One, I am not merely hushed and respectful; I am shaken and very nearly annihilated.

For Pam, it's true that some of the holy fear is rooted in the sense of oppression associated with all of her recollections of the coma:

> *I'm so glad you took me to a church the day an alter call was given. It was then when I asked Jesus into my heart I burst out crying remembering what had happened to me while I was in my coma. . . . Satan is real and either him or demon's had stayed with me freaking me out in my coma.* [2014]

> *When I fell into that COMA I changed. What a scary world this changed into.* [2012]

Still, in her heart and mind, even the most vividly experienced demons are overmatched. The Lord fills heaven and earth, and even the highest heavens cannot contain Him; yet all His fullness dwells in Jesus our

---

[120] *Webster's*, 736.

[121] Rudolf Otto, *The Idea of the Holy: An Inquiry into the Non-Rational Factor in the Idea of the Divine and Its Relation to the Rational* (1917), trans. John W. Harvey (1923), 2nd edition (1950; Oxford: Oxford, 1958), 8-32. This sacred presence, which Otto calls "the numinous," is a much better starting point for a science of religion than Jonathan Haidt's well-meaning but reductive efforts to ground sanctity and religion in feelings of disgust and vague "uplift" or "elevation." See Jonathan Haidt, *The Happiness Hypothesis: Finding Modern Truth in Ancient Wisdom* (New York: Basic-Perseus, 2006), 185-99; Haidt, *The Righteous Mind: Why Good People Are Divided by Politics and Religion* (New York: Pantheon-Random House, 2012), 13, 146-53. See also my blog entry on this subject at *Bible Weigh Station*, https://bibleweighstation. wordpress.com/2015/03/10/jonathan-haidt-and-the-possibility-of-moral-instruction/.

Champion.[122] When He rises, all the powers of darkness flee like little insects (Nah. 3:17). Pam knows this well; as early as 2011, she was writing, *Evil has come against us but You God are here forever and ever.*

Our "express lane" Christianity seizes on the promise that "perfect love casts out fear" (1 John 4:18, NRSV) and seeks to dismiss the fear of God—just as we rush to Easter without stopping at Good Friday, and clamor for selfies in the throne room without ever seeing Christ crucified before our eyes (Gal. 3:1). Deep down, we know better. Perhaps one day, perfected in love, we shall be strengthened to stand in the presence, but for now our faith is permeated with the fear of God.[123] The news that Christ is risen never ceases to awaken in us "fear and great joy"; we "delight in the fear of the LORD" and "rejoice with trembling."[124]

We see this often in people who have survived strokes, aneurysms, brain injuries: all intermingled with confusion and cognitive impairment, they show a heightened sensitivity to spiritual realities. They know their lives are trajectories on a vast canvas, and it frustrates them when others set the frame so small. There are visions in their thoughts, images that we are too quick to scorn. Pam wrote:

> *I had a godly dream today.*
>
> *I was outside with others. I felt you were there. One man did something bad causing the upset guy to begin a horrific fight. I tried to get another man to break up the serious beating. I began crying in fear. Why wasn't somebody help the man was continuing to be too weak to help himself, so why I was thinking, why wasn't that stronger man being stopped by any of the other guys? No one would help. While I was still watching this I say those 2 stop their fighting. They were laughing at me. I had*

[122] Jer. 23:24; 1 Kings 8:27; Col. 1:19; 2:9.

[123] Rev. 1:17; Ezek. 1:28-2:2; and, e.g., Acts 9:31; 2 Cor. 5:11; 7:1; 1 Peter 1:17.

[124] Matt. 28:8, NRSV; Isa. 11:3; Neh. 1:11; Ps. 2:11, NIV84.

tear's falling down my face. They seemed a bit surprise by my reaction—as if they were the one's who never though I'd react the way I was. Confused . . . I woke up.

People these days, don't seen to see things the way I see them in life.

The same Pam who once received a word that "We need to stop hurting our brothers" now sees in dreams the wounds we vainly laugh off.

God has planted eternity in Pam's heart (Eccl. 3:11); in consequence, she hungers for much more than consumer happiness or old memories and a return to "normal." She longs for holiness, and grieves for sin:

I have been spending a lot of time talking out loud (quietly) to God about a lot of things. It leave's me crying till I fall asleep. I do wake up feeling much better.

Such tears and conversations are accepted in God's temple as holy offerings. It is only at our moneychangers' tables, where words are currency and reasoning the balance, that groans and sighs are accounted of no value.

c. Her heart is open before God.

The person who is most at home in the kingdom of God is not the one who has life all figured out, but the one who has learned to trust the Father. Even after great loss, even in the midst of pain, we look to Him. Fredrik Wisloff suggests that in sickness we are like Elijah at the brook, and all our troubles and difficulties are the ravens sent to feed us. We can relax and welcome them:

The black birds did not come to rob you. They came with blessings from God. In their beaks they had gifts from your

Heavenly Father. When the birds left, you were richer than ever before.

Do not be afraid of "bad things." God never gives anything bad to His children. That which God sends or which He allows to come, is always for good, even if it is brought to you on black wings.[125]

This is not quite "all our pain is good";[126] rather, it asserts that, even when we stand in agony and anguish, we are visited by a good God.

What we call the mind—the intellect—is led by the heart. We labor to develop, educate, train, fill, enrich, and apply our minds; as we age and encounter people with dementia, we ask God to preserve our minds; after stroke or injury, we earnestly beseech Him to restore our minds. But God, who addresses as "mind" our entire consciousness[127]— intuitive knowing as well as discursive reason—God is more concerned with *renewing* the mind, adjusting our "moral and spiritual vision and thinking to the mind of God."[128] Paul indicates that this happens particularly as we walk before Him wide open, offering our entire beings as "living sacrifices" (Rom. 12:1-2).

In Pam, I have witnessed a shift: Despite periods of grieving, more and more she regards herself as yielded to God. She is less preoccupied with what has been taken from her, or missed opportunities, because of a conviction that every real or potential crown is hers only in order that she may cast it at His feet (Rev. 4:10). She has just surrendered some of hers ahead of time.

---

[125] Fredrik Wisloff, *On Our Father's Knee* (Oslo: Nordstrand, 1962), 14-15.

[126] N. T. Wright objects to these "dreadful" words in an old hymn, on the grounds that they induce "moral chaos." Wright, "9/11, Tsunamis, and the New Problem of Evil" (2005), in Wright, *Surprised by Scripture: Engaging Contemporary Issues* (New York: HarperOne, 2014), 114-15.

[127] *Vine's*, New Testament section, 408 (*mind*).

[128] *Vine's*, New Testament section, 524 (*renew*).

Last year, she shared that she no longer likes violent stories. I suggested to her that this indicates a measure of healing from trauma, from the impulse to reenact. Those memories in her have reached some resolution; they no longer command her attention.

On the best days, her heart is set on the joy of His presence, just as it was years ago:

> *I laid next to you for a long time last night as you first fell asleep. I prayed along with the music you've been turning turned on every day for me ever since I was in Baultimore. The Presence of the Holy Spirit was heavy on me. I was crying so much I was affraid I'd keep weaking you up so I finally had to leave into here. I put the other music I'd found yesterday . . . within seconds the presence of the Holy Spirit covered me. What a Blessing. . . .*
>
> *I guess you were right me—God has had me set aside as a worship lover of God.*

One night she found a worship song with special relevance to aphasia:

> I'm finding myself at a loss for words
> And the funny thing is it's okay
> The last thing I need is to be heard
> But to hear what You would say.[129]

Sometimes worship flows seamlessly into evangelism:

> *The gift's of God are irrezokable. Holy Holy Holy is the Lamb of God—the whole earth is filled with His Glory and Beauty. I have my gift's as does John. I can sing and write music. People are*

---

[129] Peter Kipley and Bart Millard, "Word of God Speak" (Curb Wordspring Music, Songs From the Indigo Room, Simpleville Music, 2002).

drawn to them as Holy Spirit is. He was sent to me year's ago. I have Beauty because God is Beautiful! Hallelujah. Another gift is my belief in Jesus.

I have joy unspeakable. My Father draws people to me to share Jesus. Jesus is amazing. God is patient and kind. He will set people free if they ask him into their lives. He doesn't want anyone to die and end up in Hell. . . .

GOD IS A MOTIVATOR and so am I, now.

All suffering, all pain, all emptiness, all disappointment is seed: sow it in God and he will, finally, bring a crop of joy from it. — Eugene Peterson[130]

d. She reveals and unlocks other people's hearts.

Humiliation is the great unnamed component of any stroke recovery. Pam needs help where once she was independent, competent. She must go back and learn basic abilities all over again. People misunderstand her, and sometimes treat her poorly. And I face new demands, and a schedule that every day is shot down in flames. I meet accusations and anger, and can either speak and raise the tatters of my pride or stand with Jesus and with Pam, silent and defenseless, clothed only in the seamless tunic of humility.

Pam goes before me through this valley. I saw the first glimmers of reawakening humility in her desire to exalt God, her appreciation of small kindnesses, and—of all things—her humor: her willingness not to take herself too seriously. One year after the stroke, she spoke up at an AA meeting, telling her story. "The doctors took out part of

---

[130] Eugene H. Peterson, *A Long Obedience in the Same Direction: Discipleship in an Instant Society* (1980), 20th anniversary edition (Downers Grove, IL: InterVarsity, 2000), 100.

my brain," she said. Then, her deadpan yielding to a mischievous grin, "But that's okay—I wasn't using it anyway!"

Affliction creates weakness, and that weakness has the power to expose the spiritual or moral strengths and weaknesses of those it meets. Dan Hamann has described how his brother Paul, who has Down's syndrome, "unlocks" the warmth and compassion in the hearts of others. Pam unlocks people almost every day, opening ancient doors, long-rusted locks. She helped me find the key to my own abandoned tears.

> We all need to be unlocked. It is a question of who has the key. — Dan Hamann[131]

Periodically she needs to see new doctors. Invariably, they quickly assign themselves to one of two categories: either the kind and helpful or the impatient. The latter, despite their paper credentials and their "in network" status, we try very hard to discard and never see again. But the odd thing is that, by myself, I can't tell one from the other. It takes Pam to summon the distinction, and she does it within minutes.

From the onset of her coma, Pam has called forth faith and love from many hearts—as Paul did among the Galatians when he was ailing (Gal. 4:13-15). People prayed, sometimes surprising themselves. Others came, or wrote, or called. And once we were done with hospitals, some reacted to their perception of pain or of need, often turning away as I once averted my heart from beggars. Sometimes Pam startles one of these, making them laugh and so see past their sight.

How much greater her impact is when she pursues holiness, when she worships, when she manifests joy in the midst of pain, when she shares her faith. If weakness disarms, weakness that spills goodness utterly conquers. David Roper has said:

---

[131] Qtd. in Christopher de Vinck, *The Power of the Powerless* (1988; New York: Doubleday, 1990), 122-23.

Though we may seem to be doing nothing worthwhile in this world, we can be doing everything worthwhile if our lives are being styled by God's grace. Set aside through sickness or seclusion, we can still be immensely prolific. Though we may be bedridden or housebound, our holiness by itself can yet bear fruit. To be useful, we don't have to be good for anything—just good. Good people do more good than they ever know. Lighthouse keepers never know how many ships they have turned away from the rocks. Their duty is to shine, not to look for results.[132]

And still more. As if it were not enough to reveal the thoughts of many hearts (Luke 2:35), I believe that some Christians—one might call them "spiritual barometers"[133]—reflect and bear the conditions of the churches and communities around them. In the New Testament, the paralyzed, leprous, demonized, deaf, and blind who come to Jesus each present both a personal physical affliction and the spiritual condition of many. So today, some believers bear in their bodies the warfare that surrounds them, interceding, and lifting it to God. They deserve honor and aid, because they are a first battleground.

Pam has been unvanquished like Baltimore, inconsolable like Washington, DC, and especially unhealed like Lawrence. Sometimes she has even struggled with unbelief because Jesus didn't come to help. Yet, since coming home from the hospitals, her picture of divine

---

[132] David Roper, *Elijah: A Man Like Us* (1995; Grand Rapids, MI: Discovery House, 1997), 88. Original title *Seeing Through*.

[133] The term is an old one, dating back at least to 1856 when James Morrison, a Scottish minister, was given a barometer by his students. He remarked "that there are other storms and tempests than those of wind and rain to which they as well as all the rest of mankind are by nature exposed, and it was only by becoming spiritual barometers they could properly know the fearful character of the storms, realise the true symptoms of the impending danger, and thus be led to flee for safety." "News of the Church," *The Reformed Presbyterian Magazine*, Edinburgh (March 1856), 86; available at *Google Books*, accessed December 19, 2021, https://books.google.com/books?id=iy4EAAAAQAAJ.

intervention has broadened, and her eyes have been opened to see that He does come, faithfully, daily: *You have healed me in ways I never could imagine. . . . You have brought back to me more than I ever could have dreamed.*

> Though God's ways of expressing his faithfulness are sometimes unexpected and bewildering, looking indeed to the casual observer and in the short term more like unfaithfulness, the final testimony of those who walk with God through life's ups and downs is that "every promise has been fulfilled; not one has failed" (Josh. 23:14-15). — J. I. Packer[134]

The Book of Acts describes an instance of an entire town turning to Jesus after one bedridden Christian, Aeneas, is healed (Acts 9:32-35). When his physical paralysis departs, so does his community's spiritual paralysis. If churches took this to heart, we would pray earnestly, perseveringly, for each afflicted believer in our midst, either until they were healed or until we received insight into their gifts and callings, and into anything they may have to teach us about our neighbors and our own hearts.

e. She enters into others' pain, and brings them comfort.

Love may not keep score (1 Cor. 13:5, Msg), but every husband thinks he knows the amount of grace or "wiggle room" he has left. And love may not insist on its own way (1 Cor. 13:5, NRSV), but husbands can tell how far out of their way they have journeyed. I write in brokenness and partial knowledge.

I both love and appreciate Pam, but from the days we first dated I would gladly have enrolled her—and she me—in Empathy School.

---

[134] J. I. Packer, *Concise Theology: A Guide to Historic Christian Beliefs* (Wheaton, IL: Tyndale House, 1993), 47.

When we were ten years married, on a trip to see her mother, we stayed in a motel, and something I'd eaten for supper made me ill. The whole time I was in the bathroom, upchucking, my ears were filled with the *Diners, Drive-Ins, and Dives* marathon Pam was watching in the next room. She actually turned up the volume to overthrow the sounds of my distress. Just when I thought I'd hit empty, someone asked host Guy Fieri if he'd like a raw egg on top of his corned beef hash—and I finally did what all the coaches and gym teachers of my youth had urged in vain: I reached deeper and found something more in me.

Later, after the stroke, I would have traded all the therapies—PT and OT, speech and even music therapy—to put Pam through Empathy Therapy. Perhaps then I could have been spared the indignities of her hard, cackling laugh when I fell for her "nasty stuff, makes you poop" concoction, or underwent a hissy fit, or was suddenly awakened from my hard-earned slumbers by a leg cramp.

And still I remain her comic butt, her queen's jester. But where others are concerned, I at times glimpse something wonderful. All of her sensitivity, that once turned only inward to plumb her own pain, and then with an artist's grace released it to dance on her face, and to pray in her songs—this wordless awareness now has become a key that unlocks other hearts.

One Father's Day a pastor, busy with his kids, asked whether we could stop by the hospital to visit his mother. We didn't know her, but were happy to oblige. I sent Pam in first, and after a minute she sang out to me to join her. I stepped in and saw the two women sitting together, holding hands, both in tears. Pam asked me to pray, but they were already praying in deep concord; I only added words.

> And if anyone gives even a cup of cold water to one of these little ones because he is my disciple, I tell you the truth, he will certainly not lose his reward. — Matt. 10:42, NIV84

God isn't careful in His measurements: what He fills, overflows. The consolation and encouragement we've received is meant to spill over into others' lives (2 Cor. 1:3-5), and Pam has learned to watch for spillway opportunities, in person and in prayer:

> *Tonight I pray to You, God, to strenghtn the hearts that grow weary. You said that when we are weak You will be our strength.*

Sometimes for whole days together, she seems to be lost in her own pain and grief; and then all at once, through channels I can't perceive, great wondrous tides of empathy rise and wash out over others.

How is this possible? Pascal wisely says, "The heart has its reasons of which reason knows nothing"; and, more, "The heart has its order," different from the mind's.[135]

f. She hungers both to fill up Christ's afflictions and to be healed.

Once, as I listened to Handel's *Messiah*, one passage leapt out at me with the force of a present and personal promise, specifically for Pam:

> Comfort ye, comfort ye my people,
> saith your God.
> Speak ye comfortably to Jerusalem,
> and cry unto her,
> that her warfare is accomplished,
> that her iniquity is pardoned:
> for she hath received of the LORD's hand
> double for all her sins. — Isa. 40:1-2, KJV

---

[135] Blaise Pascal, *Pensees* (written 1656?-62, published 1670), transl. A. J. Krailsheimer (1966; Harmondsworth, England: Penguin: 1970), #423, 154, and #298, 122. Also available at *Christian Classics Ethereal Library*, accessed December 19, 2021, https://ccel.org/ccel/pascal/pensees.

Impressionistic and eager to believe, I took this to mean that some trial in Pam's life had come to full term. In fact, we had five good months—and then things got rough again. We were besieged once more, and now I felt betrayed as well.

How then am I to read these words? Isaiah wrote, I believe, before Jerusalem's "warfare" (or "hard service") had fairly started—before the destruction of the city, and the exile; certainly he wrote before the nightmare had concluded, if indeed it yet has. The word translated "accomplished" or "ended" (Hebrew *male*) is literally "fill," even "fill to overflowing."[136] The prophet's message, in effect, is "One day your fight will reach its fullness and come to an end," and the almighty God has already set its limits. This is no less comforting a promise than my first reading; it just isn't one that I can seize and hold apart from God and His daily quickening of my eye of hope, my ear of faith. I still need to ask Him to train my hands for battle (Ps. 18:34; 144:1), including the battles whose victory is spoken and assured.

And I need to declare it—to Pam, my Jerusalem, my walled city.[137] I am summoned to speak to her, to prophesy over her, *Receive encouragement and strength, my dear one; lift up your head, because your victory is certain, and your Champion stands at the gate. Jesus endured the cross till all was finished, and He now gives you grace to persevere in Him. All of your sins have been taken away, and, in Calvary's great exchange, you have received much more: a robe of righteousness, a ring of authority, sandals of protection, the name that signifies adoption, and acceptance with fullness and joy (Luke 15:22-23). Drink deeply of His life and strength; look for His coming and the full revealing of His glory (Isa. 40:1-5).*

Sometimes I stammer some of this, for a day or even a week. Eventually I fall silent. Why? It is hard to hang on for healing; Bob Sorge

---

[136] *Vine's*, Old Testament section, 81 (*to fill*).

[137] Song 4:4, 12; 6:4; 8:10.

compares it to Jacob, wrestling the angel, grappling and straining, refusing to let go even as the pain gets worse.[138]

But I think there is also another reason. Much as we hunger for healing, we also long to see the purpose in our pain. If only there may be fruit, we want to endure to the end; though our nerves scream, in our hearts we don't ask too soon a deliverance into a barren ease.

> All human nature vigorously resists grace because grace changes us and the change is painful. — Flannery O'Connor[139]

One of the Old Testament words for pain is *hil*, which pictures an awful dance: twisting and writhing in pain or anguish or contrition or anxiety—or childbirth.[140] Isaiah records an astonishing prayer, whispered (or yet to be whispered) by Israel in the depths of affliction, drawing near to God:

> As a pregnant woman about to give birth
> writhes [*hil*] and cries out in her pain,
> so were we in your presence, LORD.
> We were with child, we writhed [*hil*] in labor,
> but we gave birth to wind.
> We have not brought salvation to the earth,

---

[138] Bob Sorge, *Pain, Perplexity and Promotion: A Prophetic Interpretation of the Book of Job* (1999; Grandview, MO: Oasis House, 2009), 101-04. He contrasts this tenacious "Jacob theology" with "microwave theology," which expects instant healing and, if it doesn't receive it, concludes I'm being punished for sin, and gives up; and with "Martha theology," which assumes we won't be healed till the last day, and so has a perfect excuse never to wrestle with unbelief.

[139] Flannery O'Connor, *The Habit of Being* (New York: Vintage, 1979), 307; qtd. in Henri J. M. Nouwen, *Home Tonight: Further Reflections on the Parable of the Prodigal Son*, ed. Sue Mosteller (New York: Doubleday-Random House, 2009), 17.

[140] Francis Brown, S. R. Driver, and Charles A. Briggs, *A Hebrew and English Lexicon of the Old Testament* (1907), revised edition (Oxford: Clarendon, 1975), 296-97. (Hereafter *BDB.*)

and the people of the world have not come to life.
— Isa. 26:17-18

I see this sense of futility in Pam, but also this dogged (or, better, per-severing) determination, that cries, *Let my suffering not be in vain*. Even if I must endure longer, even if I must fill up Christ's afflictions (Col. 1:24), let me see offspring (Isa. 53:10). To this end, and only for this, she blessed me to tell her story. "It might encourage someone," she says. "Someone might get saved."

We—I—demand victory without perseverance; when we walk down a road, we want to twirl a baton, not carry a cross. We point to prophecies about childbirth without labor pains (Isa. 54:1; 66:7-8)—and fail to see that these passages promise, not no pain, but no *additional* pain; for the mother is "desolate" Jerusalem, who has writhed on the rack many years. God will not waste pain: when it is filled full, He will bring deliverance, suddenly, speedily; and the fruitfulness will be abundant. This is the Christian hope in suffering; this is Pam's courage.

*   *   *

Sometimes this world is an ocean of pain, engulfing life and beauty; and, like Noah's dove, we find no place of rest apart from Christ. When the waters subside for a while, we can see the rainbow: God disarming Himself, setting His bow in the clouds, pledging a limit to suffering, and an end.[141]

Through the wind and the night we glimpse Jesus, able to tread upon the waves (Matt. 14:25), yet willing to descend, past even Jonah's sounding, into the deep.

And we see Peter. Like us, at first he bravely, gamely aspires to triumph over suffering with his rough, unwashed feet; to rise above (Matt. 14:28-29). Later—when his flesh fails, when he endures a dark night of losing his Lord through his own lips, when he is sifted and

---

[141] Gen. 8:8-9; 1 Peter 3:17-22; Gen. 9:12-17; Isa. 54:9.

humbled, when even resurrection brings accusing pain—later, seeing Jesus, he has no appetite for wave-walking, nor any leisure. Hearing "It is the Lord!" he embraces the lower passage. Out of respect, he robes himself, then plunges into the sea of affliction, fully immersed now (John 21:7; 13:9-10), and strikes out for shore.

Pam, too, is in the waters, learning to crawl; stroking toward the direction of the remembered voice. Often she sees only flood:

> *I'm remember too much about all the things I've lost because I agreed to have my tumor removed. I've been in more pain then I recall. I've rested a lot yet I still feel broken and exhauted. I want a miracle so I can walk around outside and enjoy the warm weather and look to see the beauty of flower's blooming, hear the variety of the birds or even the various people walking their dogs. I have to accept the truth that I can't read books, things on the computers, and my memory seem's worse than it had been.*

Then, even in mid-stroke, she'll gasp acceptance and submission:

> *I'm sorry I reacted so inappropriately. You were accurate in saying "God was keeping me on a short leash." That is His amazing blessing.*

God give me grace to cheer the swimmer on.

WHAT SORT OF SHEPHERD

What sort of Shepherd goes wandering off
And abandons His sheep to the heat of the day?
You scowl at me when I doubt and I scoff—
The fact is, I'm steady, and You are the stray.
I have to dodge wolves and set out on Your track,
Miss meals, chase You down, pick You up, bring You back.

What sort of Shepherd breaks half a sheep's bones
By wielding His stick with a ponderous zeal?
Then Your ordained dogs gather, drawn by my groans,
To nip at the one they're appointed to heal.
And yet, after hating and fearing Your ways,
I have to anoint You by singing Your praise.

What sort of Shepherd comes with a sweet voice
And promises meadows and life-giving streams,
Then chooses steep valleys—yet says to rejoice,
Ignoring the death-smell, the dark, the lost dreams?
I stagger—yet You expect me, all the same,
To spread a sparse table and bless Your good name.

What sort of Shepherd has vowed to restore,
But only withholds, till I've nothing to lose?
If Your hand protects me, it wounds me still more:
You lie, change, deceive, disappoint, and confuse.
My head's always turned to look back at the path
For I'm stalked by Your changeableness and Your wrath.

Yet You say I'm stubborn, a calf or a mule,
Not lamblike enough to lead gently along.
You say that my heart is the heart of a fool
That needs a stout cudgel to learn right from wrong.

You say You prod me to flee from attack
And my deepest wounds come because I kick back.

You say my own folly prompts me to stray
And then I blame You—yet You bear with me still.
You say the desires of my heart don't obey
While You work to purge them and strengthen my will.
You say the state of my heart makes You cry—
You still hope for me, though I still let You die.

You say You trust me, to call forth my trust,
And hide Yourself only to make me pursue.
You view me with mercy, not with my disgust,
And call me and feed me and bind me to You.
You say that You love me and share in my pain
And meekly stand by while I cruelly complain.

You watch over me when I run from Your voice
To drink from the wells that are clotted and gross.
Each time You see me—even there—You rejoice
And You gather me up and You carry me close.
In all the dark places You stay by my side,
Your patience unbounded, Your heart opened wide.

How often, when I've done my best to resist,
Your pierced hand has forced me to lie down and rest.
I've snapped at You, only to find myself kissed;
I've blasphemed Your name, and been gently caressed.
Your goodness astounds even my darkened mind
And even the blows of Your mercy are kind.

Each day I'm anointed by tears from Your eyes;
I'm fed by Your body, upheld by Your prayers;
I drink the refreshment that Your Word supplies;
Your blood takes my sins, and Your presence my cares.

I want for nothing, it is true,
So long as I want only You.

What sort of Shepherd is faithful to me
Because not to be so would make You a lie?
Your nature, Your pleasure, Your identity
Are bound up with my life, my learning to die.
You long for the morning when I can run free—
Then bind me up; hobble me; Lord, shepherd me.

6
ANGER

The Overbearing Murmur

When my heart was grieved
and my spirit embittered,
I was senseless and ignorant;
I was a brute beast before you. — Ps. 73:21-22

One day in 2013, two and a half years after her stroke, Pam went to
one of her safe oases: the chiropractor's office where she once worked.
The doctor and his assistant are good friends and always welcome her.
On this occasion, though, she came home frantic. After some rapid
conversation with me—and a few choice epithets—she abruptly realized
that she was in pain. Even then, she couldn't pinpoint the location of
the problem until I guided her through a process of elimination, which
determined that her eyeglasses were chafing her nose. She told me that
she had known for three weeks that "something" was going on, and
that she had blamed me, and considered running away. We discussed
self-awareness of pain, but when we finished she still believed I should
be the first to notice.

How can we not know that we're hurting? How can our anger be
more accessible to consciousness than our pain? The truth is that we are
all accomplished at hoodwinking ourselves:

> The heart is deceitful above all things,
> and desperately corrupt;
> who can understand it? — Jer. 17:9, RSV

The heart deceives, not least in what it chooses to send to the surface. Many a time, pain presents as anger.

I am not a huge fan of Phil McGraw: TV's "Dr. Phil." I've never liked bullies, even the ones that occasionally pick on other bullies; I don't believe that people can or should be browbeaten into the kingdom of heaven—or out of addictions and into healthy relationships. Mixing in "folksy" assertions—"This is not mah first rodeo!"; "Ah did not just fall off a turnip truck!"—doesn't help much.

But I saw one episode that contained an illuminating moment. Having put all the screws to one man, and taken a commercial break, Dr. Phil asked him what he was feeling. Fuming, the man replied, "I'm really angry." But the veteran of many rodeos wouldn't allow this to pass. "Ya know," he said, "ah find, when people say they're angry, they're usually either hurt, scared, or frustrated. So which is it?" And the man had to pick one.

Anger is often described as a *secondary emotion*. What this means is that we experience emotions—anguish, fear, anxiety, shame, guilt, and more—that are so uncomfortable that, rather than stay in them, we fly at once to anger. Sometimes, the passage is so quick that we aren't even fully aware of our *primary emotions*. We never stand in them and explore them, never really allow ourselves to feel them. We just get mad. We go through life mad, in whatever degrees and ways we can get away with.

> I may not find you as I want you to be, and you may not find me as you want me to be. I fear that there may be quarreling, jealousy, outbursts of anger, . . . — 2 Cor. 12:20, NIV84

For the survivor of a stroke or brain injury, this tendency is reinforced. The other emotions may be impossible to articulate; heck, you may not even recognize that you're feeling *pain*. Anger remains familiar, and straightforward. It finds expression.[142]

Pam—and I—endured months and years of almost daily rage. Anger often hijacked our plans and dominated our domestic life. Yet, if I pause now to describe this, my purpose is in part to encourage other stroke and brain-injury survivors, and their families, that one can persevere; there can be an end to anger, and even the cultivation of a deep inner peace, abiding and joyful even when its surface strives with storms.

Here then is a brief calendar of her most outstanding flare-ups and outbursts—mine, less excusable, will come up later:

2010

- October (soon after our return home from the hospitals): I answer a phone call from Pam's daughter. Pam gets furious, storms out of the house, and walks about; she won't return or talk with me. Later, she's contrite, but still believes she overheard something unkind.

- October: Pam asks a companion to take her out in the car, but can't find the words to explain where she wants to go. She becomes upset and angry.

- November: She takes offense at something her speech therapist says, and cancels all upcoming appointments. Once home, she takes up scissors and cuts her hair—though not

---

[142] The mother of a young man who suffered a devastating brain injury writes of her own coping stratagems, "Anger helps, as it always does; the tears stop coming . . ." Spinney, *Beyond the High Blue Air*, 249. Compare a prisoner of war: "I hardly knew it then, but I had begun the process of shutting down my emotions, pulling back into cold anger at the first sign of confrontation rather than expressing myself." Eric Lomax, *The Railway Man: A POW's Searing Account of War, Brutality and Forgiveness* (New York and London: W. W. Norton, 1995), 205.

too badly. Then she says I think she's crazy, throws things, and storms out.

- November: We go to the hospital for a follow-up MRI, this one with a gadolinium contrast. The injection of the dye is painful, and she bolts as soon as the procedure is finished, forcing me to cancel her occupational therapy appointment.

- November: Pam fires her last companion, essentially for asking too many "What do you mean?" and "Is that really what you want?" questions. Pam's verdict is "That's how I learned not to be an a—h—!" After she calms down, I suggest she consider a refresher course.

- December: Our primary care doctor suggests I take Pam for a psych evaluation. She absolutely refuses to go.

2011

- January: A small breakthrough: Pam acknowledges that she has been prone to fits of anger—usually directed at me, she says, because I'm there. But this isn't who she is, or wants to be; and she has the insight to identify it as the pain and rage of her childhood, of powerlessness. I encourage her that, if God is allowing all of these painful memories to surface, He must want to accomplish a work of healing in her. Privately, I seize upon her strong sense that the recent behavior "isn't her"; the "real" Pam is still in there, unchanged.

- February: Pam quarrels with a neighbor and calls the police.

- March: We travel to Texas to investigate an intensive aphasia program. At the airport, she becomes furious when there's a flight delay.

- March: I'm late getting home, and she breaks her cell phone.

- April: Pam writes on the walls and threatens divorce.

- May: She's angry and abusive, sitting in my office and pelting me with bits of bread. Later, she dreams that I drive off and leave her, and takes this as a warning from God to treat me better.

- May: She develops poison ivy, and the itching makes her frantic. Convinced I've hidden her medications, she goes through the house turning on every light.

- May: She won't sit still in the car, and, when I try to restrain her, claims I hit her. She barricades herself in the bathroom, and tells a pastor that she loves me but wants a divorce.

- May: I make breakfast, but she becomes difficult and throws the food at me.

- June: The conflicts and contradictions keep escalating. In a moment of remorse, Pam writes:

    I'm not sure why I keep saying angry things to you. I'd be lost without you. I'm so sorry for the pain I've caused you. Please forgive me. Thank you for saving me again.

Two nights later, she gets angry as we eat out to celebrate our anniversary; she leaves and walks home—and then writes:

Dear John,

I'm sorry for the way I behaved today. I'm grateful for your patience with me once I left. That was wrong.

Would you mind if I go ahead a ask you to use as much time to keep away from me as long as you need to for your own calm, too.

*Maybe we'd be better if we move in a different areas to
sleep. As long as I'll be needing to have to go to bed so
early and awake whenever I need to.*

- June: I have to travel for my job, and can't take her along.
She orders me to move out. I refuse, and the next day she
acknowledges, *None of my angerness really isn't because of
you.* But the following week, after bringing up the topic
again, she leaves abruptly and stays at a motel for a few
days.

- June: She quarrels again with a neighbor, and writes to me,
*You don't seem to be strong enough to stick up for your sick wife
in her coma who didn't know you.*

- July: Pam throws food and breaks my father's cane. The
next day, she writes me an apologetic letter:

  *I'm afraid I may have already lost you, John. . . .
  I'm so sorry for all the things I've put you through.
  Please, will you help me any way you feel now?
  I'll trust you for anything to help me live. What now?*

- July: I have my own blowout, described later in this chapter. As a result I lose Pam's trust, and things get even worse
for a little while.

- August: Pam says herself that sometimes she acts like a two-
year-old who needs to nap but fights it. Indeed, she resists
and resents my efforts to "manage" her.

- August: In the driveway outside, she locks her keys in the
car—all of them. I don't hear the doorbell, so she turns on
the hose and sprays water everywhere.

- August: As we drive home from Kansas City, she starts
coughing, and then is angry when I don't treat it as an

emergency. She gets out of the car, right where we are in a strange neighborhood, and walks away.

- August: I wake to find her angry. She's lost her keys, but eventually we figure out that the main issue is pain: a chiropractor taped her feet too tightly. I find her keys in the shower, but my work day is pretty much lost.

- August: Late in the summer, things start to improve. Her outbursts blow over more quickly, and she now stops to ask, "Why did I do that?" Her new pet dogs probably exert a calming influence, but she credits cooler weather, stating several times that really hot days make her cranky. She writes:

  My Goodness. I am so very sorry for all those things I've said or written these last 11 month's. Will you please help me get better, honey? Honestly, I really don't know why I behave this way, John.

- October: As I drive Pam to visual therapy in Kansas City, she keeps asking for "refills." I don't know what this means. As we near the end of the trip, I finally catch on that she wants to stop at a gas station with a mini-mart that sells snacks. I suggest Burger King and she agrees, but when we get there it turns out that she was thinking of McDonalds, and now she says dramatically that she'd rather be dead. When we're calmer, I propose this as Burger King's new advertising slogan. After all the tension, I look into the possibility of hiring a driver to take her to these appointments, but she writes:

  I'm difficult. I can see why you'd prefer to hire someone to drive me to KC to help me with my disabilities. I'm afraid to go with anyone else to drive me. They won't like me or be as good as you've been. . . .

I'm sorry I was so mad that last week you drove me to KC. Please forgive me for my behavior.

- December: After family visits for Christmas, Pam tears up some of her journals. I think she is grieving all that's been lost, and the gulfs that appear to surround her now. She is also hurt that I didn't write more in my Christmas card to her.

2012

- January: I'm exhausted one evening, but Pam wants to go to Walgreens, and threatens to walk if I don't take her.

- February: We learn that the University of Kansas is charging us for Pam's speech therapy sessions with students last semester, and she explodes. At least this episode results in a clarification: the bill is a mistake.

- April: At the grocery store, I start to feel overwhelmed by the press of people and noise, and hurry Pam along. Once we're home, she gets angry and again talks of divorce. Then, more calmly, she says she hates my driving. My tension makes her tense, so much so that she no longer learns anything when I drive her to appointments.

- May: She wants to go grocery shopping but storms off twice, once in the store and again on the drive home, hopping out of the car at a traffic light. After a time she calls, and I pick her up.

- May: Rage following a panic attack. She flushes some meds down the toilet.

- July: Pam insists on shopping for a moped, saying that she *will* get out without depending on me. Soon after, she begins riding the bus to some appointments.

- August: I take Pam to Wendy's for lunch after church. She seems happy, but suddenly insists that she can't eat unless I make conversation. I try, but almost at once she's angry and says, if I won't talk, she can't eat and will wait outside. Then she doesn't wait, but takes off in her wheelchair. I search for her for an hour before she answers her phone.

- August: Also this month, we have the incident of Pam experiencing an aura and then panicking as I drive her to the ER. When I stop at a red light, she's out of the car and walking. We lose quite a bit of time before I can coax her back into the car, and she's that much more disoriented and weak when we finally reach the hospital. Still, her takeaway is that I should beep the horn and never slow or stop in these situations.

- September: Pam acts subdued with me but goes to see a lawyer, saying that I'm causing her stress and panic attacks. A police officer comes to our apartment with a Temporary Order of Protection, and I have to leave for a time. He warns that I'll go to jail at the next offense. Pam is alarmed that her complaint has such large consequences, and cancels the Order of Protection.

- October: Another big flap when she learns I've stored some photographs in the apartment garage.

- November: More clashes as I finish moving the last of our belongings out of the house. She leaves a church supper abruptly, taking the car; I walk home, carrying her plate of food, but she's gone to bed.

- December: I drive to Walgreens for Pam's prescriptions and have to wait—and completely forget that she has a physical therapy appointment. She's furious and won't get in the car when I go to the therapist's to pick her up. So I leave the car with her, but she still calls the police on me. We remain apart all day.

2013

- February: Pam tells me she is going to babysit for a friend, but stays overnight at a domestic violence shelter. She hates it there and is glad to come home. During her absence, I am again visited by the police. I'm mystified, clueless, as we had no argument that day.

- March: Pam abruptly fires the contractor renovating the house and hires a different firm. I have to write them a check, and transfer funds between accounts in order to cover it. She interprets this as a theft of "her" money and files a Temporary Order of Protection from Abuse, stating in her complaint, *Always hurting me.* As a result, one evening after 8:00, two sheriffs show up at the apartment and order me to leave at once and to initiate no contact with Pam until a court date eighteen days away (on Good Friday). They seem surprised that I can think of no friend to call, to stay with, but drive me to a motel. Pam sends me an email: *May the Lord help you.*

- March: We have a difficult couple of weeks. She keeps the car and the apartment; I stay at a motel and walk everywhere. She calls to say she misses me, and tries to share a TV sitcom with me over the phone. Another day, she picks me up in the car and takes me back to the apartment for lunch; I make sandwiches, but by this time she's angry and threatens to call the police unless I leave. I walk back to the motel, but that night, after a nightmare, she calls. At last she invites me to move home, and dismisses her complaint against me.

- June: Pam records this prayer:

  Father, please heal me so I can be the wife he deserves.
  Deliver me from this anger and rage. I see why John is

afraid of me. Have mercy on us both so we can share your gospel through the Gift's that are earezokable—soon, father.

2014

- March: Stressing over our efforts to sell the renovated house, Pam again threatens to divorce me.

- November: Pam writes in one of her letters to me, *Sorry I've been such a mean creep lately. Pain does that to me.* But, really, with the house sold, and Pam able to drive, and more of a settled routine, the outbursts have grown fewer and shorter.

2015

- March: With headaches and pain in her feet, back, arm, and eye, Pam still takes time to write, *John, I was passing [on] my anger from this variety of the pain I've been having—mad words around you.*

- June: Again, a quick apology after an understandable reaction:

  Please forgive me for the way I reacted when I realized I'd just broken my right toe last night. The pain was excruciating and I freaked out. As usual I took it out 100% on you, John. I was wrong. . . . [I] did not have the right words to tell you what had just happened to me. As "they" say at AA I should have counted to ten before I even opened my mouth. I also should have first prayed to God down on my knee's as asked God to help me. Instead, as you observed, I screamed at you when I felt you didn't understand what had just happened.

A tapering off, and then . . . peace. There have been flare-ups since, especially when there's underlying pain—in 2017, she wrote to me, *Ever since I injured my right foot at church I've been behaving awful.*

Today I've been realizing I've had a migraine. It also helps that she takes a mood-regulating medication; in 2018, after we had a quarrelsome day, she realized that she'd forgotten to take it. But the change is still extraordinary. If survivors and families glean nothing else from this chapter, perhaps it may at least kindle hope that the season of storms may come to an end, and, ultimately, that there is a possibility of emotional growth surpassing mere restoration, as some survivors attest:

> Instead of steeling myself when I felt sad like I used to before the stroke, I had to allow myself to cry. I allowed myself to feel sad. And this changed the landscape of my emotions. Over the years I became a less angry person, because my anger had actually been a cover for sadness and vulnerability.[143]

Still, this is quite a chronology. Some episodes seem to have obvious roots in pain or fear, in times of pressure, or in my foolishness and insensitivity. Others appear to be somewhat seasonal—perhaps, as Pam suspected, intensifying in hot weather.

Two patterns stand out, and each raises a compelling question:

1. Each flare-up tended to blaze till it became an inferno. Leaving, throwing or breaking things, threatening divorce, calling the police are extreme expressions. When family members say that a stroke or brain-injury survivor isn't the same person—when Pam herself wonders who she is—behaviors like these are often in view. Why does brain-injured anger swell to such heights?

2. The episodes continue without much abatement for several years, and reach their climax in 2013. Still, at last there is a dramatic falling off. What on earth caused it? Can all survivors of stroke or traumatic brain injury reasonably hope for anger to diminish over time?

---

[143] Lee, *Tell Me Everything You Don't Remember*, 48.

We will look at both of these topics. I warn you in advance that I know more of the stamina of anger; its dying away remains largely a mystery to me.

DISINHIBITION

He who has no rule over his own spirit is like a city that is broken down and without walls. — Prov. 25:28, Ampl

Think of anger as an elevator.[144] It ascends, perhaps, through five floors; I call mine:

1. Annoyance,
2. Resentment,
3. Irritability,
4. Anger, and
5. Rage.

Each time my car rises to a new floor, I hear the dinging of a little bell: something in my subconscious sends me a little warning, so that I can prepare myself; because the world looks vastly different, and I come forth very differently, when the doors open on 5 rather than on 2.

This system works reasonably well. But then there are those periods in life when I start the day at 3. For weeks on end, I may wake each morning already at Irritability; I may never once touch down at the ground floor, the calm state that AA and Al-Anon folks might call Serenity. And this "elevated" response, this always-irritable condition, is fine, and perhaps unavoidable. But it's good for me to be aware that, when I live this way, when anger becomes "normal," I stop hearing the warning bells. I just react.

----

[144] I owe this illustration to Glenda Young, a friend and a wise counselor.

Since we are often told that depression is anger turned inward, I conceive that my elevator is built to travel down as well as up. I picture a series of subbasement levels, mirroring the above-ground floors, and call them:

−1. Sadness,

−2. Gloom,

−3. Bitterness,

−4. Depression, and

−5. Despair.

The descending car, no less than the ascending, is equipped with warning bells, and these cease to sound when -2 or lower becomes my daily starting point.

There is one additional wrinkle: the elevator often runs as an express. Over the course of the day, as circumstances and triggers change, we may go directly from -2 to 2, or from 3 to -3, and so on. This means, again, no alarms.

Following a stroke or a TBI, every day can seem like a ride on an express elevator. No bells, and no intermediate stops. With no map or memory of our primary emotions, we practically live in this bobbing, windowless capsule. We shoot from 0 to -5, and from there directly to 5. Then, with a little awareness, back at once to -5.

Why does this happen? Consider the flow of current through an electrical wire. After generating electricity, we are able to harness its power, to guide and use the energy, so long as we wrap the wire in layers of insulation. Since these layers are made of materials that conduct electricity poorly, the current flows through the wire. But if the insulation is torn or stripped, a short circuit may occur—and, depending on the surrounding materials, may result in a fire or even an explosion.

. . . a rage that reaches to heaven. — 2 Chron. 28:9

Much of our social training in childhood is a form of electrical engineering. Parents and teachers lay wire as they channel and direct the emotional energy we so often express as anger. The layers of insulation are social norms: *Don't hit. Don't kick. Count to ten before you get angry. Don't use certain words.*

Stroke and brain injury strip the insulation and leave the wires of our emotion bare. Survivors short-circuit, often destructively, sometimes spectacularly. They frequently say that the "filters" that once softened their impressions and regulated their expressions have all been swept aside—as in this account:

> There was, for me, a peculiar emotional quality to having a stroke. It felt as if a protective layer had been stripped away from me—as if I were exposed to the world without a buffer. I'd been in the hospital before for surgery. After surgery, for a while I'd regress and experience life in a more childlike state of helplessness. But having a stroke wasn't like that experience at all. Having a stroke was raw, as if my filters weren't in place.[145]

Though she describes this state as "emotional soup" and "emotional incontinence,"[146] the same author comments that it isn't all bad,

---

[145] Shapiro, *Healing into Possibility*, 117. Here is a more scientific explanation: "Anger interrupts the functioning of your frontal lobes. Not only do you lose the ability to be rational, you lose the awareness that you're acting in an irrational way. When your frontal lobes shut down, it's impossible to listen to the other person, let alone feel empathy or compassion. Instead, you are likely to feel self-justified and self-righteous, and when that happens the communication process falls apart. Anger also releases a cascade of neurochemicals that actually destroy those parts of the brain that control emotional reactivity." Andrew Newberg and Mark Robert Waldman, *How God Changes Your Brain: Breakthrough Findings from a Leading Neuroscientist* (2009; New York: Ballantine, 2010), 19-20.

[146] Shapiro, 119, 117. See also Joel Stein, *Stroke and the Family: A New Guide* (Cambridge, MA and London: Harvard, 2004), 163-65.

citing the example of her friend Carol, who is a therapist as well as a stroke survivor:

> She can use that increased sensitivity to experience emotions, both her own and other people's, as a tool in her group therapy sessions. Her ability to be so in touch with feelings gives permission and space for others to work with their own.[147]

The removal of society's careful filters, of politeness and modulation, leaves a kind of wildness. There is, first, an emotional *lability* or instability, a powerless feeling of one's feelings. If Post-Traumatic Stress Disorder (PTSD) is characterized partly by dissociation,[148] one striking feature of many stroke and TBI survivors (though in time they may progress to PTSD) is that they *cannot* dissociate. They are largely at the mercy of the emotions coursing through them:

> When anger comes on me, it's not typical anger. When I become stressed, the anger instantly takes over. I cannot control my emotions.[149]

And there are many emotions. Jason Padgett especially experienced disabling fear, even agoraphobia[150]—granted, his TBI was brought on by a savage beating. More commonly, one reads of pain and grief and frustration. Following her stroke, Corrie ten Boom sometimes wept

---

[147] Shapiro, 122.

[148] Judith Herman, *Trauma and Recovery: The Aftermath of Violence—From Domestic Abuse to Political Terror* (1992; New York: Basic-Perseus, 2015), 34-35, 239-40; Kirby Farrell, *Posttraumatic Culture: Injury and Interpretation in the Nineties* (Baltimore and London: Johns Hopkins, 1998), 11.

[149] Laura and Bruce Allen, *Brain Storm: A Journey of Faith through Brain Injury* (Bloomington, IN: WestBow-Thomas Nelson, 2012), 73.

[150] Jason Padgett and Maureen Seaberg, *Struck by Genius: How a Brain Injury Made Me a Mathematical Marvel* (Boston and New York: Houghton Mifflin Harcourt, 2014), 41-42, 48.

just because life had become so difficult.[151] Mark McEwen, a news anchorman who sustained a massive stroke, wept "tears of triumph and joy" the first time he could walk the length of a hospital corridor without assistance, "but somewhere in the mix there were also tears of frustration."[152]

Again, this vulnerability can be positive and healing. Cathy Crimmins, whose husband suffered a brain injury in a boating accident, describes one of his "inappropriate" responses:

> Yet sometimes I can understand why the rest of the world finds Alan's new softness more appealing. He has no defenses. He is an open book and seems very emotionally available to people. One night, a year after his injury, we go out with Valerie and Jon, dear friends of ours who run a café, and a few other neighbors. Valerie has just found out that a rare lung disease is likely to kill her in the next few years. Valerie is French and cultivates a cynical Gallic affect. She drops her news casually in the middle of dinner, so offhandedly that we think she is kidding. "Oh, yes, I am dying!" she insists merrily, and takes another sip of champagne. The rest of us sit there, shocked and trying not to overreact. Alan, who has no social filters left on his reactions, bursts into loud sobs. Valerie turns to me: "It is not like Alan to be so upset!" Yet I can tell that Al has disarmed her, that his sobs are the only adequate reaction to finding out that someone you love might soon die. Everyone at the table feels this way but cannot express it so immediately. This is what people mean, I think, when they say that brain-injured people, in

---

[151] Pamela Rosewell Moore, *The Five Silent Years of Corrie ten Boom* (Grand Rapids, MI: Zondervan-HarperCollins, 1986), 155-56.

[152] Mark McEwen with Daniel Paisner, *Change in the Weather: Life after Stroke* (New York: Gotham-Penguin, 2008), 120-21.

their childlike openness, are examples of what the rest of us should be.[153]

Secondly, once one feels, one expresses:

> I had no restraint in my unkindness. I was unable to keep my insults inside my mind.[154]

Disinhibition means that many of the rules and norms of behavior, carefully instilled through years of socialization, are simply gone, leaving one uninhibited. This quality is often abetted by *impulsivity*, "an inability to delay action while considering the consequences."[155] Of course, certain sleep-talking bungee-jumpers might already have a head start down this particular highway.

After surgery, some people return to consciousness "cussing up a storm."[156] This is embarrassing to Christians. Linda Barrick notes that her daughter Jen never used swear words, adding, a bit smugly, "When you're shaken, whatever you're full of spills out."[157] Losses, frustrations, and difficulty in expressing oneself make for unpredictable utterances; particularly after brain injury, "Under stress, an obscenity may be the

---

[153] Cathy Crimmins, *Where Is the Mango Princess?: A Journey Back from Brain Injury* (2000; New York: Vintage-Random House, 2001), 227-28.

[154] Lee, *Tell Me Everything You Don't Remember*, 228.

[155] Stein, *Stroke and the Family*, 145.

[156] Marks, *A Stitch of Time*, 243.

[157] Linda Barrick with John Perry, *Miracle for Jen: A Tragic Accident, a Mother's Desperate Prayer, and Heaven's Extraordinary Answer* (Carol Stream, IL: Tyndale House, 2012), 82. On the other hand, "When she's moody, she gets very abrupt and insistent, though never mean" (211). Barrick quotes Jesus: "What you say flows from what is in your heart" (Luke 6:45, NLT)— missing His point, which is that our hearts are mixed and muddied (even as our vision is clouded, 6:41-42). Elsewhere in the New Testament, we read, "Out of the same mouth come praise and cursing. My brothers and sisters, this should not be" (James 3:10). Should not, but is, so long as you and I are less than perfected in Christ.

first word the brain supplies."[158] Bruce Allen is perhaps more typical: although he was a former pastor who didn't curse, following a brain injury he found himself using certain choice words when he became angry.[159] Pam's personal playlist of imprecations came back all at once, never again to desert her.

An apocryphal story[160] has a couple of English ladies approaching Samuel Johnson, following the publication of his *Dictionary*, to commend him for leaving out all "the indelicate and objectionable words." Shrewdly if not kindly, Johnson replies, "What, my dears! Have you been searching for them?" In a mind affected by stroke or TBI, the situation is almost the reverse: many words have been excised from this dictionary, but those used for cursing—perhaps just because they are such strong, sharp sounds—are all retained, and the user browsing for plainer language keeps lighting on them. If *The Pam Unabridged Dictionary of the English Language* is ever printed, I am convinced, you'll be able to turn to the letter "J" and find, under "john," compounds beginning with *d—* and *s—*. Search for *ice* and you'll locate *dollar amount*.

With or without four-letter words, with the filters down, what comes pouring out is usually anger. Paul West, himself a stroke survivor, writes:

> Most of the stroke victims you will meet will strike you as agitated beings in whom the very slightest setback will produce explosions of rage and shock at the poor innocent in the outside world who has again failed to understand them.[161]

---

[158] Claudia L. Osborn, *Over My Head: A Doctor's Own Story of Head Injury from the Inside Looking Out* (Kansas City, MO: Andrews McMeel, 1998), 187.

[159] Allen and Allen, *Brain Storm*, 73-74.

[160] See versions and discussion in "Improper Words: Have You Been Searching for Them?" at *Quote Investigator*, accessed December 19, 2021, https://quoteinvestigator.com/2013/09/22/improper-search/.

[161] Paul West, *The Shadow Factory* (Santa Fe, NM: Lumen, 2008), 111.

West, a professional writer, goes on to say that the survivor's

> sudden irritability . . . is very largely the result of pure
> frustration. . . . [T]hese bouts of irritability have an imper-
> sonal bouquet, not aimed at anybody in particular but
> rather directed at the full panoply of language that has been
> denied. It is not irritability as much as a consuming desire
> to do better.[162]

But others describe a generalized anger, even a rage, that extends far
beyond communication difficulties. Following a stroke, May Sarton
wrote, "I am on the edge of anger all the time. . . . I seem to be an
impossible person."[163] Some experience a virtually unending series of
outbursts. Former football player Terry Evanshen received his brain
injury in a car accident:

> . . . damage to the frontal lobes of Terry's brain had disrupted
> his anger controls. Terry had no ability to suppress rage, or
> moderate it, or direct it harmlessly into vigorous activity or
> work, as most adults do. None of his tantrums would last
> long, . . . and when they dissipated Terry would forget they
> had happened.[164]

As others confronted him, Evanshen came to think of himself as an
angry person. When a counselor assured him that character persists,
that he was still basically his old self,

---

[162] West, 177-78. West's wife, Diane Ackerman, duly notes his "childlike tantrums" and "angry
outbursts," but also describes a change as he begins to communicate more successfully, and
as he starts taking an antidepressant: "Surprisingly, his temper vanished a few weeks after the
stroke, when he became mellower, more patient, deeply appreciative, . . ." *One Hundred Names
for Love*, 32, 61, 212.

[163] May Sarton, *After the Stroke: A Journal* (New York and London: W. W. Norton, 1988), 54.

[164] June Callwood, *The Man Who Lost Himself: The Terry Evanshen Story* (Toronto: McClelland
& Stewart, 2000), 114.

Terry didn't believe her. It had been three years since the accident and he could see little sign of any former character coming through, unless his former self was a miserable, explosive jerk.[165]

Kevin Sorbo takes us back to the elevator that starts each day already at the third floor:

> . . . the most common symptom for a head-injured patient is an enhanced or uncontrollable temper, an accelerated rage response. I had that one, for sure. Basically, my emotions were not my own. I have always been impatient, but now, with my temper constantly burning at medium-high, I was rude and overly critical much of the time.[166]

Sometimes temper flare-ups alternate with crippling remorse, shame, and fear of the person one is becoming. Krickitt Carpenter was brain-injured in a car accident. Her husband Kim writes:

> We would have sweet times of companionship and rebuilding that were suddenly interrupted by the temper outbursts of an unruly teenager. There would be instances when she completely lost control, quickly followed by periods of fear and confusion about her behavior.[167]

Kim summarizes: "When it came to Krickitt's emotions, anything could happen at any moment."[168]

[165] Callwood, 199.
[166] Sorbo, *True Strength*, 205.
[167] Kim and Krickitt Carpenter with Dana Wilkerson, *The Vow* (2000), revised edition (Nashville: B & H, 2012), 122.
[168] Carpenter and Carpenter, 110.

The survivor is also thrust into a condition of childlike dependence, at least at first. By some perverse logic, this neediness can make one demanding, prone to tantrums:

> One of the most trying aspects of being sick is being cared for, as counterintuitive and thankless as that may sound. Nothing makes a person feel out of control . . . like having to cede it to another person. All the cooking and cleaning and being ministered to was, I felt, turning me into a whiny, overgrown baby. — Amanda Fortini[169]

> And I was, emotionally, very much a child and needed constant reassurance and attention. When I didn't get it, I could conjure the blackest of moods.[170]

Paradoxically, some stroke and TBI survivors experience the *opposite* of disinhibition: a lack of animation and emotional connection, almost a vacancy, known as *adynamia*. (This is not Pam's problem; one day when she can't sit still, she tells me, "I'm dynamic—it's called itching!") This state has affinities with PTSD. The adynamic person may have difficulty conversing or even thinking, may appear to others to be sleepwalking—except in moments of desperation, or when the emotions rush in, overwhelming and paralyzing, producing a condition of confused awareness called *flooding*. Adynamia and flooding are vividly described by Claudia Osborn in her memoir of struggling back to a full emotional life.[171]

---

[169] Amanda Fortini, "The Vital Role," in Nell Casey, ed., *An Uncertain Inheritance: Writers on Caring for Family* (New York: William Morrow-HarperCollins, 2007), 196.

[170] Patricia Neal with Richard DeNeut, *As I Am: An Autobiography* (New York: Simon and Schuster, 1988), 311.

[171] Osborn, *Over My Head*, 92-98, 61-62, 166, 212-13, 235-36. She still had her moments of disinhibited outrage, and was grateful she lived in New York City, where such outbursts passed unnoticed (177)!

Pam certainly experienced both emotional instability and disinhibition. And while I sometimes bore the brunt of her pain and anger, I can testify that she also felt an admirable empathy and experienced powerful compassion. The stripping of her wires led to a kind of hot-wiring; it prepared her to unlock others.

There has also been a heartening progression:

- Six months after her stroke, Pam was raging at me every day, usually several times a day. Often she seemed to be reliving and reenacting old traumas, dating back even to childhood. An insightful counselor suggested that Pam's lability and disinhibition extended to her memories—that she couldn't choose NOT to remember, and couldn't redirect her thoughts.

- By the time we reached the year-and-a-half mark, some self-control was possible. Pam was furious at me, but she desperately wanted company. One evening I told her that, since she wouldn't stop raging, I would go back into my office and shut the door. Plaintively, she replied, "No, I'll calm down"—and she did.

- Two years after the stroke, during a counseling session, our pastor observed that Pam had gone into "attack mode" and was no longer listening. She calmed right down, and afterward was happier and lighter. It helped that the critique was balanced; the pastor also found fault with my passivity. Still, she demonstrated that she could set a check on venting and blurting.

- At just under four years, when she paused in scolding me, I said, "You know, you treat absolutely everyone better than you treat me." She fell silent and, as I added some details, listened closely. The letter she wrote me a couple of days later shows that, while she still had trouble holding on to a train of thought, she could evaluate feelings and reject possible expressions:

Beautiful John, Good Morning. Thank you for telling me that "I testested (?) no (TREATed) any one better then I treated you. Ouch. No. I was very grateful for you telling that DEMON scaring us daily. . . . . What was I jusust writting?

I LOVE you, John. You have helped me live! I'm out of that coffin filled with one large demon terrozing me 4 Days—left when you, John, wrote via internet telling million's to pray 4 Pam. They did.

*   *   *

To some, disinhibition is divine. Job charges, "God does not restrain his anger" (Job 9:13), and while this is wildly inaccurate—later, he will complain that God is too soft on the wicked[172]—we understand: he feels utterly crushed. Others fear, in the midst of affliction, that God may be "angry with us beyond measure."[173] But the consistent testimony of Scripture is that the Lord is "slow to anger" (Ex. 34:6). Though His anger has tremendous, near-annihilating power—"Who can stand before you when you are angry?"[174]—He saves it as a last resort. When the psalmist warns, "Kiss the Son, lest he be angry and you be destroyed in your way, for his wrath can flare up in a moment" (Ps. 2:12, NIV84; NRSV "for his wrath is quickly kindled"), he is not describing a God who is quick-tempered and capricious. Rather, this is the "suddenly" of God, when, after much correction and many pleadings, all at once He acts. We see this, for example, when His anger burns against Moses only after He has patiently answered every

---

[172] Job 21:17-21. Elihu notices this flaw in Job's reasoning (Job 35:15); Jonah echoes it (Jonah 4:1-3).

[173] Lam. 5:22; compare Isa. 64:9; Jer. 10:24, NRSV.

[174] Ps. 76:7; Nah. 1:6; Rev. 6:15-17.

objection to the prophet's call, and Moses still asks Him to send someone else (Ex. 4:13-14).

So far from being hotheaded, God sets an extraordinary example of loving, long-suffering patience. "Time after time he restrained his anger and did not stir up his full wrath" (Ps. 78:38). Because He is our very breath, those who feel abandoned cry out, asking if He will be angry forever (Ps. 79:5; 85:5; Jer. 3:5); yet the faithful also testify, "his anger lasts only a moment" (Ps. 30:5; compare Isa. 54:8), and the Lord Himself graciously sets a limit to His anger because He is conscious of our frailty:

> I will not accuse forever,
> nor will I always be angry,
> for then the spirit of man would grow faint before me—
> the breath of man that I have created. — Isa. 57:16, NIV84

The anger of God is always utterly overwhelming, impossible to fathom or long endure. But the pledge of God's character, as revealed to Moses in Exodus 34, is that anger, though strong, comes slowly; that mercy and grace come first; and that anger is followed by steadfast love.

ANGER AS ENERGY AND HOPE

> Samson said to them, "Since you've acted like this, I swear that I won't stop until I get my revenge on you." . . . His parents did not know that this was from the LORD, who was seeking an occasion to confront the Philistines. — Judg. 15:7; 14:4

> When Saul heard their words, the Spirit of God came powerfully upon him, and he burned with anger. — 1 Sam. 11:6; compare Judg. 14:19

She would have spoken further, to have enlarged and confirmed her discourse, when Pamela, whose cheeks were dyed in the beautifulest grain of virtuous anger, with eyes which glistered forth beams of disdain, thus interrupted her.
— Philip Sidney[175]

One day in 2015, Pam announced to me, "I need to join a fight club." Okay, so a cop show on TV had planted the idea. Still, as her frequent sparring partner, I grasped just how much the idea resonated with her. Heck, I'd have to bet on her. She was saying that she had too much energy—and angry energy, at that.

Can the generator of anger drive recovery? Should it? I have to admit that I'm torn. I remember my father after his heart attack, politely impervious to all the pleadings and prodding of nurses and therapists, and I think: *Anything is better than giving up*. I admire Pam's spirited determination, even if the byproduct—or the fuel, or the engine itself—is rage.

The massive stroke suffered by Jean-Dominique Bauby left him with locked-in syndrome, able to communicate only by blinking his left eyelid. Helpless as he was, a fire burned; and he believed it was essential to tune and lubricate all his other emotions:

> I need to feel strongly, to love and to admire, just as desperately as I need to breathe. . . . But to keep my mind sharp, to avoid descending into resigned indifference, I maintain a level of resentment and anger, neither too much nor too little, just as a pressure cooker has a safety valve to keep it from exploding.[176]

---

[175] Philip Sidney, *The Countess of Pembroke's Arcadia* (1593), Book 3 (London: Sampson Low Marston, 1898), 281. Also available at *Luminarium*, accessed December 19, 2021, http://www.luminarium.org/renascence-editions/arcadia1.html.

[176] Jean-Dominique Bauby, *The Diving Bell and the Butterfly: A Memoir of Life in Death* (1997), transl. Jeremy Leggatt (New York: Vintage-Random House, 1998), 55. Pann Baltz, who suffered

Speech-language pathologist Mark Ittleman suggests that the patient "must have a junkyard dog mentality to dig into the language stimulation process and never give up, even if it takes a lifetime."[177]

Some of us make an idol of our anger. Like the Israelites with the golden calf, we prize it as a mindless force of power and vitality. Half blindly, at any least provocation, we lower our heads and charge, tossing people aside, goring and trampling them; then we justify our behavior by saying that we were "just being honest." This is a grievous distortion. *Honesty* is allied with *honor*; it can be revealed or disclosed in an instant; it does not escalate, but burns steadily like a candle flame. Fierce anger is to honesty as madness is to character: not a summation but an abrogation or a lapse. A bull is not honest, but wild. A forest fire is not honest but furious, raging out of control; so far from revealing truth, it combusts it; so far from reconciling lives, it smothers and incinerates; the air it boasts of clearing, it annihilates.

It is one of the mysteries of God that He, whose strength is inexhaustible, can speak of being energized by anger:

> I looked, but there was no one to help,
> I was appalled that no one gave support;
> so my own arm achieved salvation for me,
> and my own wrath sustained me

---

seven strokes (but who was not locked-in), went further, expecting some explosions: "It was important for us to understand that anger is a natural by-product of a long and critical illness. The person who is sick is going to lash out in frustration and fear, and even feel resentment because those around her are healthy and pain-free. And the family will occasionally be angry at the person who is sick. It's all part of the normal response, and you must be able to confront those feelings in an honest and constructive way. I think a lot of relationships split up because there is so much guilt about how people are feeling." Qtd. in Marilee Dunker, *A Braver Song to Sing* (Grand Rapids, MI: Zondervan, 1987), 140.

[177] Mark A. Ittleman, *The Teaching of Talking: Learn to Do Expert Speech Therapy at Home with Children and Adults* (New York: Morgan James, 2013), 113. Nevertheless, Ittleman opposes any "stimulation" that challenges survivors to the point of frustration. He regards frustration as a sign that "the task presented is too difficult," and advises the therapist or caregiver to make an adjustment (47).

[Msg "I went ahead and did it myself, fed and fueled by my rage"]. — Isa. 63:5

What is striking is that, in a parallel passage, the word "wrath" is replaced, and we read, "his own righteousness sustained him" (Isa. 59:16). With God, the two are synonymous. His anger is a zealous regard for justice and purity. When He acts in anger, we see, not powerful petulance, but the majesty of holiness, the vindication of innocence, the beauty of humility, an end to evil, and universal relief and rejoicing at the establishment of just rule.

These qualities are rarely on display in our tantrums and hissy fits. We are advised, "Everyone should be quick to listen, slow to speak and slow to become angry, because human anger does not produce the righteousness that God desires" (James 1:19-20). Matthew Henry says, "To be angry at nothing but sin is the way not to sin in anger"[178]—but our anger is not so righteous and so pure. To be sure, we see glimpses: Moses's "hot anger" at obdurate Pharaoh is appropriate (Ex. 11:8, NRSV), while Jonathan's "fierce anger" at his father's "shameful" injustice represents a decisive—if imperfect—break with evil (1 Sam. 20:34).

Even Jesus redirects His anger more often than He gives vent to it. In one memorable encounter, He knows that the people around Him value Sabbath observance above the manifestation of God's life-giving power. He attempts to reason with them about this, but they won't engage. "He looked around at them with anger; he was grieved at their hardness of heart [Msg "furious at their hard-nosed religion"] . . ." (Mark 3:5, NRSV). His face registers anger and pain, but He goes on to act in a way that shows compassion and mercy.

Anger is like a suit of clothes. When God does act in anger, He doesn't adopt a disguise or don a mask; He chooses the uniform that

---

[178] Matthew Henry, *Commentary on the Whole Bible* (1708-10; Grand Rapids, MI: Christian Classics Ethereal Library, n.d.), 1:567, on Ex. 11:8; available at *Christian Classics Ethereal Library*, accessed December 19, 2021, https://ccel.org/ccel/henry.

expresses an aspect of His righteous and holy nature. One biblical writer says, "You have covered [NRSV "wrapped"] yourself with anger and pursued us" (Lam. 3:43). At other times—most times—He takes off His anger and sets it aside. We might say that God "wears many hats." He puts each one on deliberately, ever true to His character and to His long-range purposes.

In contrast, we who brag of honesty refuse to stand exposed in pain and fear, in frustration and shame and anxiety. We rush to bolt ourselves in thick-smithed anger as our armor and stumble into life half-hidden and inflexible. Hear what the psalmist declares of the wicked man, adding a hope that his dissimulation will become his inescapable truth:

> He clothed himself with cursing as his coat,
> may it soak into his body like water,
> like oil into his bones. — Ps. 109:18, NRSV

We catch Peter in the act of donning this same chain mail: "He began to call down curses on himself, and he swore to them, 'I don't know this man you're talking about'" (Mark 14:71, NIV84).

So Paul urges us to "put off" anger, wrath, and malice, as one sheds last season's clothes (Col. 3:8, KJV; compare Eph. 4:31); one paraphrase even specifies "cast off and throw away all these rotten garments" (Living).

We may admire the idea of unfiltered rage, but we're appalled when we actually meet it. People get stuck in anger; like a charging rhino, they go on and on, past all memory of cause or purpose. The prophet says of Israel's southern neighbor Edom, "his anger raged continually and his fury flamed unchecked" (Amos 1:11). This is not strength but psychosis. Almost every episode of the TV show *The Dog Whisperer* features at least one dog that routinely rises to a yapping frenzy, making life unbearable for itself and others till Cesar Millan defuses the dog's anger by breaking its obsessive concentration and rectifying a root issue.

Anger rarely "clears the air"; usually it calls forth others' anger so that we "keep on biting and devouring each other" (Gal. 5:15, NIV84), until finally the angriest voice wins, while everyone else is cowed. We try to wait it out, but it doesn't end, or not for long: tantrums are habit-forming. When Jacob flees from Esau's murderous rage, their mother Rebekah promises him, "When your brother is no longer angry with you and forgets what you did to him, I'll send word for you to come back" (Gen. 27:45). The message never comes; presumably, by the time Esau does calm down (Gen. 33:1-9), Rebekah has died.

The Bible has a name for anyone whose moral compass is personal vanity, with the needle shifting at once as honor is flattered or insulted. The name is *fool*; the several Hebrew and Greek words bring out different nuances, but they come pretty much to the same unsightly character. Such people are practical atheists, living as if there is no God but self (Ps. 14:1; 53:1), no honor save my own. We call them thin-skinned, but it is just as accurate to say heavy-plated: no matter how deep we probe, we find only fresh layers of angry pretense. This is the man who is always ready to fight to the death for a parking space. "He who foams up quickly *and* flies into a passion deals foolishly" (Prov. 14:17, Ampl).[179]

Angry though she was, Pam never became this fool. Her pain was always evident; anger was not her armor so much as the walker or cane she leaned upon to step out of the hospital. Because she had long since given herself to God, she had little left to defend. She was not the elder brother from the parable of the prodigal son, standing with a chip on her shoulder, refusing the Father's invitation until every party should be in her honor. She was Job, desperately reaching after the God who receded; grasping at anything, even lobbing stones to get His attention.

Her rage was stronger for being inarticulate. It was a long time before she could entrust her missiles to words; for months and years,

---

[179] Compare Prov. 12:16; 20:3; 29:11; Eccl. 7:9; Job 5:2. The fool has only contempt for godly wisdom: Prov. 23:9; 29:9; Matt. 7:6.

the guns of her language jammed. So she threw food and stepped out of cars, releasing energy in ways that couldn't heal, dissipating it wastefully, alienating people. And still she was sometimes checked and cowed by others' anger, or what she took for anger—as when, at National Rehab, she asked why the loud nurse was angry with her.

Against all expectation, a few times I have seen Pam's anger clear the air. Once, at a church, we attended a marriage "simulcast," a series of teaching sessions broadcast from another state. Our minister had to leave; in charge was an elder, a Mexican American man who spoke English with halting formality and great courtesy. When the simulcast ended, he announced that he would close the meeting with a prayer. I froze as I heard Pam boil up beside me, felt the high curling scorn of her words: "So that's it?! There's nothing?!" It was the voice I had heard each time I lifted the lid on her hospital lunch tray. This time, she managed to get out that we needed help in our marriage, and the ambushed elder handled it well, assuring her that of course anyone who wished could stay and talk. My embarrassment ebbed as I saw other couples speak up, seeking counsel. Despite her choice of words and tone, apparently Pam's honesty had opened a door.

Afterward, while Pam was in the bathroom, I ran into the elder in an aisle. Around us, couples still were deep in conversation. He looked both ways, with the furtiveness of the once-bitten, and then commented, "Wow, your wife—she is a firecracker!"

"You don't know the half of it," I answered, smiling. Later, I passed this along to Pam, and for some days she proudly referred to herself as a "firehouse."

She had insight and perspective regarding her flare-ups, as a fool rarely does. Once we watched as a TV preacher, Creflo Dollar, reminded Christians, "Don't kick your brother when he's down." Pam protested, "But that's what I'm good at!" and we shared a hearty laugh.

*   *   *

Beginning a couple of months after we came home, she asked me to sue the doctors. I wasn't enamored of the idea; we had our hands full with recovery, I pictured a huge expenditure of time and energy, I had little hope of either compensation or answers, and I could easily imagine the two of us getting stuck in anger. I simply wanted to forgive and move on—though by "forgive" I meant only burying my questions and trying to shrug off my resentments.

Pam was not so easily deterred. The Holy Spirit must have been working, because she came to me with a dim memory of a woman demanding help from a judge. I read her the parable, with the widow's plea: "Grant me justice against my adversary" (Luke 18:3). Then I tried again to dissuade her from pursuing it. But she, with the very persistence enjoined in the parable, began calling lawyers. And so I followed her into a tangled wood.

We soon were advised that Kansas is a "one cause of action" state, meaning that you can't sue two parties seeking remuneration for one set of damages. Who then to blame? Pam's worst outcomes were from the stroke, which occurred while she was a patient at Hopkins, and which they tried to downplay as simply a "seizure." We found a Maryland law firm that was willing to obtain her hospital records and have them reviewed by three neurosurgery forensic experts. This turned out to be a lengthy process—for one thing, the experts had to be far away, removed from collegial and referral relationships with Hopkins doctors. The process dragged on from February to September 2011. It produced no smoking gun, and no explanation as to why Pam's brain hemorrhage occurred.

This left the separate matter of the Kansas ophthalmologist whom Pam had consulted many times as the vision in her left eye deteriorated, with increasing pain and sensitivity to light. He had misdiagnosed the problem, while admitting that his preferred culprit should affect only people in high-stress jobs and should resolve itself quickly. He had also pooh-poohed her suffering and, worst, failed even to suggest scanning for a tumor—which prompted our neuro-ophthalmologist to call him grossly incompetent. At the very least, he put her through two and a half years of pain and decline, which ended only in May 2010, when her car accident revealed the tumor.

In Kansas, the statute of limitations on medical negligence cases is two years, which I figured gave us until May 2012, exactly two years after we first became aware of the tumor. But we learned that there is a separate, four-year "statute of repose," meaning that doctors can only be held accountable for negligence within the last four years. This still seems incredible to me, a codified refuge of scoundrels. Since the misdiagnosis was recorded in December 2007, this window was about to expire. In the end, none of the several firms we consulted would take our case.

I was relieved, in late 2011, to drop the matter and walk away; I have always felt the poorer for living in a litigious society. But Pam was despondent at each closing door, and she kept contacting new lawyers. She didn't want a windfall; she had become like Jesus's widow, crying out for some sort of vindication and justice. At the outset, on the same day she called the first lawyer, she asked me someday to write something about what it's like to have a stroke and how one would like to be treated. In June 2011, she drafted a letter to her mother:

> *John + me, Pam, have already inached a lawyer to find out doctor's tried to blind me, keep me bushed down, lied to my realitives, friends and many others that I just had a seizure. . . . Lies! Lots of lie's to me. Pam Espy tired of being lied to. I only want the truth. Especially concerning my brain and all the medications I told to swallow.*

The same desire for "truth" informs a letter to me in September, a list in which ultimate questions jostle side by side with practical concerns:

> *Who am I? Question's I still wonder—Some I may understand*
>
> *Why am I exhausted most of the time anymore?*

Why did my eye's get so bad after medication was raised up?

What really happened to me Aug 24, 2010 in Baultimore?

Why didn't I know I had a husband, children, neighbor's or anyone?

Why can't I read, color's, name's, number's, age's and anything I had none before I flew to Baultimore, MD? Is that normal for most opperations? It's been over a year now and I'm still confused.

She also wrote, *This crazy Brain shure wishe's we had gotten that law suit.*

I have mixed feelings about this period of dipping our toes into the current of legal action. Some of the lawyers were kind, even empathetic; others formed one more set of cold professionals, like the doctors who spoke only to me. Our case could only be a long shot; still, if Pam could have received answers, some sort of explanation or apology—from a judge, or a lawyer; from the doctors, leveling with her about mistakes; from God—would her day-to-day anger have melted away?

God told her, "Ask." She did, in this process, communicating with lawyers and with me. Still, the takeaway from the parable of the persistent widow, the "how much more" that Jesus underscores, is that we should cry out to God day and night for justice. And He challenges us: Will we have the faith to persevere in this? (Luke 18:7-8). From this standpoint, the lawyers were a huge distraction.

*   *   *

Can anger drive recovery? To first steps, perhaps, but not to wholeness. Anger is a self-indulgent misuse of freedom, a shiv stabbed into the soft underbelly of love (Gal. 5:13-15). It leads to evil (Ps. 37:8) and gives the devil a foothold (Eph. 4:26-27). According to Jesus's high standard, it is always incipient murder (Matt. 5:22, Msg).

There is, I think, a better model. It starts when God sets us a problem—challenging and, to a degree, frustrating us. (Some doctors worry when a stroke survivor is *not* frustrated.)[180] God calls out, in the night, to the young Samuel—simply speaking his name. He could have sent an angel, presented a burning bush, written on a wall, or spoken the entire message; instead He calls and waits, calls and waits. By the time Samuel sorts out what is happening, God has his full attention, and that of the high priest Eli (1 Sam. 3:1-10).

Again, looking out over a large crowd, Jesus challenges His disciples, "You give them something to eat" (Mark 6:37); He tests Philip by asking him where they should buy bread (John 6:5-6). He is not abandoning them to their own devices; He is prompting them to consider the power and provision of God, and to reflect on the significance of the miraculous work He is about to do.

So, too, when God plunks His prophet down in a Death Valley of bleached bones, scattered and long dead, He doesn't simply show what He can do. He initiates a dialogue, and makes Ezekiel an active participant:

> He asked me, "Son of man, can these bones live?"
>
> I said, "Sovereign LORD, you alone know." [By this time Zeke has seen a few things, and has enough faith not to trust his common sense.]
>
> Then he said to me, "Prophesy to these bones . . ."
>
> — Ezek. 37:3-4

The Lord guides each of us along, through an obstacle course of challenges and tests, until we are prepared to speak into a situation in faith. He trains our hands for battle (Ps. 18:34; 144:1).

---

[180] Hale, *The Man Who Lost His Language*, 78.

Occupational therapists sometimes use a technique called *con-straint-induced movement therapy*. If a left-brain stroke makes it difficult for me to move my right hand, I may compensate by reaching and grasping with my left hand. The therapist, wishing to coax me into practicing with my right hand, may temporarily slip a light restraint over my left wrist—in effect, forcing me to work with my damaged hand.[181] Jesus does something like this when He says to a man with a withered hand, before his entire synagogue, "Stretch out your hand" (Luke 6:10). As I once heard a TV preacher remark, the man could have stretched out his good hand! But he recognized that Jesus was summoning him out of shame and fear.

Some of God's constraints are more forceful, more intense:

> He has blocked my way so I cannot pass;
> he has shrouded my paths in darkness. — Job 19:8

> He has walled me in so I cannot escape;
> he has weighed me down with chains. . . .
> He has barred my way with blocks of stone;
> he has made my paths crooked. — Lam. 3:7, 9

As with any therapy or training, the question is whether we trust the intent behind the obstacle.

"God helps those who help themselves," says Kevin Sorbo of his recovery.[182] This isn't precisely true, of course—Jesus wasn't really asking the twelve to feed the multitude without Him—but God will set a problem and wait for faith to rise up in us: faith that first cries to Him,

---

[181] See the account of constraint-induced therapy in Doidge, *The Brain's Way of Healing*, 86-87, 102; also Doidge, *The Brain That Changes Itself*, 132-63. There have been some attempts to apply a constraint-induced model to speech therapy, for instance by requiring the patient to omit gestures, to repeat target words, or to ask for objects by name. See Doidge, *The Brain That Changes Itself*, 154-56; Ackerman, *One Hundred Names for Love*, 305-06; Ittleman, *The Teaching of Talking*, 50, 130, 163.

[182] Sorbo, *True Strength*, 217.

but then faith that takes a step. When the people of Israel are trapped between the sea and the pursuing Egyptian army, Moses bravely announces in the face of the available evidence that all will be well:

> And Moses said to the people, "Fear not, stand firm, and see the salvation of the LORD, which he will work for you today; for the Egyptians whom you see today, you shall never see again. The LORD will fight for you, and you have only to be still." The LORD said to Moses, "Why do you cry to me? Tell the people of Israel to go forward." — Ex. 14:13-15, RSV

It is a surprising rebuke, but sometimes "being still" is not all God has for us to do. He challenges us to step out of paralyzing fear—not in blind willfulness, but as He directs. At the sea, as at the miraculous feeding, detailed instructions follow, but faith must be set in motion.

Often, we react to God's challenges and constraints with intemperate and partisan anger. We feel threatened, and anger rises up in us to defend our position, the rights and pleasures to which we believe we're entitled (what we call "justice"), and even our pain: we diligently dress our wounds of rejection, and nurse our resentments. Most of all, we defend our reputation and sense of self-importance; Johnson says wisely, "Anger is excited principally by pride."[183]

These are the idols of our hearts. They sap our life; our proud outbursts of anger are only the spasms of spiritual death. We stew and sputter, till God grants us grace to say, "Is not this thing in my right hand a lie?" (Isa. 44:20).

*   *   *

Anger may be my idols' Monster Truck Rally, but at times it's also . . . comical. I recall one day when I drove Pam to her physical therapy appointment. In accordance with our customary brilliant division

---

[183] Boswell, *The Life of Samuel Johnson LL.D.*, 220.

of labor this late in her recovery, I sat in the waiting room reading a magazine while she did the actual work, going through her exercises. Broad is the highway that leads to PT, but just at the end there's a narrow doorway, and you can't see what's going on inside. The small crowd in the waiting room only heard a disembodied male voice, crying out above the clack of machines and the reassuring staccato of instructions: "Ow! . . . Owww!"

We were already separate and subdued, but now a great hush settled, sympathetic and also embarrassed. We avoided each other's gaze. Pain is private, and we had inadvertently intruded; pain is urgent, piercing the confident pipe dreams of therapy.

Then, in the silence, the same voice erupted: "Goddammit! I *told* you not to do that!" And suddenly we were all laughing, nervously, guiltily, and the wisecracks began: "Something tells me they're not filming a commercial in there." Because, while pain isn't funny, frustration and the proud illusion of control are.

Pam's anger is rarely funny—there is in it too much raw pain, and defenseless vulnerability—though, later, we find some of her angry verbal expressions amusing. Mostly, it's my flare-ups that give us comic relief. Once, driving her to an appointment, I indulged in my usual stream-of-consciousness tirade about the other vehicles, all piloted, in my humble opinion, by proud graduates of the Look Out For Me School Of Driving. "Let's allll wait for Chuckles," I ranted, as some guy up ahead executed the World's Slowest Right Turn. Pam has heard all this a thousand times—and, more often than not, my mechanism for releasing tension succeeds only in making her tense. But on this day, early in her recovery, she started laughing. "Chuckles!" she said. "Hahaha!" The mere sound of the word delighted her, but I think she also recognized how foolishly I was behaving. Her merriment lightened both our moods.

Another time, shortly after her release from the hospitals, she became furious with me because she was hungry and I had a long phone conversation with one of her sisters. On and on she went, saying terrible things—"There is no God"—and describing how glad she would be at last to be dead. Then something in my face—frustration or fuming resentment—caught her eye, and she began laughing really hard. "You're just like a little boy!" she exclaimed, hugging me, happy. Not exactly a flattering outcome, but grace all the same.

Remember how Shakespeare describes us in life's middle stage:

> Jealous in honor, sudden and quick in quarrel,
> Seeking the bubble reputation
> Even in the cannon's mouth.[184]

Stroke bursts the bubble, for the survivor and for anyone around. Yet something in us still rushes to battle, enlists in a fight club. We may as well laugh, however uneasily.

*　　*　　*

Does anger fuel recovery? Ideally, I think not—though orneriness helps a little. A wise word says, "The laborer's appetite works for him; his hunger drives him on" (Prov. 16:26, NIV84). There is an energy that lashes back, and it is powerful, if unfocused. And then there is an energy that is yearning, expectant, diligent, and positive. This is the deer panting for freshets, a soul thirsting for God (Ps. 42:1-2); this is the motive force of God's one-word invitation to Pam: "Ask." It requires hope, and the birth of hope is messy, often accompanied by anger at God.

We are uncomfortable admitting it, but most human love begins in need. We are hollowed shells of craving, and only when love finds and fills us can we become overflowing cups. Even then, we are empty at our core, full only as we are filled afresh. This is the rhythm of healing, and of life.

---

[184] William Shakespeare, *As You Like It* (1599?), 2.7.154-56; available at *The Folger Shakespeare*, accessed December 19, 2021, https://shakespeare.folger.edu/shakespeares-works/as-you-like-it/.

Looking back over the long years of wilderness wandering, the whole course of God's dealings with Israel, Moses offers a succinct summary:

> He humbled you, causing you to hunger and then feeding you with manna, . . . to teach you that man does not live on bread alone but on every word that comes from the mouth of the LORD. — Deut. 8:3

Humility and grace, hunger and fullness, silence and the voice of God, emptiness and life. I used to think that anger was the strongest force on earth. Crowds part for angry people; they sweep all before them, and plunder as they please. But now I see only the tracks of our destruction, the broad bare swaths where nothing grows. Now I believe that the strongest force is love, love that begins in weakness and hunger, that cries and hears, hopes and trusts, and takes a step.

> I glory in infirmity,
> That Christ's own power may rest on me:
> When I am weak, then am I strong,
> Grace is my shield, and Christ my song. — Isaac Watts[185]

A year after the stroke, following an angry episode, Pam wrote to me of pain and fear and forward-looking hope:

> *Dear John, I'm sorry. Remember the little boy that cried wolf? Is it possible that I'm remembering myself as a little girl how I always's cry'd and cryed for mom to help me but she rarely would. . . .*
>
> *Will I ever really feel safe anywher? The time I finally felt safe was when Dad died. . . .*

---

[185] Watts, Hymn #1.15, in *Psalms and Hymns*, 538.

I know you've told me you'd never leave me and you haven't. Would you please forgive me, honey. I need to get well enough to forgive everyone again and again. I need to believe you and stop behaving the way I used to. Maybe I'm not really believing anything again and keep staying on my knees and just pray. "I'll leave you before you leave me" wasn't that what I'd believed before I go saved. Something awful like that. . . .

Maybe it will take year's to know that God's truth will set me free. I still don't feel free anyway. I do know how sorry I am for treating you the way I did last night. Please forgive this new pam. Who am I know anyway? Any idea? I do know how I felt when you first brough me back away from Baultimore. That was so kind of you. . . . Why wouldn't Jesus just cause me to only remember you and me so in love with each other and only one another like I'd been in Baultimore and before then.

You may be filled with rage, and it may be the dynamic center of your stricken life. Still, anger is not the deepest thing in you. Nor the strongest.

THE SIN I'D NEVER COMMIT

Love . . . is not easily angered [Ampl "is not touchy *or* fretful *or* resentful"] . . . — 1 Cor. 13:4-5

My untried heart thus seemed to me,
(So little of myself I knew)
Smooth as the calm unruffled sea,
But ah! it proved as treach'rous too! — John Newton[186]

We snap suddenly. Like a wall, overburdened, that bulges and cracks, and then in an instant collapses (Isa. 30:13-14); like a nail driven into

---

[186] Newton, #2.87, in *Olney Hymns*, 454.

a wall, that faithfully and for years together supports the good china, and then all at once gives way (Isa. 22:23-25)—so our human strength, ever brittle at best, eventually fails us, and others.

In retrospect, I had plenty of warnings. I knew that Pam was easily startled and frightened. Lost in a half-familiar world, coping as best she could, she struggled to interpret others' emotions. On one cold night soon after we came home, I plugged in an electric blanket. It never heated up because, in our old house, that outlet wasn't working. I became frustrated (Level 1 or 2 of my elevator), and Pam concluded that I must be angry (Level 4) at her—and slept on the floor all night.

I knew that she needed me to be calm. But instead of embracing this as the problem God was setting me—instead of accepting the situation as His invitation to a higher standard of Spirit-filled self-control—I wallowed in self-pity. *She can have any mood she likes, and express it without inhibitions*, I thought, *but I'm not even allowed to have a bad day.*

A medication caused Pam's skin to bruise easily, and her right-side visual impairment (hemianopsia) resulted in frequent collisions with furniture. More than once, well-meaning if overzealous nurses and therapists decided that I "must be" hitting her, and reported me. A social worker began showing up just to check on us. She wouldn't accept Pam's denials, let alone mine. A bruise was a bruise, and it must signify abuse. If the bruising continued, she said, I would go to jail.

Despite better things to do and much to be thankful for, I wasted some energy in sputtering indignation and idle resentment. And then I very nearly lived up to the labels plastered on me.

Retaining even righteous anger is dangerous to the soul.
— Rose Marie Miller[187]

---

[187] Rose Marie Miller, *From Fear to Freedom: Living as Sons and Daughters of God* (Wheaton, IL: Harold Shaw, 1994), 143.

July 14, 2011: a hot day, the kind that Pam would later recognize as making her cranky. During the morning my job kept me tied up on the phone. By the time I was able to go downstairs to make her lunch, she was getting frantic; she asked that we go out for something, since that would be faster. In the car on the way to Sonic, she got worse. As soon as our food arrived, I started to drive us home. She unwrapped her sandwich and saw cheese—usually not a problem—and, in the car, threw her food at me, screamed out the window, and began taking off her clothes. I parked in our driveway and went into the house, hoping we both could cool off, but her anger continued. She took the key and scratched paint from the front door in bold, stabbing strokes; turned to key the car, but thought better of it; strode from room to room, turning on lights; entered my office, went up to the computer, and began typing aimlessly.

And I lost it.

I seized her wrists, backed her away from my desk and against a wall, holding her there. "Calm down!" I shouted, again and again, idiotically, like one who turns on a flame thrower to put out a kitchen fire.

She faced me with a twisted smile. "Go on," she dared, "hit me."

Were we even dealing with each other any longer? Or was she once more on a playground at some new school, defying the accumulated bullies of a lifetime? Did I even want to restore calm, or only to lash out?

She strove and raged, but I held tight. All at once she surrendered and sank down. I released her wrists; she rose and ran. On her way downstairs, she drew her cell phone, pressing 9-1-1. When a voice answered, she hung up, and threw the phone down. Continuing out of the house, despite a sore foot, she ran off.

How had we come to this? It was easy to blame the social worker, and others, for speaking into being something that hadn't existed (Rom. 4:17). Call someone an abuser long enough and loudly enough, and you'll get your wish: the tag becomes a self-fulfilling prophecy. This is what it means to do the work of the accuser (Rev. 12:10), and angry, jaded people do it well.

And yet . . . what if I had been humble enough to heed a warning? The lash of criticism stung; I never allowed it to pierce and penetrate.

> For if we searchingly examined ourselves [detecting our shortcomings and recognizing our own condition], we should not be judged *and* penalty decreed [by the divine judgment]. But when we [fall short and] are judged by the Lord, we are disciplined *and* chastened, so that we may not [finally] be condemned [to eternal punishment along] with the world. — 1 Cor. 11:31-32, Ampl; compare 2 Cor. 13:5

I was not grieved to repentance by my own anger. Two weeks before this incident, I had written:

> Pam's language and vision keep getting better . . . slowly. Emotionally she is fragile and defensive, and we have some tough days. But her squalls tend to pass like weather; I am trying to learn to wait them out. I am learning just how prickly and defensive I am!

But I had long since exceeded "prickly." Each day I prayed for supernatural patience, only to blow it all over again, in lapses small or large. Still, I only dusted myself off and did it again—rinse and repeat. I wasn't hearing the elevator bells of my own escalating anger; my ears were bent on monitoring Pam's rises and falls. Even after she ran out the door, I stood numb in the empty house, with every light switched on, and only resolved to feed her lunch earlier.

A police officer came, polite but suspicious. When I said that Pam had left, he insisted on walking through the entire house, explaining that he had to make sure that I didn't have her body stashed in one of the rooms. But when he saw deep scratches on the front door, and angry epithets scrawled on the inside walls, he set it down as *her* committing domestic violence. I asked him to let it go, but 911 had been called and the wheels set in motion.

Pam came home at 11:15 at night, but only to rant and leave. The next day she wrote me a letter, breathtaking in its desire to forgive, poignant in the sheer terror it revealed, the fear of being left utterly on her own:

> *Dear John, I'm so sorry for the way I behaved toward you yesterday. I was wrong. You didn't really do anything wrong to me. . . .*
>
> *How can I ever help you now that I've behaved so horribly? I miss you, John. Please don't leave me, OK? I'd die if I really ever lost you, John.*

She stayed, but wanted me to rent office space somewhere and be gone all day. I resisted, arguing that this arrangement would be dangerous for her, that she was already lonely and overwhelmed. Uneasily, we resumed our unsteady routine—except that she went impulsively to a Salvation Army store and bought massive pieces of furniture, as if ballast could bring stability.

And then the police officer returned to check on things. Pam remained compliant in his presence, but was quietly furious when she realized that he "sided" with me. Once he was gone, she left, taking the car though she wasn't supposed to drive, leaving an angry letter:

> *Hit Me Once -- Shame on hard.*
>
> *Hit Me Twice -- It's Over -- J. Espy. . . .*
>
> *Thx for all you've done for me since my coma. I don't know you anymore.*

After some threatening voicemails, she called in simple despondency, lost in Topeka and unable to read the road signs. When she arrived home, she was angry all evening, yet still wanted me to lie beside her and hold her hand as she went to sleep.

Emotionally, her ensuing letters to me were both raw and changeable:

July 21:

I do love you. Unfortunately I'm not sure if you love me anymore. Truth. . . .

Your wife is too sad. I miss the man you used to be that took me to Baultimore. You've changed -- so have I.

July 21, later in the day:

JOHN ESPY

MOVE OUT NOW

I Filed for Divorce. If You Wait You Will Receive this Notice when the Police Leave it on My Door . . . By then they will Make You Move Out

August 1:

A week + ago you pushed me against your company wall upstairs twice. In return I tried to get away from you by fighting back. . . .

I fialled for my 4th Divorce because of the way you've treated me ever since I got well enuf to understand who you are and when I could speak a little better so other's could understand me. . . .

I'm tired of being married to a man who treat's me the way you've acted the last 14 years you've been married to me, John.

August ? (undated):

I'm in so much pain in both my feet. . . .

I'm now not sure what is real and what is not. This change in my brain has confused me in so many ways. . . .

Over the year's of our marriage I've really gotten closer 2 you than anyone.

But why did you really hate me enough to beat me up last month? Now I am afraid of you, John. . . .

Should I go ahead and divorce you, John. I don't believe your in love with me anymore.

Why didn't you help me to find out what was growing inside my brain all these years? I tried my best to help you get better. . . . You've been so busy with your job's I've had to take care of myself alone even when we lived together. . . . We were so in love with each other leading up till my car accident last year. I'm so grateful I came out of that coma.

So I did fall in love with a stranger. But you were so easy to fall in love with again.

Another policeman came, remarking to me, "I see what you have to contend with." I was shallow enough to feel gratified by this—as also when our primary care doctor, hearing the social worker's charges, said, "Boy, do they have a wrong number." I knew that I had let Pam down, not once but many times; I saw that she was isolated and often misunderstood. Yet part of me craved vindication, even at her expense. With relief I kept an official letter from the social worker, stating that my name would not be entered into the Adult Protective Services Registry of confirmed perpetrators.

Vindication isn't what I needed or deserved. I was not John Stone, stable and dependable. I had dropped the protective, shielding cloak;

deserted my post as a husband. Her anger and my worse anger together revealed my ugly, sinful heart.

How does one come back from such a sight? My rationalizations sounded lame even to my ears. So I confessed my sin to God and to my pastor. I apologized to Pam. I tried to retreat more quickly when tempers flared. And, eventually, I read a statement by another broken man.

Jean Vanier was a Canadian Catholic who devoted his life to serving, and learning from, people with severe intellectual disabilities. He founded the first L'Arche ("The Ark") community in France in 1964; today there are 156 communities in thirty-eight countries.[188] In *Befriending the Stranger*, Vanier describes Lucien, a man unable to speak. Disoriented and afraid when he was brought to L'Arche, he resorted to constant screaming. A calming touch or gentle words served only to increase his anguish. Listening, Vanier writes,

> I could sense anger, violence, and even hatred rising up within me. I would have been capable of hurting him to keep him quiet.[189]

At this time, Vanier had been living in the communities for fifteen years. He might have concluded that he wasn't cut out for it. Instead, with profound insight, he suggests that our brothers and sisters who have severe disabilities become our teachers by revealing to us "our inner limits and brokenness,"[190] so that we may live together in a more honest dependence on the God who is our loving Father.

---

[188] See the websites of *L'Arche International*, accessed December 19, 2021, https://www.larche.org/what-we-do, and *L'Arche USA*, accessed December 19, 2021, https://www.larcheusa.org/about/story-people/.

[189] Jean Vanier, *Befriending the Stranger* (2005; New York and Mahwah, NJ: Paulist, 2010), 62. See also Cathy Crimmins's account of her "least proud moment" as her husband's caregiver: *Where Is the Mango Princess?* 221-22.

[190] Vanier, *Befriending the Stranger*, 63.

Understandably, we want to set any fence we can between ourselves and sin. But our best resolve and the full force of our disapproval are flimsy barricades. Peter vowed to stand by Jesus even if it meant death (Matt. 26:33, 35), only to deny his Lord three times before morning. As Paul says, "Therefore let anyone who thinks he stands [who feels sure that he has a steadfast mind and is standing firm]"—who says, "Oh, I would never behave like that" (Living)—"take heed lest he fall [into sin]" (1 Cor. 10:12, Ampl). *The Message* adds, "Forget about self-confidence; it's useless. Cultivate God-confidence."

Certainly we can make progress. Peter lived to write about the possibility of never falling. Paul changed from a merciless and violent man to behaving as gently as a mother with young children. But we can't dare to entertain the thought that we've arrived.[191]

I hardly have that luxury. My heart continues to betray itself, as does my mouth; at every turn I hear the tell-tale cough of sin's infection. In October 2012, when Pam became angry that I had stored some photographs in the garage, she moved to retrieve them, and I, to prevent her, to keep her away from precarious piles of boxes, . . . I foolishly grabbed her wrists once more. We got through that incident, and the earlier one, but, except in God's eyes, I am not sure that they are ever fully gone. Five months later, when she had me removed from the apartment for a time, her complaint said, *Always hurting me.*

When God tells me to "get rid" of anger (Eph. 4:31), I cannot get by with a rapid-fire prayer for patience. I need to take my rage to God, camping out at that place of shame, the cross (Heb. 13:13); crying out to God to put to death in me what I am unable to master or to kill.

Do not be quickly provoked in your spirit,
for anger resides in the lap [NRSV "bosom"] of fools.
— Eccl. 7:9

---

[191] 2 Peter 1:10; 1 Tim. 1:13; Gal. 1:13; Acts 9:1; 1 Thess. 2:7; Phil. 3:12-16.

Here, frankly, church is of little help. Most days, at church, we are all fine folks; it's the sins of others that are dragging the country down. Nothing so alienates a community as smugly scolding Christians, and nothing so draws the broken and promotes reconciliation as heartfelt repentance. Yet no sooner do I squint to see these faults than I relumber my line of sight (Luke 6:41-42). Why on earth am I not looking at Jesus, standing silent and defenseless?

In Luke 18:9-14, the self-righteous man is sincere in thanking God that he hasn't stolen money or committed adultery. He is saying, in effect, "There, but for the grace of God, go I." Yet he is not justified in God's sight; he is really exalting himself, not magnifying grace. In contrast, God hears the flagrant sinner who has the humility to plead only the divine mercy.

The first man in this parable excuses himself by focusing on "especially bad" sins. Some sins may indeed be worse than others, but God's rating scale isn't necessarily the same as ours. At least in some respects, the consequences meted out to David for adultery and murder are less severe than those that follow the arrogance of numbering his troops (2 Sam. 12:10-14; 24:13-15).

In this life, we may never get beyond the position of the second man, confessing our sins, clutching a holy dread of sinning.[192] In the presence of the holy God, we always stand "at a distance" (Luke 18:13), "far off" (NRSV), by drawing near to that other holy site, the place of death and disgrace, the cross (Heb. 13:11-13).

When I was accused, I was quick to defend myself. I thought that I was maintaining my integrity and my Christian witness. What if, at least in private, I had seen an opportunity for self-examination, repentance, and healing? "Come to terms quickly with your accuser," says Jesus (Matt. 5:25, Ampl). We "come to terms" not through bluster and bravado, but by confessing honestly and pleading the cleansing blood of Jesus.

---

[192] Confession: 1 John 1:8-10. Dread: Jude v.23; 1 Cor. 9:27; Rom. 11:20; 1 Peter 1:17.

I am a confirmed perpetrator, capable of any sin; I am not better than others; apart from Jesus, I can make no claim of heart innocence. Only as I embrace these truths can I live and walk "in Christ."

PROTECTION AGAINST ANGER

One day in 2013, Pam got out her guitar and played, from memory, the Larry Norman apocalyptic song "I Wish We'd All Been Ready."[193] I supplied some altered lyrics:

> Life was filled with guns and war
> And everyone got trampled on the floor—
> I guess that Pam got angry!

The truth is that we both harbor destructive anger. Pam is waging a long uphill fight to regain her language and her life; I get overwhelmed, and I am overprotective of her and of myself—even of my silly job; significantly, I snapped when she started typing on the laptop I use for work.

She has disinhibition's open firing range, but I am not fundamentally and predictably any calmer. I pride myself on my long fuse, but it seems to spark and sputter a lot. And we each feed off the other, reacting to anger with "pre-anger" or muffled and festering bitterness. When her elevator reaches +5, mine drops at once to -3, and I barricade the doors.

Caregivers are urged to practice *self-care*, and to *set boundaries*. In a blog post, I discuss my reservations about these strategies.[194] Mostly, I find, I just need to die—again and yet again, at the cross, with the help of God.

---

[193] Larry Norman, "I Wish We'd All Been Ready" (Beechwood Music and J. C. Love Publishing, 1969).

[194] "On Defenses against Anger," at https://irrevocablebook.wordpress.com/.

One day, perhaps, I can be John Stone, steadfast and calm. I can stand upright, no longer pinned down, but strong against any impulse to pin. I can say, "I will never leave you"[195] and still, like Kim Carpenter, grant her the freedom to live separately "if that's what it took to bring her peace."[196]

ANGER AT GOD

> The godless in heart harbor resentment;
> even when he fetters them, they do not cry for help.
> — Job 36:13

Pam has a healthy fear of God—a sense of His majesty and a conviction of His utter goodness. She goes to Him with praise, even when this requires some work on her part. She tries, even now, to make light of her resentments: one day she quoted, flawlessly, "The LORD is my shepherd, I shall not want" (Ps. 23:1, NRSV), and then paused a beat, and added, "But I DO want!"

Long before her stroke, when I suggested that the wounds of her childhood had probably implanted a deep level of rage against God—and that she might benefit from bringing Him her anger, perhaps by throwing plates against a wall—the thought terrified her, and she wept. After the hospitals, a well of bitterness opened, casting up long-soured pain, day after day. Much of this sludge she directed at me—and, as the worst of caregivers, I often agreed that I richly deserved her ire. And what could I say to her now—"Go throw plates at God"?

> Beware lest wrath entice you into scoffing.
> — Job 36:18, RSV

---

[195] See Hugh and Gayle Prather, *I Will Never Leave You: How Couples Can Achieve the Power of Lasting Love* (New York: Bantam, 1995).
[196] Carpenter and Carpenter, *The Vow*, 131.

Brain injury is almost sure to bring anger at God. It seems to be a cruel infliction; how can we not rebel? By allowing us to experience confusion, delusion, mood swings, scattered emotions, shattered relationships, lost income, ongoing stigma, and much more, the God who is supposed to love us has defied all of our expectations concerning how a loving and compassionate God who cares for us should behave.

Patricia Neal was an accomplished actress, and just thirty-nine years old, when an aneurysm led to three strokes. Later, she wrote:

> I can remember what was left of my shambled brain bitterly reminding me that God had done this to me. And I hated God for that. I was angry and I would be angry for a very long time.[197]

Over the course of two decades, she found her way to a convent in Connecticut, became a Catholic, and found a new perspective and a resilient peace:

> I was deeply impressed that God was using my life far beyond any merit of my own making. The stroke had been a means of allowing me to reach so many who were suffering. He had not given me the stroke. He was giving me the strength and love to move with it. I learned that my damaged brain cannot reclaim what is dead. It has to create totally new pathways that will allow me to make choices I would never have made had I not suffered that stroke—choices that an infallible voice assures me will be blessed.

> But perhaps what stays with me most significantly is that conversation with Lady Abbess in her garden. She said there is a way to love that remains after everything else is taken from us. I am seeking that way and I know, in fact, its blessing surely works.[198]

---

[197] Neal, *As I Am*, 258.
[198] Neal, 370.

This was no quick life lesson, but a slow growth, unperceived by most.

I have my own problems with anger at God. Mine are worse than Pam's, because I am willing to believe lies about Him. Deep down, I question His goodness. At one Christian men's retreat, when I obeyed a direction simply to ask the Holy Spirit to reveal to me my core lie, writing down whatever thought I received, what emerged was *There isn't enough God to go around.* Unlike Paul, who was sure that the grace of Christ is sufficient (2 Cor. 12:9), and the Canaanite woman, who knew that God's table groans with such overflowing abundance that even the dogs feast and suffer no want (Matt. 15:27), I get stuck in a scarcity mentality.

Once, I made all the arrangements to get mad at God. I hoarded old plates, chose a time when Pam would be out, set aside a broom and dustpan for the mess, even started a list. But I threw four plates, and stopped. My heart wasn't in it. I felt self-conscious.

Fact is, I'd rather hum along indefinitely, nursing resentment. The New Testament warns us not to "grumble, murmur, complain," and the very sound of the Greek word *gonguzo* suggests muttering under one's breath.[199] The Israelites succumb to "constant grumbling," even rewriting history.[200] In His kindness, God desires to correct and instruct even complainers (Isa. 29:24), like them and me, but He esteems the one who "speaks *and* thinks the truth in his heart" (Ps. 15:2, Ampl), even when this is honest anger.

> I truly believe I could have saved myself a lot of pain and even physical complications if I had believed that God loved me enough to hear my anger. — Pann Baltz[201]

---

[199] 1 Cor. 10:10; Phil. 2:14; 1 Peter 4:9; *Vine's*, New Testament section, 422 (*murmur, murmuring*).

[200] Num. 17:5; Ex. 16:2-3; compare Num. 11:4-6.

[201] Qtd. in Dunker, *A Braver Song to Sing*, 105.

I harbor rage at God, percolating as constant resentment, when my hopes and expectations are frustrated. I want God to grant my wishes and fulfill my agenda, while validating my slights and booboos; when He doesn't, I'm offended. Like a stubborn five-year-old, or the prophet Jonah when God won't annihilate his enemies, I snap at God: "I do well to be angry, angry enough to die!" (Jonah 4:9, Ampl). How much more, when I survey the losses of Pam's life, capped by a stroke, do I feel she's received a raw deal.

So I stew, until God calls me out. He always does. Jesus seeks out a man who's been stuck at a day spa for thirty-eight years, obsessed with one treatment process and convinced that God acts only arbitrarily and sporadically. Even with the Author of Life standing before him, he's fixated on the healing waters, upset that God still hasn't sent him a pool boy. Jesus must bring him up short, asking, "Do you want to get well?" (John 5:6).

Resentment is nattering passivity and living death. God will not leave us there. Even a stroke is better. He raises us to rage and healing.

*   *   *

A dear friend, a Kenyan evangelist, told me a true story about his work among fierce warrior peoples in the northern part of his country. One man lost all his cows in a terrible flood. Brooding, he concluded that God was responsible, and decided that he would get his revenge by killing God. Never having attended Sunday school, this man knew only that God lived in the sky. Taking his spear, he went outside and hurled it up, as hard as he could. It disappeared from view, and he kicked up one foot and declared, "Ehe! I have killed Him!" At that moment, the spear came hurtling down, impaling his leg and sticking fast in the ground. He let out a terrible scream—of pain, rage, frustration, despair—and passed out. His neighbors carried him to a hospital, where a nurse said, "Put him with the . . ."

"With the idiots?!" Pam interjects, when I tell her this story. I smile appreciatively, and pick up where I left off when I was so rudely interrupted: ". . . with the warriors who took poison when their cows died."

When the evangelist visited the hospital ward, he found this man saying, "God is great!" He had seen God's power, and feared Him; he recognized that God could easily have killed him. And so the evangelist began with the story of Job: another man who lost everything and was angry at God. From there he went on to some parables, and then introduced Jesus.

C. S. Lewis famously said, "God whispers to us in our pleasures, speaks in our conscience, but shouts in our pains: it is His megaphone to rouse a deaf world."[202] I have never much liked this thought, as it seems to imply that the people who suffer most must be especially hard of hearing, which simply is not true.

I think it may be more accurate to say that, in our pain, *we* shout to God. Whatever may have held us back in the past—whether we bit our tongues out of reverence or unbelief, contempt or faith—now we release our verbal spears. And, against all better judgment, we listen.

Speaking from his own experience, Douglas James Miller regards anger as one of the last effects of a stroke to show itself; he sees it as a sign of recovery. Frustration develops into anger at oneself. Last of all, some survivors become angry with God:[203]

> For these people, anger at God is not what you would
> expect. It is not anger that he allowed the stroke to happen
> to them or even (in their worst moments) that he did it
> to them on purpose. . . . They are stymied by the fact that
> they cannot connect with him because the stroke simply

---

[202] C. S. Lewis, *The Problem of Pain* (New York: Macmillan, 1962), 116. Philip Yancey proposes altering the metaphor from a megaphone to a hearing aid (*The Question That Never Goes Away*, 49-50).
[203] [Miller], *Stroke*, 17-20.

strips them of this physical/spiritual ability. They have been unable to feel his comforting presence at all during the worst experience of their lives. They quite understandably think that God has abandoned them, that he has refused to give them even a few moments of peace, that he has refused to come to their aid. They don't even feel like the same person anymore and begin to doubt whether their spiritual experiences in the past are even applicable anymore or valid. . . . [W]hat they don't realize is that the reason for this is their brain and soul have been fried enough to block their ability to sense him, not that he isn't there or isn't concerned.[204]

This is the anger of Job rather than Jonah; the sufferer shouts, not, "What on earth are You doing?" but, as Pam cried, "Where are You?" This is hunger for His presence. It may be messy, angry, disinhibited, but it is also holy. Amid such rages, God has a way of making Himself known.

*   *   *

How has Pam's rage diminished over time? God's process baffles me. In vain I can point to the basic decency of character, long established in her by the Holy Spirit; to increasing mastery, and the importance of routine. The pieces remain fragmentary.

But something started when God spoke to her, inviting her into dialogue: "Ask." He has called her into something greater than a restoration of pre-stroke conditions. He is determined to heal every vestige of underlying rage.

It began with increasing awareness. Two months after God called her to ask, she wrote this query: *Why do I get mad so easily?* The desire was there to stop, turn around, and move in a new direction.

---

[204] [Miller], 21.

Four years later, she wrote to me:

I don't think I ever stay mad at you following our own ups and downs episodes. By the eve. we both apologive, pray and continue to get better.

Another four years passed. She snapped at me one night, and the next day recognized that she was angry at God, not me. There is a growing self-awareness.

Trust faces God empty-handed:

I desire then that in every place the men should pray, lifting holy hands without anger or quarreling [Msg "not shaking angry fists at enemies but raising holy hands to God"]; . . .
— 1 Tim. 2:8, RSV

More and more, I see that she has let go of anger. Silently she challenges me to follow suit.

Pam was told, "God's going to keep you on a short leash for a time." The leash is pain, but it's also faith. Like a dog restrained, and straining, our first response to the leash is anger. Stubbornness rising to frenzy, we continue to pull away toward the world of our expectations and desires. Then all at once we come to our senses, recognizing the futility of our striving. Rage turns us round, and we discover that God stands at the other end of the leash, holding us close because He loves us. He's waiting for us to stop fighting and enter into His joy.

*   *   *

We turn from the emotions of recovery to examine some of its processes,[205] and then to outcomes and tentative lessons.

---

[205] See the separate essays "Therapies" and "Doctors," at https://irrevocablebook.wordpress.com/.

CONSTANCY

O faithful God who does not change
Yet who makes all things new,
Remind us, when Your ways seem strange,
That You are always true.

You have a time for scattering stones,
A time to make stones live,
A time when You break all our bones,
A time when You forgive.

There is a time You show Your face,
A time You disappear,
A time when You do not embrace,
A time when You draw near.

At times Your angry arm is bent
To brush us from life's path;
At times, with weeping, You relent
And mercy conquers wrath.

You beckon us to come and rest
But, as we turn aside,
Your heart goes out to the oppressed
To see their wants supplied.

Lord, we are weak and tossed about
With whitecaps for our will,
Distracted and possessed by doubt
Unless You make us still.

Help us to welcome each surprise
As life, which You impart,
The leaping fire which never dies—
Love, always in Your heart.

7

UTTERANCE

POWER AND SILENCE, PRAISE AND PROTEST

> If anyone speaks, he should do it as one speaking the very
> words of God. — 1 Peter 4:11, NIV84

God speaks, and His every utterance is a word of power and of bedrock truth. His words unlock ours—particularly Jesus, the perfect expression, the Word who came to us as no word has ever come. The Word of God in us produces life; cleanses and sanctifies; guides, guards, and disciplines; heals physically and also spiritually. Made in the image of God, we also speak with power, for good or ill; but the apparent efficacy of sinful talk turns in the end to frenzied babbling, while the weak cry of faith is fruitful.

> A famine of the gospel word
> Would be a stroke indeed! — John Newton[206]

Silence feels to us like a punishment, or at best a painful discipline. Much of the life of a follower of Jesus can be described as learning to speak suitably: not blurting and venting, but giving voice to honest praise; when appropriate, shifting to protest, yet crying out in

---

[206] Newton, #2.49, in *Olney Hymns*, 387.

faith as well as in pain; lamenting and grieving, but not grumbling or complaining.[207]

Perhaps more than most people, Pam struggles with her words. She is eager to say what is right—to make sense, and to connect. Here I will look mostly at some of her slips along the way, but let's also try to discern the path she is on, and in.

MISSTEPS

> . . . a dumb ass spoke with human voice . . . — 2 Peter 2:16, RSV

> He did not recognize him, . . . so he blessed him. — Gen. 27:23, NRSV

We are sloppy with our words. It takes devotion and much practice to use them responsibly; along the way, we wound others, and shoot ourselves in the feet. We can be merely cleaning them, and they go off.

The Word in us is mighty, and yet we misspeak. Part of the suspense of Scripture, and much of its humor, lie in discovering all the ways in which we can trip over words:

- Peter is the great filterless talker of the New Testament. He's in especially fine form on the Mount of Transfiguration, when he pipes up—interrupting a conversation between Jesus, Moses, and Elijah—to share his notion of putting up tents or shrines. "He blurted this out without thinking, stunned as they all were by what they were seeing" (Mark 9:5-6, Msg). Like us, Peter has the wrong concept of permanence. He thinks he can stay where he is, freezing a moment, staking out a hallowed spot, while running his mouth. In God's plan, though, Moses and Elijah will disappear, and Jesus will lead His followers back

---

[207] I have enlarged on these themes in a blog post: "Call and Response," at https://irrevocable-book.wordpress.com/.

down the mountain. Peter's calling is to listen, and witness, and remember. Decades later, what stays with him from this event is what God said, and nothing of his own commentary (2 Peter 1:16-18).

- The brothers James and John have their own impulsive episode when a Samaritan village is inhospitable to Jesus. "Lord," they say, "do you want us to call fire down from heaven to destroy them?" (Luke 9:54). There is no lack of faith here, nor zeal; but, like us, they come up short in the areas of love, humility, and patience to persuade.

- And then, in other cases, faith is wanting. When Peter is arrested, the early church begins "earnestly praying to God for him." Released miraculously by an angel, he shows up at one of the prayer meetings. A servant girl breathlessly reports his coming, and the roomful of prayer warriors replies with deep-knit unity, "You're out of your mind" (Acts 12:5, 15). Do we believe the words of our own prayers?

- Then again, how easy it is to trust mere words, to make of them a formula. Seven Jewish exorcists try using the name of Jesus, but the evil spirit replies, "Jesus I know, and Paul I know, but who are you?" and the demonized man strips and wounds them all, putting them to flight (Acts 19:12-16, NRSV). Not the Word of God taken on our lips, but the Word dwelling richly in our hearts, has power to heal.

- The power of the Word appears in a different light in the tale of Eutychus, a young man in the city of Troas who is present at one of Paul's lengthier sermons. As Paul talks "on and on," Eutychus is on the edge of his seat—the back edge; he falls sound asleep, becoming the unofficial patron saint of a mighty, snoring host of churchgoers ever since. Eutychus is unwisely perched on a windowsill; as he drifts into dreamland, he falls from the third floor and dies. But the apostle embraces him, and he comes back to life—and Paul, undeterred, keeps preaching all night (Acts 20:7-12). I guess there's no stopping a sermon once a congregation learns that they can't escape, either in sleep or in death.

- James takes a jab at powerless words within the church. When a believer sees a brother or sister in need, and says, "Well, goodbye and God bless you; stay warm and eat hearty," this word has neither faith nor power, but is "dead and useless" (James 2:15-17, Living). We say such things, in our own self-seeking strength, to throw up a protective shield and keep people and problems at a distance. The Word of Christ is not dwelling in us richly (Col. 3:16) while we are spouting words like these.

It's delightful, and also amusing, to watch toddlers just starting to walk. They go wrong so suddenly, and in so many ways. We can't help marveling: they are so determined. God has put it in them to stand and walk and run, and they will do it. We root for them, and we also laugh at the pratfalls.

> Our hearts break when we see injustices and feel overwhelmed by sadness all around. But in the kingdom of God, the melody of heaven persistently breaks into a dark world. So we will choose subversive joy. — Osheta Moore[208]

In the same way, there are comical elements in these New Testament accounts. We laugh ruefully, shake our heads, and recall our own slips. "For all of us make many mistakes" with our words (James 3:2, NRSV). We also are equipped to learn more by making mistakes and receiving correction than we could from an unbroken chain of brilliant successes.

---

[208] Osheta Moore, *Shalom Sistas: Living Wholeheartedly in a Brokenhearted World* (Harrisonburg, VA: Herald, 2017), 56.

Pam has had to relearn language, almost entirely. There have been many gaffes and howlers; there still are. But this hard road is not a sign that she is disqualified from speaking words of God. It is, rather, a path to a new authority.

Strong Sounds

Early on, the sounds seemed to be as significant to her as the sense; when she was tired, or following a seizure, her speech sometimes degenerated into a fairly random "word salad." She showed a fondness for long vowels and hard, guttural consonants. So she once called her tumor a "stoover," and, after I mentioned freezing rain, echoed it back as "creevy rain." After a nap, she said she'd been "nozing" and "dazing." One day she called the TV remote first "mooshing" and then "mcdrinky." An orange became a "gritchy," ointment "oink," butter unappetizing "snotup," a clothespin a "tob." I was surprised, one morning, when she offered me a cup of "shtupple" (coffee), and I laughed out loud when she pounded her fist (rock, paper, scissors) and intoned, "Stone, pecker, shtupple."

> Rest and laughter are the most spiritual and subversive acts of all. — Anne Lamott[209]

At times she even appeared to hear the sounds she liked. When I sarcastically called something brilliant, Pam laughed and asked, "What was that word?" I repeated it: "Brilliant." She was disappointed: "Oh. I thought you said *skraydid*." After she listened to TV, as she tried to describe what she was learning, "Barack Obama" turned into "Tonka Tinky," a "filibuster" into a "rizzle dizzle," and "crocodiles" into "crackracketers." When we visited a Chuck E. Cheese restaurant, its name became "Chucky Chicken" and the oddly appropriate "Mucky Micker."

---

[209] Anne Lamott, *Plan B: Further Thoughts on Faith* (New York: Riverhead-Penguin, 2005), 308.

And then some days the hard consonants just poured out of her without even a prompt. As we played an "A to Z" game, I asked her to name things found in church, and she instantly replied, "Gorts." Once she heard the word "alleged" on a news broadcast; it caught her fancy, and she kept repeating it. So I told her the story about Mark Twain as a young cub reporter, instructed by his newspaper editor to use such careful language; he then submitted an account of a party attended by "a number of alleged ladies."[210] She laughed appreciatively, and then commented, "They could have been barkburgers."

A lot of hard consonants traveled in my direction. I emailed my boss, "Pam told me the other day that I am getting 'cricky.' I don't know what that means, but it doesn't sound good." Or she might call me "perfecal" or journal that I was a "volzer" (lover) of God. And then one day she denounced me as an "erk-jay"—and was astonished and indignant when I cracked the code.

At least she applied the same standard to herself, admitting that she'd been "granchy" (grouchy) or, on a happy day, saying that she felt "rum." I particularly like her one-word summary of her personality: "I'm gibby." Sounds right to me.

Pam is also a skilled user of onomatopoeia. She wrote to me, *Please forgive me for the way I over reacted to the driver on Kasold st. that cut you off. I was wrong. You'd already given them your honk.* Later, she expressed concern because she smelled a "horrible yick" in the fridge. There is a wonderful phrase: every husband would take "bad smells" more seriously if they were presented to him as "horrible yicks."

Numbers

Diane Ackerman writes of her husband, Paul West: "Numbers no longer made any sense to him at all. . . . He didn't know his address,

---

[210] This story is repeated, for example, in Clifton Fadiman and Andre Bernard, gen. eds., *Bartlett's Book of Anecdotes* (1985), revised edition (Boston: Little, Brown, 2000), 543.

phone number, birthday." He seemed to think that 50 was more than 400.[211]

Conceptually, numbers have been difficult for Pam, no matter whether she hears them, reads them, or writes them. When I told her that something had happened fifteen years ago, she exploded with, "That's a lie!" because she processed what she heard as "twenty." Weighing herself, she announced, "I am two-oh-oh!"; she meant not 200 but 120, but this was also a misreading of the digits displayed. And after speaking on the phone, she relayed to me the message that Cheri and Pat would pick us up for supper at 3:50. Knowing this couldn't be correct, I asked her to write it, and it came out as 6:30. A later note to me declares rather helplessly:

Now it's close to ? 1, 2, 3, 4, 5, 6, 7, 8:30? pm?

And just last month, she told me she'd be ready for music therapy "at W p.m."

Sometimes it's anyone's guess whether the mix-up has to do with numbers, words, or just being hungry. "John," she tells me, "they have a deal at McDonalds: two for the price of one. So we have to buy three!" On another day, she catches herself substituting a plural for a singular form: "You know where all the computers are? Which means all one of them?"

Other terms relating to quantities, times, and seasons have also proved challenging. When some cheese in the fridge got old, she warned me not to eat it or I'd throw up in "two months" (hours). As we passed a sign displaying the temperature in degrees F (Fahrenheit), she read the digits correctly but improvised the unit: "It's 82 Fubboff." Urged on by a craving for pizza, she instructed me to heat the oven to "40 mph." Hearing a reference to "roman numerals," she made a completely nonmathematical association and said she was hungry for

---

[211] Ackerman, *One Hundred Names for Love*, 159.

Ramen noodles. And sometimes her quantitative reasoning is simply delightful, as when she confided, "Morning is the best time of the year."

> . . . where morning dawns, where evening fades,
> you call forth songs of joy. — Ps. 65:8

Opposites

Following his stroke, Paul West sometimes spoke the exact opposite of what he had in mind—for instance, "Boy, do I have a story for you!" for "I have nothing new to say."[212] This seems to be a common outcome in aphasia, and it can create confusion and conflict. Pam once said, "I kept the car going" in an effort to tell me that she had parked it in the garage. And on one particularly bad night, she woke me abruptly to ask if she could hold me. I was startled, but said yes, only to have her storm off in a fury because she wanted *me* to hold *her*. I went after her and coaxed her back into bed, but we both slept poorly, and she remained angry all the next day.

Or again, we were in a restaurant, and she offered me an abandoned newspaper. "I'd rather listen to you," I said. What happened next surprised me: "You jerk!" she exclaimed; "I'm outta here." It took quite some time for us to figure out that she thought I had looked at the paper and said, "Better than listening to you."

Is there a conceptual reversal going on, or is it syntactical (in the ordering of words within a sentence), or is there a lower-level confusion about specific word meanings? If I knew, I think I could detect and defuse these episodes more quickly. Certainly some statements show a simple switching of consonant sounds, as when she called to say that she was bringing me "molane" (lo mein), or complained that her tacos were "creep chap" (cheap crap), or empathized with my "let jag," or

---

[212] Ackerman, *One Hundred Names for Love*, 289.

admitted that she was "deing bifficult." Other statements swap words, as when she recognized Genesis as "the first Bible of the book." For some reason, many of these word exchanges seem to be directed at me: she has kindly acknowledged that I needed "stuff for my time," warned that I was "bruisin' for a cruisin'," and threatened to "butt [me] in the bite." These reversals still occur today: recently Pam acknowledged that she accomplished little in physical therapy because "All I do is stop non-talk," and one morning she greeted me by asking, "How sleep did you long?"

Usually, when Pam opens her mouth, one may safely predict that the outcome will be like her description of a TV cop show when a new suspect was introduced: "The thot plickens."

Anomia

From the first, Pam's form of aphasia has depleted her store of nouns. Many of her sentences are constructed perfectly, but she must struggle to name even familiar objects. After I took her out to gaze at a full moon, as we said our prayers she thanked God for "the round thing." Her vocabulary improves, slowly but steadily; still, more than four years after the stroke, when she had a sore back, I suggested that she sleep with her feet elevated, and she asked, "Where are my feet?" In the car, gesturing for me to turn right, she advised me to "make a rectal." Though that may have been purely an insult.

> "What's the use of their having names," the Gnat said, "if they won't answer to them?" — Lewis Carroll[213]

Adjectives are also shaky. One counselor asked Pam how she remembered school; she answered, "It's ambiguous." The counselor probed a

---

[213] Lewis Carroll, *Through the Looking-Glass, and What Alice Found There* (London: Macmillan, 1871), chap. 3; available at *Project Gutenberg*, accessed December 19, 2021, https://www.gutenberg.org/files/12/12-h/12-h.htm.

little: "And what do you mean by 'ambiguous'?" Pam: "That's when you waste my time." Later, she asked me to define "ambiguous," and I used the example of a TV weather guy predicting "variable cloudiness," leaving the viewer with only a vague expectation. "Oh," she said, satisfied, "it's what I call BS."

Adventures in Reading

Some way into recovery, I became aware of a pattern. When she read, Pam no longer labored over each syllable of a word, sounding it out phonetically. She had discovered a shortcut: she would read the first three or four letters and then guess. This proved mildly amusing when I showed her the word "butterfly" and she read it as "buttocks," or when, in a store, she studied a Promaster wallet and asked why it was named "Promiscuity." But she really gave me a jolt on the day when we were driving through town and she spotted the sign of a title company. "John," she said, "does that say 'titty bar'?" I nearly swallowed my tongue, and redoubled my efforts to steer the car in a straight line; then I spluttered, "No, Pam!"—an increasingly common opening in my statements to her—"First of all, we don't say those words; and secondly, even when a place is that, I don't think they put it on the sign"—still laughing and shaking my head in disbelief.

Sometimes she reads the letters of a word out loud, with unfortunate results. She was in good voice the day she decided to tackle a grocery store receipt; right there in the checkout lane, she projected well as she deciphered *Fuel Points*: "F-U-. . . ." Mothers covered their children's ears.

There are other reading challenges. We drove past a sign for the town of Eudora, and Pam struggled to sound it out. At last I helped and said it for her. She repeated it, and considered a moment. Then: Pam, indignant: "So the E does nothing!" Me: "Yes, it's a silent letter." Pam: "I know what that means! Screw the E!"

Near Misses

Pam comes within a hair of some words and idioms—and still creates consternation. I have to admit, though, that some of her alterations just may be improvements. There is an arresting poetry in her statement, "It's raining like mustard." On the other hand, when she told me on another day that it was raining "buttholes and bunks," I could only reply that I try to stay in when it's raining buttholes.

Many words are born or reimagined as Pam struggles to describe her own perceived failings, acknowledging her "craziosity" or her "erotic [erratic] behavior" or her "fouthy [*foul* plus *filthy*?] mouth," reflecting that she must watch what she says or she will be "humidified" (humiliated), or making the distinction that what she did wasn't "internal" (intentional). "Are you sorry?" I ask; she replies, "Yes, hugibly." She also has a keen eye for others' faults: she has "no respection" for one person, while another must be "completely alcoholed." Children making sidewalk drawings are "chalkoholics." A doctor's office is "short-sighted" (-handed). And of course I annoy her; she has told me to "bite off" and offered to give me the "flipbird."

"You sarcasted me!" she accuses. (I did.) On the other hand, when I praise her reading ability, she rolls out this affirmation: "I am a quick fixer-upper!" When I raise my voice, she becomes indignant: "I can hear you. I'm not blind." Usually, though, she wants me "to be force and center."

She continues to rewrite world music and make it her own, singing, "Another one bites the bus," "Where the deer and the cantaloupe play," "I can do anything you can do better," "And the sign said, 'Long-haired creepy [freaky] people need not apply,'" or even "They all ran after the Bible verse." Once she came out with: "When I find myself in times of trouble, Mother Mary works for me." I answered, "Yeah, well, she works hard for her money."

Usually it's the right noun that is missing in action, but sometimes the deserter proves to be a verb, as when she recalled her mother showing her how to nurse: "She taught me how to pay the baby. Give money to the baby." And sometimes it's an adjective, as when she said of a small juicer, "It's not too heavy; it's light-headed."

Some of her shifts are delightfully logical. Just after February 14, she told friends that we had been "Valentating." She observed that she keeps dropping things, and needs to hire someone to "undrop" them. At other times, particularly when she is writing, her changes may reflect haste; she drafted a letter to "Holly Spirit" and reminded me, "Rest Is a Reapon [Weapon]."

With proverbs, clichés, and idiomatic phrases, she may seize on just one word. Trying for "sound bite," she came up with "height bite" and then "bite head." Or she may miss just one word: she can't think of something "off the top of my back," but sees that a comment is "right on the tongue of your throat." Once she acknowledged that she was "making a mountain out of a nailhole."

Remembering their chaotic childhood, her sister comments that they were "raised by wolves"; Pam changes this to "raised by monkeys," and later states, "I was brought up by organ donors."

She keeps going back to some proverbs. "An apple a day keeps the pregnant away," she informed me in 2013; another time, "An apple a day makes the heart go down"; later still, "An apple a day makes farts"; the other day, "A doctor a day keeps the apples away." Other bits of wisdom include "Don't bite the house that feeds you"; "The one who felt it belt it"; "Different flolks in different chokes"; "One does not steal Peter to marry Paul"; "You bruise it, you lose it"; "No shoes, no foot, no service"; and her musical complaint to me, "You don't sing me suck-songs anymore." Surely she spoke a pithy, summarizing truth when she told me, "I tell it like I feel it."

Compliments

From the day in hospital when Pam beamed to see me and, turning to a nurse, exclaimed, "I love my wife!" she has been the queen of the backhanded compliment. Our friends seem especially to enjoy this category of utterances, and the light they shine on what Pam calls my "personal diddity [dignity]."

You R perfect in His sigh, she wrote me. She has called me "cuddable" (cuddly). Another day: "You're a do-able man." Pause. "Adorable."

She recognizes clearly that I am an intellectual giant, saying happily, "I'm not great, but I'm smart enough for you." Or another time, to others: "I'm not very smart. That's why I like to hang out with my husband."

I was more surprised than gratified to be told, "I didn't have to go through bad things—I had you!" It turned out that she had left out a key word, "alone." She hadn't had to go through bad things *alone*.

On the other hand, I could not fail to be deeply stirred when she began a new day with the words, "I don't wanna wake up when I'm sleeping with you."

In a birthday card, she flattered me: *Today you woke up 65 years old. Impressive. You don't look over 41 pm.*

She tried to tell me that I do a perfect job of taking care of her, only it came out backward: "You can't do things better." And she kindly assured me that she didn't need anything, and I should enjoy a day off: "You're the one I don't want."

She has gratefully acknowledged that I am her "hairtaker"—I wish I could—and "car taker," as well as her "desiccated driver." She finds my habits "quite enduring." Attempting to tell a friend that we can harmonize, she said, "John and I violate each other." When I took her out in her wheelchair, she called me her "pusher"—this fits rather well with a note she left me about a visit to the chiropractor: "John, went to Dr. K for crack." Once, she confided that she had been testing me; I asked whether I had passed, and she replied, "With dying duffers [flying colors]." I am honored to stand and be recognized with the other dying duffers.

[In South Africa under apartheid] I recalled what I had also noticed in the Middle East: the oppressors are grim

while the oppressed laugh and tell jokes. — Nicholas P.
Wolterstorff[214]

She encourages my job skills, writing, *Thanks so hard for working.*
When I'm searching for employment, she asks, "What are you going
to apologize [apply] for today?" And when I get home from a business
trip, she says thoughtfully, "You need time to decompose."

I told her I loved her one day, and she answered, "I love you acci-
dentally." A puzzled discussion ensued; it turned out that her statement
might be loosely translated, "What a coincidence! I love you too." Or,
as she praised me on another occasion, "I love you, John. You're a cred-
dor." She has also called me "a light in a shining world," which sounds
glorious but redundant. She explained to a nurse that she married me
because I was "under public domain." Apparently I was attractive only
because my copyright had expired.

I play many vital roles in Pam's life. Once, while I was traveling for
work, her clock radio came unplugged. She reconnected it, but could not
reset it; so, when I called at night, she asked me to give her a wake-up
call the next morning. When I did, she said she needed another fifteen
minutes. Just like that, she turned me into her snooze button.

One evening she looks at me, beaming, and pronounces, "When
the shoe fits, marry it!" So now I'm footwear.

I sleep in one morning, and wake to find her gazing at me, no
doubt in silent and rapt adoration. "How are you?" she asks. "You're
my ride."

It's not always sweetness and light. I wrote to my brother, "Pam
called me a Monkey Head today. It is good to see her vocabulary
improving, if not her wifely submission and respect." She has
pronounced me a "lazy billybam," a "willowbluster," a "megabugger,"
an "ackhole," "easily pronsegated," "stupidic," "gullilible," and "full of

---

[214] Nicholas P. Wolterstorff, *Journey toward Justice: Personal Encounters in the Global South*
(Grand Rapids, MI: Baker Academic, 2013), 145.

trinks [tricks]." Watching me drink a second cup of coffee, she staged an intervention, informing me that I am a "hooker." When I reminded her that I'm ticklish, she replied, "You're everything-ish." She shared with me a particularly gruesome *Dr. Oz* segment about fecal matter on food, and later called me "Mr. Fecal Mango Butt." She is sorry, she said, that people "skip me out," but she sees why: I'm basically a "trunky guy." I have taken these words to heart, and will try to improve—but I'm not optimistic, since she tells me that I am "slow on the upkeep [uptake]." And to make matters worse, I have a "battitude" (bad attitude).

Inspecting the groceries I've brought home, she declares of one frozen dinner: "I wouldn't buy that by mistake!"—meaning that on her *worst* day, at her *weakest* moment, she would not pick out *by mistake* the item that I have selected on purpose. Little wonder, then, if she calls me a "shorthead," or renders a severe verdict when I'm five minutes late: "You have been charged and found wetting."

Sometimes I fight back, at least half-heartedly. When she boasts, "I am a danger waiting to happen," I let her know that, in my considered opinion, that ship has already sailed. These disputes are risky: she may call me a "Patty Cathy," or accuse me of "riverjacking" (jibberjabber). She has even told me that I am a "pigot" (*pig* plus *bigot*?). Once, comparing me to the villain on a TV cop show, she told me that I am a "startfighter."

"Don't fart on my side of the couch," I lecture; she retorts, "I might do it to depite [defy? spite?] you." Another time, she says confidently, "You have the fear of Pam." And once, when I resist her, she only gives me a pitying look, and then speaks to me as if I were a child: "You know I'll win." As she sagely advised me on another occasion, "You should lose while you're ahead."

For good measure, sometimes, she scolds me in advance. Once when I teased her, she responded, "Be quiet and leave me alone!"—then added, "And the next time also!" Her overall plan for a happy marriage found expression in a single pithy statement: "I will tell you what and when you should do."

Emerging from my office, I ask, "Would you like company?" Pam, with an evil grin: "Do you have someone to send me?"

I like to think that all our interactions contribute to her recovery of language. So I often press for clarification, which can be a bit like prodding a powder keg. One day she declared in exasperation, "I don't know names of things, butthead!" Yeah, she knew *that* name.

"You men!" she exclaims to me; "you think you're indescribable [indestructible]!" At a doctor's office, she reminds me where the bathrooms are: "There's a men's room on the other side, and a women's room for you." She kindly buys me some T-shirts, which she purchased without being able to read them; I stop short at one depicting a small band of protesters, one apparently lying dead, and the caption is, "Bullets Can't Stop Ideas." I tell her she should just paint a target on me, and then I send the shirt on to my boss, Jim.

Sometimes a word just slips out. During the coronavirus pandemic, her AA sponsor called and asked Pam, "Has John set you up to attend meetings on Zoom?" "Yeah," she replied, "the b—." Pam herself was taken by surprise, but her friend couldn't stop laughing.

Yet I mustn't be ungrateful—or falsely humble, assuming THAT opportunity ever arises. Once, Pam catches me refusing a compliment, and calls me on it: "You're just pidding down the lane." And I suppose I was.

Occasionally, her heavy artillery backfires a little. The other day, when I teased her, she retorted, "I am not going to dignify myself with a response." And—I have to hand it to her—she was as good as her word.

Secondary Aphasia

A fact little noted in the medical literature is that aphasia can be contagious. In some of our conversations, I make far less sense than she does. Recently, in the kitchen, I complained that she was getting in my way. She was undeterred: "I was being a helper." Frazzled as I was, I would not back down, insisting, "That's not that helper!" Another time, I called her attention to a dog that was "waving its tag" (wagging its tail).

In the summer of 2017, a new job took me on a wonderful trip to Africa. I laughed when Pam told me that she had said to a friend, "My husband just got back from Avocado." But the tables were turned when, during a conversation, she kept pleading with me to make her a sandwich, and at last I came out with, "When I was in Peanut Butter . . .". I also described a book I'd read, "*When Hurting Helps.*"[215]

And when I was tired, quietly dozing, and she burst in from the kitchen to announce that we were out of bananas, I protested, "I don't wanna go to the banana store!" The *banana store?*

Recently I tried to enlist her help in completing a survey from her social worker, listing some of the ways he's assisted her. Unfortunately, she was more interested in a hole in my shoe. As I was writing, on her behalf, "and helping me to ride buses," she made a grab for my foot. "Stop it!" I cried, yanking my foot away. "Big baby!" she declared; "you big baby!" "I'm doing this for you," I protested, and caught myself writing "and helping me to ride big babies."

When I worked out a plan to complete two errands in one trip, I exulted aloud: "I'll take care of two eggs with one stone." And once, when she asked what I was up to, I called from the bathroom, "I'm waking up and peeing." "What?" she asked. Still groggy, I called back: "I'm peeing up!"

It's just as Pam said once: aphasia "livens up our light."[216]

---

[215] Steve Corbett and Brian Fikkert, *When Helping Hurts: How to Alleviate Poverty without Hurting the Poor . . . and Yourself* (Chicago: Moody, 2009, 2012).

[216] A further collection of Pam's verbal "missteps" appears in "Call and Response," at https://irrevocablebook.wordpress.com/.

AUTHORITY

> A voice says, "Cry out."
> And I said, "What shall I cry?" — Isa. 40:6

> I'll tell Thee All — how Bald it grew —
> How Midnight felt, at first — to me —
> How all the Clocks stopped in the World —
> And Sunshine pinched me — 'Twas so cold —

> Then how the Grief got sleepy — some —
> As if my Soul were deaf and dumb —
> Just making signs — across — to Thee —
> That this way — thou could'st notice me —

> I'll tell you how I tried to keep
> A smile, to show you, when this Deep
> All Waded — We look back for Play,
> At those Old Times — in Calvary. — Emily Dickinson[217]

In one of his most personal letters, the apostle Paul allows the presence of boastful "super-apostles" (2 Cor. 11:5) to provoke him into presenting his own credentials. For two full chapters, he appears to engage in foolish bragging, only to conclude:

> Have you been thinking all along that we have been defending ourselves before you? It is in the sight of God that we have been speaking in Christ, and all for your upbuilding, beloved. — 2 Cor. 12:19, RSV

Paul has been at work to expose the emptiness of boasting in our cravings, of "mere words" of self-promotion; and he shows that the power

---

[217] Dickinson, from #577 (ca. 1862), *Complete Poems*, 282. Also available at *Wikisource*, accessed December 19, 2021, https://en.wikisource.org/wiki/If_I_may_have_it,_when_it%27s_dead,.

of Christ fills us when our fleshly strivings are put to death and we stand in weakness. He might say, with Chrysostom, "Need alone is the poor man's worthiness."[218]

In a similar spirit, I have not recorded Pam's verbal missteps in order to mock her, or (solely) for the purpose of making you laugh. I hope that you have also experienced a force and freshness in her utterances. She has a directness that often touches people, draws them in, in a way that my logic cannot. Corrie ten Boom wrote:

> In 1 Corinthians 1 and 2 we read about the "foolishness" of God and the "wisdom of the wise." Two realms they are: The wisdom of the wise is all we can grasp with our logical thinking, with our brains; the foolishness of God, the greatest wisdom, we can touch only with our faith knowledge.[219]

Like Corrie ten Boom, and like the men and women of biblical times who experienced divine deliverances, Pam tells her story again and again. There is power in the tale itself, but even more in the telling; as Paul says:

> However, we possess this precious treasure [the divine Light of the Gospel] in [frail, human] vessels of earth, that the grandeur *and* exceeding greatness of the power may be shown to be from God and not from ourselves.
>
> — 2 Cor. 4:7, Ampl

Immediately before and after this image, Paul mentions utterance— speaking by faith (v. 13), allowing the Word in us to make our lives an "open statement [*phanerosis*: KJV "manifestation"] of the truth"

---

[218] John Chrysostom, *On Wealth and Poverty* (388-90), transl. Catherine P. Roth (Crestwood, NY: St. Vladimir's Seminary, 1984); qtd. in Wolterstorff, *Journey toward Justice*, 67.

[219] Corrie ten Boom, 1968; qtd. in Pam Rosewell Moore, *Life Lessons from the Hiding Place: Discovering the Heart of Corrie ten Boom* (Grand Rapids, MI: Chosen-Baker, 2004, 2005), 168.

(v. 2, NRSV). We are crockery that bears witness, the Word of God in a handful of dust. We crack unto epiphany, taking our place among the mysteries and manifestations of God.

*   *   *

There is a power in impeded speech. A story is told of Emerson—in middle life, not yet aphasic—speaking in Cambridge, Massachusetts against the Fugitive Slave Law in 1850. Some Harvard students came to shout him down, and largely succeeded, but one observer felt a heightened impact:

> The hisses, shouts, and cat-calls made it impossible for Mr. Emerson to go on. Through all this there never was a finer spectacle of dignity and composure than he presented. He stood with perfect quietness until the hubbub was over, and then went on with the next word. It was as if nothing had happened: there was no repetition, no sign that he was moved, and I cannot describe with what added weight the next words fell.[220]

The same effect may be seen in the climactic scene of the film *The King's Speech*. King George VI ("Bertie"), who has struggled for years to overcome a paralyzing stammer, addresses by radio a nation, an empire, that has exhausted diplomatic remedies and finds itself at war. Many of the auditors can vividly remember the horrors of the first Great War; this is not an hour when glib assurances or patriotic hoo-rah can calm and motivate. Rather, the stately, self-conscious procession of the monarch's

---

[220] James B. Thayer, qtd. in James Elliot Cabot, *A Memoir of Ralph Waldo Emerson*, 2 vols. (1887; Boston and New York: Houghton Mifflin, 1893), 2:586; available at *Internet Archive*, accessed December 19, 2021, https://archive.org/details/amemoirralphwal11cabogoog.

phrases, which clearly do not come easily, is balm to the people's spirit; they hang on every word, united.[221]

So it is with brain injury. In January 2013, two years after a bullet ravaged her brain, Gabby Giffords testified on gun violence before the Senate Judiciary Committee. Her husband describes the event:

> Gabby was speaking in her deliberate, halting cadence. In that setting, her short speech was all the more powerful and affecting. Gabby's struggle with each word became everyone's struggle. The whole country was pulling for her.[222]

Terry Evanshen's car accident left him with a severely impaired memory, and yet, in time, he found a new life as a public speaker:

> Magic happens when Terry Evanshen gives a speech. . . . Terry is touchingly open and vulnerable as he describes the grief of living with deep damage to his memory, and his daily struggle to be proud of himself. It touches a place in most people's souls: loss and self-doubt are the common currency of everyone's reality.[223]

One who has heard Evanshen speak many times adds, "His story is pretty extraordinary, but he reaches people most with his honesty." In one engagement, after he addressed high school students, they eagerly filled out response cards, "anguished youngsters pouring out their

---

[221] *The King's Speech*, written by David Seidler, directed by Tom Hooper; 2010. For the text of the September 3, 1939 address, see Mark Logue and Peter Conradi, *The King's Speech* (New York: Sterling, 2010), 165-66.

[222] Gabrielle Giffords and Mark Kelly with Harry Jaffe, *Enough: Our Fight to Keep America Safe from Gun Violence* (New York: Scribner-Simon & Schuster, 2014), 200. Compare David Talbot's account of his "passionate eloquence" in a speech on behalf of a mayoral candidate while he was still recovering language: *Between Heaven and Hell*, chap. 11.

[223] Callwood, *The Man Who Lost Himself*, 239.

hearts to an anguished man." He connects with the "depth of sorrow" in adults, too; one said with emotion, "This guy tries so hard."[224]

Moses is a broken man, hiding in a desert; a fugitive from his past, from life, regarding himself as "a stranger *and* a sojourner in a foreign land" (Ex. 2:22, Ampl). Among many other failings, he is deeply conscious that he is "slow of speech and ha[s] a heavy *and* awkward tongue" (4:10, Ampl). But the Lord seeks him out, and says, "Who gave man his mouth? Who makes him deaf or mute? . . . Now go; I will help you speak and will teach you what to say" (4:11-12, NIV84). It seems that the Lord cares less for eloquence than for humility, a humility grounded in earth and clay.[225]

God sets His words in a prophet's mouth. Sometimes they come as a scroll to be ingested, sweet to the taste though perhaps (as they bring judgment on unbelief) sour to the stomach.[226] We are apt to imagine this process as one of uninterrupted glory, an unmediated enjoyment of the face of God. But the biblical writers taste the clay along with the honey.

> To throw a line out to someone who has been beaten down, you must first encourage that person to open up a little and dare to express a few thoughts, which will reveal the knots of inner anxiety. My strategy for that is simple. I approach that person, I observe a little moment of silence, I begin to talk, and I say, "I, too, am a survivor." — Sylvie Umubyeyi[227]

The Word from God's mouth never returns empty or fruitless (Isa. 55:10-11). There even are grace-shaded stretches of time, summoning faith, when no word falls to the ground (1 Sam. 3:19); but these are unusual, for the Word is seed (Luke 8:11), a seed that dies (John

---

[224] Callwood, 240, 216, 229.

[225] Num. 12:3; Zeph. 2:3, NASB; *Vine's*, Old Testament section, 119 (*to be humbled, afflicted*).

[226] Deut. 18:18; Jer. 1:9; Isa. 51:16; 59:21; Rev. 10:9-11; Ezek. 2:8-3:3.

[227] Sylvie Umubyeyi, qtd. in Jean Hatzfeld, *Life Laid Bare: The Survivors in Rwanda Speak* (2000), transl. Linda Coverdale (New York: Other, 2006, 2007), 216.

12:24-25). Again and again in salvation history, the Word of God has gone to ground, vanished from sight, broken apart into tiny pieces, and continued its work unseen, inglorious; finally to rise, no longer expected, with earth clinging to its shoots. It is resurrected, brought to light by God "at his appointed season" (Titus 1:3).

Isaiah's Servant sounds exultant:

> The Lord God has given me
> the tongue of those who are taught,
> that I may know how to sustain with a word
> him that is weary. — Isa. 50:4, RSV

Dig deeper: the Speaker has been beaten, mocked, accused; He knows what it means to walk in darkness unrelieved by light (vv. 6-10). He has earned something more precious by far than "street cred": he has valley cred, wilderness cred. The one who is weary receives and thirstily drinks in the Word of One who has been there. And "the tongue of those who are taught" may be precisely the tongue that struggles to find and form its words—even as Moses, educated in Egypt to be "mighty in his words and deeds" (Acts 7:22, RSV), never spoke with divine force until he was "slow of speech and tongue" (Ex. 4:10).

The effect is unplanned by the speaker, even unsought. Karl Barth, who amid the devastation and darkness following World War I wrote a commentary on Romans that became influential, later compared himself to

> a man climbing in the darkness a winding staircase in the steeple of an ancient cathedral. In the blackness he reached out to steady himself, and his hand laid hold of a rope. He was startled to hear the clanging of a bell.[228]

---

[228] Roland H. Bainton, *Here I Stand: A Life of Martin Luther* (1950; Nashville: Abingdon, 1990), 64. Bainton applies the metaphor to Luther.

Can one's survival hinge on utterance? It certainly feels that way. Silence, muteness, is a kind of death. Pain cries out; the heart finds its words and, even without words, finds its way to God. And then faith speaks; it *must* speak, it cannot remain silent. But see with what lowliness it speaks:

> Brought low, you will speak from the ground;
> your speech will mumble out of the dust.
> Your voice will come ghostlike from the earth;
> out of the dust your speech will whisper. — Isa. 29:4

Richard Mollica, a psychiatrist who worked with refugees, came to value the trauma survivor as a teacher, as someone whose story can guide and heal society.[229] Perhaps this process can only begin in a circle of survivors. Leymah Gbowee was leading trauma healing workshops for women in Liberia; she had a full agenda of topics to cover, but the participants kept interrupting, wanting to share personal stories. At last she set aside some evening time for this:

> I expected to hear about the war. But as would happen again and again in the future, the stories the women needed to share that night started long before the fighting did. . . . Each speaker wept with relief when she finished; each spoke the same words: "This is the first time I have ever told this story." The women talked for five straight hours, until 3 A.M.[230]

It may seem fanciful or presumptuous to compare the narratives of stroke recovery with accounts of the traumas of poverty and war. Yet, as Gbowee discovered, given an opportunity, any autobiographer

[229] Richard F. Mollica, *Healing Invisible Wounds: Paths to Hope and Recovery in a Violent World* (Orlando, FL: Harcourt, 2006), 125, 37.
[230] Leymah Gbowee with Carol Mithers, *Mighty Be Our Powers: How Sisterhood, Prayer, and Sex Changed a Nation at War* (New York: Beast-Perseus, 2011), 105.

may unearth deep pain and core lies. Out of these workshops came a collective voice, leading to a reformed society with a new story.

*   *   *

Pam's statements are often arresting and quotable. A couple of years ago, she kept hearing about Black Friday, the busy holiday-shopping day after Thanksgiving; only she called it "Dark Friday." One friend loved this and went around renaming the occasion. My own favorite "Pamism" is "I'll see it when I believe it," a misquotation that improves on the original, because faith comes before sight.

But it isn't the content of her words that most batters hearts. It is the manner, and the mere fact of utterance. Undaunted, she goes on singing praise, voicing her complaint, writing love letters, and above all telling her story. She is one of the firstfruits of a seed that died. The Word of Christ dwells richly in her.

8

LIMITATIONS

REMEMBERING

> The word *memory* comes from the same root as the word *mourn*, and that should tell you something. — Abigail Thomas[231]

Since Pam's stroke, the therapies she has engaged with have primarily helped her regain lost ground, while her doctors labor more to measure the mudslides and to guard against further collapse. Progress has been slow, to the point that each plateau stretches before us to the horizon, with no sign of foothills ahead.

Through hard work, neuroplasticity, and the grace of God, Pam walks and swims, uses her right hand, drives a car, communicates clearly enough. These are noteworthy accomplishments. But her typical day is still a twilight. Physically, she is hampered by visual impairment and foot pain, and often by a migraine. More vexing is the cognitive dimension. She struggles to remember: words, first of all, but, beyond those, concepts and planning skills, the ability to think through a strategy or rein in an emotion, math, money, words on a page. She doesn't remember, and she knows that she doesn't remember.

---

[231] Abigail Thomas, *Thinking about Memoir* (New York and London: AARP Sterling, 2008), 2; emphasis in original.

In a blog post,[232] I have reflected on the mysteries of memory: that it is active, whole-bodied, relational, and characterized by yearning; that some people, losing the continuity of stories and the ordered fixity of names, retain only snapshots; that Jesus not only unlocks our hearts but keeps and holds together our memories; that God remembers us, in Christ holding us securely in His grip; that He supplies reminders, sometimes including periods of brokenness when, preparatory to receiving grace, we can remember only pain, accompanied by feelings of remorse and shame; that there are times to forget, letting go of impediments; and that God rebuilds, not in simple restoration, but interlacing us together as the temple of Christ's body, with shared and corporate memories, a process that continues until one day we shall remember as He does. Here, briefly, I apply some of those musings to Pam's story.

> Come, O thou Traveller unknown,
> whom still I hold but cannot see;
> my company before is gone,
> and I am left alone with thee;
> with thee all night I mean to stay
> and wrestle till the break of day. — Charles Wesley[233]

Human memories may wither slowly but irretrievably, as in dementia, or they may collapse abruptly, but with some hope of recovery, as in a stroke or TBI. Pam awoke one day, in the hospital, apparently without any clear recognition of the world around her, or any sure sense of her identity, her history. Today, she continues to rummage for simple words; she can't keep track even of names of colors. Her neurologist confirms that she remains impaired in long- and short-term memory,

---

[232] "The Actions of Memory," at https://irrevocablebook.wordpress.com/.

[233] Charles Wesley, "Wrestling Jacob" (1742), in Helen Gardner, ed., *A Book of Religious Verse* (New York: Oxford, 1972), 207-09. Also available at *Poetry Archive*, accessed December 19, 2021, https://www.poetry-archive.com/w/wrestling_jacob.html.

though her procedural (muscle) memory—driving and parallel parking, playing the guitar, typing—is pretty much intact.

*   *   *

One of the strangest effects of Pam's stroke, to me, appeared only after we came home. As she moved in familiar surroundings and spent time with beloved people, mostly bad memories returned. And they tyrannized her; she seemed unable to turn her attention away, to shift out of past, deep-seated pain. She reconstructed her life story, minus God, or with all of His appearances and provisions marginalized as ornamental "grace notes." She became emotionally vulnerable and volatile. As late as 2012, she wrote to me:

> *But, why would God want me to remember all so many things from my history. Now that doesn't make since to me.*

At times it seemed as if the entire building complex of memory had been bulldozed, bombed, annihilated, and only the hardiest weeds, poking through desolate ground, remained; or as if the trauma of stroke and coma and wordless early recovery were finally finding expression in masked form. Other memories failed to thrive; when I spoke to her about her anger, she was moved, but could not hold on to the emotion:

> *How may I ever let you understand how stunned I was to learn how often I've hurt you with my word's about my - oops forgot —*

When she started recovery, her swept-out heart was like a toddler's, reacting in an eternal present. She could not wait for anything, and she had little sense of time. Once, when I reminded her of a physical therapy appointment at 10:30 the next morning, she became angry, making it clear that this was incredibly early; she didn't remember complaining, one day earlier, that 3:00 p.m. was too late for her.

Even years later, many of her memories are gathered in the chamber labeled PAIN; as she wrote in 2015:

> *I'm so glad God saved you and me. We are happily married. But our life is hard.*

∗   ∗   ∗

Pam has said consistently that, when she first came out of the coma, she didn't know who I was for quite some time. Months later, when she knew to call me "John," she admitted that she had trouble remembering my "maiden name" or "lack name." Much more seriously, she sometimes struggled to recognize names or images of Jesus and the cross; she told me that she didn't hear from God or remember to worship.

And yet her identity has not been eradicated; it is not even blurred; it stands out more distinctively than ever. "I remember you!" declares the young man who met her once in a food court, months ago. Some of her memories have been left in my charge, and on good days they recall to her a sense of calling; as she wrote to me:

> *You were so right that God did have a great reason for bringing me out of the coma in this condition. I am a prayer - warrior - singer - worship, writer - like this, great lover of Father Son + Spirit. You remembered the word was spoken over me year's ago.*

Kim Carpenter writes, "My wife may have been confused, she may have lost some of her memory, but she still knew her God."[234] Once Pam started singing, worshipping, I said the same of her. And yet, months later in a Kansas church, she would recollect, or come back to herself more fully, on speaking the name "Jesus," and would ask God where He'd been. This led me to wonder: Had she forgotten God for a time? Even more troubling, did He let her slip from His mind?

---

[234] Carpenter and Carpenter, *The Vow*, 81.

I think now that she remembered, but as if through a distorting mirror and a static-laden sound system. God's words came back to her, but skewed toward condemnation. A tender conscience is one of the blessings that keeps Pam close to God, but initially her consciousness of sin, guilt, and shame paralyzed her and threatened to overwhelm her. She knew her brokenness in every attempt to think or speak, while she relearned only gradually the abundance, the sufficiency of grace. At last she wrote to me:

> *Thank you for continuing to stop me from putting myself down. You remind me I'm not stupid, a retard, etc, etc. Obviously the enemy continue's to lie to me. I'm I one who has to stop agree's with his lie's. . . . Let's continue to stop— turn around and move in the opposite direction when either one of us feel weve've we feel we've done something that can't be forgive—What's God tell us?—He forgive's us as soon as we ask Him to them he no longer remember's. We're the one's who remember something we still feel bad about so we feel like we need to appologize again. God chooses not to hold sin's against us—He hear's us ask Him to forgive us of our sins—Then He remove's those's words as far as the east + the north—south + left to never recall them again. Only evil will trick us saying God or Pam or whoever lie's + says we are still that bad person. John, I think your perfect. I have to believe I'm perfect in Gods sight also. So, I do thank you you stopping me from all that repetition I speak about myself. Lets decide to keep loving one another and appologive before the sun goes down, pray for one another to God.*

Forgetting God is not the emptying of memory's storehouse, but a turning and a betraying of allegiances: "you have forgotten me and trusted in false gods" (Jer. 13:25). In contrast, Pam could not call God to mind, but she was not shutting Him out. She had not abandoned

Him. And gradually we became convinced that He never for an instant permitted her to fade or fall away from His mind's grasp.

*   *   *

All over the apartment, we taped cards, labeling appliances and articles of furniture with their names. Pam learned to use a printed, planner-style calendar, as well as the calendar tool on her cell phone. A days-of-the-week pillbox helped her to take her meds on time. And I gave her verbal reminders, including forceful line-in-the-sand declarations that she had to let me get my work done; as she wrote:

> *This injured brain needs the gentle way you remimnd me by —*
>
> 1. *Go, I'm earning your keep*
> 2. *I'm on the phone*
> 3. *Dor's shut—Read between the lines woman . . . bathroom = equals MY prizacy etc.*

Sometimes we could joke about it. I told her, "Love does not keep score [1 Cor. 13:5, Msg], and this is the third time I've had to remind you of that."

But I was delighted, and filled with admiration, as I saw her beginning to order her world, her day, her thoughts. For hours at a time, waking and sleeping, she listens to the audio Bible, storing up God's Word in her heart—and musing, remembering, believing, praying, praising. More than the eye, her ear becomes the access road to God's construction site within (Rom. 10:17, 10).

As the doctors predicted, the memories that resurfaced came in sudden bursts. We had our share of missteps. One day in 2012, Pam abruptly remembered Pig Latin, calling me an "itchbay," and then became excited: "I want to remember more Bible stuff!" I had to break the news, as gently as I could, that this dialect that she knew so fluently was not actually one of the sacred languages.

Little by little, she began reconstructing her history with God, although now her stroke and coma became a turning point in the narrative. In April 2012, she remembered more of her conscious-ness during that period: she felt shut in, and was frequently moved around. She was waiting for someone, but no one came. I reminded her of Lazarus, shut in the grave till the fourth day (John 11:39), and pointed out that we don't know anything about his awareness or recollections.

A few months later, a TV drama featured a body under a slab of concrete; this reminded Pam of feelings of oppression during the coma. She says she was buried, held down, seized, and pulled by creatures.

In her tellings, though, the great trigger was the altar call at a church we visited, and her going forward and crying, "Jesus!" In the light of His presence, she could bear to recollect the pain and terror of His apparent absence. Indeed, her memories became vivid; in 2015 she wrote:

> *Gentle Father, you gave me a dream. Because I silently asked you "Where were you?" when I was in that coma. You showed me, I was in a coffin unable to get out. I tried to call out to people that I was alive, not dead. As I quit trying from exhaustion I looked and saw a demon. I passed out. When I woke I saw I was still alone in that coffin. In fear I cried out again to people I could hear outside. Eventually I'd be hopeless so I stopped. Quiet I now did see that same demon attacking me. This continued all 3 days in the coma.*
>
> *When I came out of the coma I had no memories of where I'd been. It wasn't until I was able to call out the name of Jesus, I finally saw myself in the coffin.*

In a journaled prayer, she connected her experience with the suffer-ings of Christ, taking Him as her key to understanding, her Savior, her Shepherd calling her on, and her Teacher:

> *I believe You loved John and me so much you did send Your only Son Jesus to go through all of that pain, beatings and death. You allowed your Son to go down to Hell so He could bring back what Satan had taken away from all the people so we could hear His Testimony. Jesus was in that "coma (or dead as most people believed) for 3 long days. John taught me that I had also been "non-responsive) so I would be able to testify that Jesus lived and so would I. Thank you Holy Spirit for coming to Earth soon after God's Son returned to be right next to his Dad + Father. I love that I began to remember your words once I spoke out loud Jesus. You're gentle and kind as you reminded me that "even before there is a word on my mouth, behold O Lord—You know them all [Ps. 139:4]. John reminds me often that God has given me many gifts that are er-revokable [Rom. 11:29]. When I was unable to speak you helped me to calm down and continue to practice.*

In another note, she rejoices that *my "slightly used brain" has been able 2 remember songs. Hallelujah.* She prefers old, familiar worship songs, and yet each becomes "a new song"[235] in every new act of remembering. The songs are merely vehicles for today's communion, today's praise; and, as she sings, she is co-laborer with God in the work of building.

*   *   *

Pam struggles to remember; her notes to me are filled with attempts to summon particulars, such as *the guy with the name I can't remember that starts with a letter.* It is hard for her to keep perspective when one

---

[235] See Ps. 33:3; 40:3; 96:1; 98:1; 144:9; 149:1; Isa. 42:10; Rev. 5:9; 14:3.

or another missing word always looms so large. Yet she does have a personal narrative, a sense of life stages. She remembers her life before and after she was saved as a teenager in Salina, and before and after she responded to an altar call and met Jesus all over again. God is the chief actor in her life, and He is good.

There is much she has forgotten about our twenty-plus years together, but on good days what was lost is mostly clutter. She regards our life with fresh simplicity, writing in an anniversary card:

> *"This is my beloved and this is my friend."* Song of Solomon 5:16
>
> *You are both, sweetheart*

We both like the Pixar animated movie *Up*, with its talking dogs that get distracted whenever a squirrel appears.[236] With newfound wisdom, she treats her memory lapses as just such harmless and amusing interruptions:

> *Memories, can be beautiful + yet, whats 2 painful 2 remember—we simply choose 2 forget. But it's the laughture we choose 2 remember in our Golden years. 'squirel—*

TESTIMONIES OF THE NOT-YET-HEALED

Now Elisha was suffering from the illness from which he died. — 2 Kings 13:14, NIV84

I have thought it necessary to send to you Epaphroditus my brother and fellow worker and fellow soldier, and your messenger and minister to my need, for he has been longing for you all, and has been distressed because you heard that he was ill. Indeed he was ill, near to death. But God

---

[236] *Up*, directed by Pete Docter, screenplay by Bob Peterson and Pete Docter, Pixar, 2009.

had mercy on him, and not only on him but on me also, lest I should have sorrow upon sorrow. I am the more eager to send him, therefore, that you may rejoice at seeing him again, and that I may be less anxious. So receive him in the Lord with all joy; and honor such men, for he nearly died for the work of Christ, risking his life to complete your service to me. — Phil. 2:25-30, RSV

We always carry around in our body the death of Jesus, so that the life of Jesus may also be revealed [RSV "manifested"] in our body. . . . Though outwardly we are wasting away, yet inwardly we are being renewed day by day. — 2 Cor. 4:10, 16

There is one story that Christians are hungry to hear. It is not precisely the gospel story, which we think we know; it is the good news made personal, made real in our bodies and before our eyes. It is the story that concludes, ". . . and then someone prayed, and I was instantly and completely healed."

In many churches, this is the only personal story that we hear. That is, if someone other than the pastor, the youth pastor, or the worship leader is allowed to speak in church, it is to tell a version of this story. Accounts of physical and emotional healing have become our only public testimonies.

These stories should be told; in fact, if you have such a testimony, you should continue to tell it and not fall silent. Psalm 145:4 says, "One generation will commend your works to another; they will tell of your mighty acts" (NIV84; compare Ps. 71:16-18). Though Jesus instructed many of those He healed not to speak of it, at least during His ministry, still He told the Gadarene demoniac, "Go home to your own people and tell them how much the Lord has done for you, and how he has had mercy on you" (Mark 5:19). He also said to questioners:

> The very works that I do by the power of My Father *and*
> in My Father's name bear witness concerning Me [they are
> My credentials and evidence in support of Me]. . . . [E]ven
> though you do not believe Me *or* have faith in Me, [at least]
> believe the works *and* have faith in what I do, in order that
> you may know and understand [clearly] that the Father is
> in Me, and I am in the Father [One with Him]. — John
> 10:25, 38, Ampl

In the book of Acts, individual healings sometimes draw entire communities to listen to the gospel.[237]

And yet we seem today to be left with two difficulties. First,
because all our sanctioned testimonies are alike, we have stopped
listening. When there is only one story, there is really no story at
all—no suspense, and no valuing of developments along the way. The
congregation isn't excited; the community isn't transformed. And soon
the voices fall silent. We listen only to the newest story, or the person
raised from death trumps the one who had a limb restored. This woman
was healed of cancer, but that was thirty years ago, and now she has a
heart condition.

> . . . even though my illness was a trial to you, you did not
> treat me with contempt or scorn. — Gal. 4:14

Which brings us to the second problem: Some of us have very different
testimonies. We have not been instantly and completely healed—at
least, not yet. Some of us are very sick indeed, requiring much help
and patience from others. Yet we still have testimonies. We strive, like
Habakkuk (3:17-18), to rejoice in God even in a time of barrenness.
We seek to serve, like Paul, despite "a physical infirmity" (Gal. 4:13,
NRSV), or, like Timothy, despite "frequent illnesses" (1 Tim. 5:23).

---

[237] Acts 3:1-11; 9:32-35, 40-42.

In all sorts of different ways, we say with the psalmist, "My comfort in my suffering is this: Your promise preserves my life" (Ps. 119:50) and "It was good for me to be afflicted so that I might learn your decrees" (119:71). We have testimonies, but, if we still smack more of brokenness than breakthrough, no one wants to hear them.

No one wants to hear such testimonies, and that is a great pity. The Book of Hebrews urges Christians to "consider *and* give attentive, continuous care to watching over one another, studying how we may stir up (stimulate and incite) to love *and* helpful deeds *and* noble activities" (10:24, Ampl). Actions speak louder than words, but testimonies surely have a part to play in encouraging and rousing one another.

To be honest, most testimonies of healing do nothing to inspire me to stand in the noble, active waiting that is hope or to walk in costly deeds of love. That is not their function; rather, the story of a brother or sister who was instantly and completely healed awakens my faith in a good and steadfastly loving God, who still performs great deeds.

But if there are testimonies to stir faith, are there none to provoke hope and love? Indeed there are—think only of Joni Eareckson Tada, whose light has been shining from a wheelchair for more than fifty years. Yet some churches would not welcome her testimony, or would allow it—in defiance of their largely unexamined belief that everyone with "genuine" faith always gets healed—only because they would make an exception for a "Christian celebrity." Other churches rightly make room for narratives of persecuted Christians and missionaries, but overlook people in their own congregations who are models of patient endurance. We forget that when Paul says to "honor such people" (Phil. 2:29, NRSV), his immediate reference is to Epaphroditus, an emissary and minister, but specifically one who fell sick and almost died. We tend to miss this, perhaps because we'd rather celebrate power than emulate long-suffering.

Of course not every story of sickness is a Christian testimony. Samuel Johnson, who knew both physical maladies and depression, observed,

"It is so *very* difficult for a sick man always not to be a scoundrel."[238] Pain makes us self-centered, grumbling, and manipulative. And yet some believers, in the midst of their trials, eventually find strength to rejoice, grace to give, and comfort to share.[239]

The truth is, we need heroes. There is much that is heroic in the lives of people who have been healed, in their preceding days or years of pain and doubt, but we rarely hear of this, because of the one story that emphasizes faith and power. We forget that the power of God also supplies hope to the one who walks in darkness and love to the one who gives from scarcity. Ultimately there is only one Hero, but how many are His stories!

Edith Schaeffer envisions a museum in heaven that contains two complementary exhibits. Each presents every difficult circumstance that Satan can devise, every trial that the accuser calls too big for God. One gallery showcases instances of God delivering from each circumstance. The other display shows believers who overcame each one because they continued to love and trust God even though He didn't deliver them.[240] Without believing that heaven literally contains such a museum, can't we acknowledge that every believer lives a story marked by trials, charged with suspense? Where are those testimonies?

My brother once attended a church with a TV ministry. Each week, the camera swept over the congregation on its way to the platform. Often it captured a man with quadriplegia, sitting in a wheelchair. One day the elders approached this man and said, in effect, "We are delighted that you come here, but this is a church that believes in healing. When viewers tune in to our broadcasts, they deserve to see

---

[238] Hester Lynch Piozzi, *Anecdotes of the Late Samuel Johnson, LL.D.. During the Last Twenty Years of His Life* (1786), in *Johnsoniana; or, Supplement to Boswell: Being, Anecdotes and Sayings of Dr. Johnson* (London: John Murray, 1836), 56; emphasis in original; available at *Internet Archive,* accessed December 19, 2021, https://archive.org/details/johnsonianaorsup00boswrich.

[239] James 1:2; 1 Peter 1:6; 2 Cor. 8:2; 1:3-5.

[240] Edith Schaeffer, *Affliction* (Old Tappan, NJ: Fleming H. Revell, 1978), 67-110.

only people who are whole and happy. Please, would you sit on the sidelines, in the shadows, just until you are healed."

Today many of our churches believe that to be a Christian, to have any testimony at all, requires that one be whole and happy. We have no Pauls with thorns in the flesh, no Timothies with frequent ailments, no terminally ill Elishas—or, if we do, we accuse them of lacking the faith to be healed, instantly and completely. We fail to perceive that, if we live long enough, this theology will banish every one of us to the shadows. We have no place for broken vessels, with Jesus's life and power revealed through cracks and amid putrescence. We will honor Epaphroditus only when he becomes camera-ready, or for an hour when he dies.

Faced with this bleak theology, perhaps the best response is Katherine Wolf's. A stroke at a young age has left her usually in a wheelchair, face partially paralyzed, one arm hanging limp; in consequence, when she is out among Christians, many offer to pray for her. She will now say, "Of course you can pray for my physical healing—thank you so much—but can you also pray for my gossipy mouth or my negative spirit of judgment and comparison or for my marriage and kids?"[241] These words express an admirable humility, but also present a challenge: Is it compassion or discomfort, faith or fear, that leads so many of us who remain relatively "able" to insist on directing spiritual energies toward only the most visible deficits?

I am as hungry as anyone to hear the stories of healing. One day I hope to stand by while Pam tells such a tale. But, God knows, I also need to be prodded and encouraged by those who haven't yet received the things promised, but still live by faith because they consider God "reliable *and* trustworthy *and* true to His word" (Heb. 11:11, Ampl). They too have a story to tell.

*   *   *

[241] Katherine and Jay Wolf, *Suffer Strong: How to Survive Anything by Redefining Everything* (Grand Rapids, MI: Zondervan, 2020), 172.

A few years ago, I posted a draft of this section at Relevant.com.[242] Some readers took issue with my statement that "no one" wants to hear testimonies of long-suffering faithfulness, and suggested that I must have been traumatized by "fringe" churches.

No doubt they are right. But I am not persuaded to modify my views or my language very much. Certainly I have attended churches where the not-yet-healed are welcomed, and sometimes even given things to do. Still, I do not find them encouraged to share their stories. The church could be fostering the authoritative utterance described in the previous chapter; instead, all too often, we make people feel even more marginalized, voiceless, dispensable. At the church Pam and I long attended, the only testimonies ever shared are at baptisms, as people begin their lives in Christ. We have quite a few mature believers; occasionally, over lunch or in a small group, one or another may be coaxed into sharing some impressions concerning what God is doing in their lives. This is good, but it falls far short of "considering" or "studying" how to stir up one another.

We are all hungry to see the hand of God in our lives. Even those without faith ask, "Where is your God?"[243]—and this is more than a taunt; behind the sneer there lurks a yearning. On any given day, some believers are over-eager, and see divine influence and blessing everywhere, while others are despondent, feeling abandoned. It takes all of us, praying, conversing, to hear and heed "what the Spirit says to the churches" and to welcome and not resist "the work of the Lord" in our midst.[244]

> [My mother's] confidence . . . made me teeter on an emo-
> tional and intellectual seesaw, balanced between my desperate

---

[242] See *Relevant*, accessed December 19, 2021, https://www.relevantmagazine.com/faith/testimonies-not-yet-healed/.

[243] Ps. 42:3, 10; 79:10; 115:2; Joel 2:17; Mic. 7:10.

[244] Rev. 2:7; 1 Thess. 5:19-21; 1 Cor. 16:9-11.

desire to be fully healed and my real-world experience of my limitations. — Claudia L. Osborn[245]

Church is more than a gathering place, or a hall for preaching the Word and singing praise; it is also a sacred space for sharing real stories, bearing witness to the truth of God in our lives. Not every believer is called to preach the gospel, but we all testify to the Word of God (Rev. 1:2), and this testimony has two distinct aspects:

> *Kerugma*, "the thing preached, the message," is objective, having especially to do with the effect on the hearers; *marturion* is mainly subjective, having to do especially with the preacher's personal experience.[246]

The apostles are witnesses (*martus*) to Jesus's resurrection and life and words; so is Paul.[247] Timothy bears witness to Jesus; so do Stephen, Antipas, and other martyrs.[248] Those who are present at certain works and words of Jesus also become witnesses to their neighbors, right in the streets: the Samaritan woman; the mourners who see Lazarus raised, and who help to summon a hosanna-shouting crowd.[249]

But the company of witnesses is larger than this list suggests; ultimately, it includes all who live by faith (Heb. 12:1). "Anyone who believes in the Son of God has this testimony [*marturia*] in his heart" (1 John 5:10, NIV84). And so, whenever the church gathers, "every one of you" has something to communicate (1 Cor. 14:26, KJV).

Over many decades, I have attended exactly one church where this was practiced. It was messy, and services didn't always end on time. The

---

[245] Osborn, *Over My Head*, 105.

[246] *Vine's*, New Testament section, 624 (*testimony*).

[247] The first apostles: Luke 24:48; John 15:27; Acts 1:8; 4:33; 10:39, 41; 1 John 1:2. Paul: Acts 22:15; 23:11; 1 Cor. 15:15. At his conversion, Paul is also called to bear witness to visions yet to come (Acts 26:16), for bearing witness is linked to prophecy (Rev. 19:10).

[248] 2 Tim. 1:8; Acts 22:20; Rev. 2:13; 6:9; 17:6.

[249] John 4:39; 12:17-18.

pastor and elders had to be vigilant to correct overgeneralizations and other misstatements. But every Sunday I rose with an eager sense of high expectancy. I had no idea what might happen at church that day; I couldn't wait to see what God would do. Often, very often, He did His work through "the least of these."

*   *   *

We are surrounded by hurting people. They have not been healed; they are not fine; they do not have a word of hope. They see, mirrored in their loved ones' eyes, that they are now diminished, defined by limitations.

For those who have suffered brain injury, this sense of loss tends to get worse over time—say, in the second half-year following their accident or stroke: "They tried to re-enter the community or the work force, and found that they were not welcome. They also became aware of their new limitations."[250] Claudia Osborn, trying to resume medical research more than a year after her brain injury, found that she had trouble focusing, that she needed a lot of help. Her neuropsychologist and coach explained, "It isn't until you try to use a skill and fail that you are conscious of how that particular limitation applies."[251]

> When is a disability a disability? In the case of a hidden impediment, such as brain injury, I conclude that it is only a disability when others recognize the deficits. And it doesn't help that it has taken me fifteen months to work out what has changed since the stroke: it is often only in new situations that I learn what I can do as before and what I cannot. It's a meandering way to find out my limits, but there is no

---

[250] Senelick and Dougherty, *Living with Brain Injury*, 98.
[251] Osborn, *Over My Head*, 168.

medical test that will work this out for me; life is the only test. — David Roland [252]

So, for months and years, the world continues to grow narrower, smaller.

Osborn's roommate Marcia stayed by her, but, in an outpouring of grief and untempered honesty, wrote that Osborn was a "shell of a person":

> . . . it's the everyday losses that get to you. Claudia is a boring conversationalist. Her language is no longer fluid and she lacks ideas to discuss with me. It doesn't occur to her to ask how my day was, and she wouldn't remember what I told her anyway.
>
> Our friendship is now a one-way street of her need. Knowing that increases the burden. I miss her support, our shared memory, and her thoughtfulness. She lacks the energy, imagination, and insight of my old friend. My time with her is lonely. . . .
>
> I cannot endlessly play the selfless, devoted friend. I do not believe the emotional truth of those who watch their relationship change from that of equals to one of parent-child without protest, sorrow, and rage.
>
> I have not the patience and this process is hell.[253]

Imagine being Claudia and reading this, or simply sensing it. Try to picture, even from a great distance, the grief and hurt, the hopelessness, the panic, the shame and guilt you would feel.

---

[252] David Roland, *How I Rescued My Brain: A Psychologist's Remarkable Recovery from Stroke and Trauma* (Melbourne and London: Scribe, 2014), 192.

[253] Marcia E. Baker, qtd. in Osborn, *Over My Head*, 46.

Each day, with shaky hands, the survivor applies the makeup of competence, and then faces a world of indignities that smudge it. Pam locks her keys in the car. She bumps into something at church, and is cut. The car won't start, and her cell phone's dying; I send a tow truck right away, but she's already stumbled off, upset. I catch her just as she's about to rinse her eyes with nail polish remover. Instead of liquid detergent, she nearly adds coffee to the washer. At the post office, she mails her handicapped driver's tag instead of her letter. Day after day, there are problems ordering food, answering the phone, handling medications, navigating.

Of course we rejoice at effort, and make light of lapses when we can. One day she purchased jock itch cream and applied it to a foot fungus. When she showed me what she had done, I told her that it was okay with me, but from now on she'd have to pee standing up.

Brain injury threatens identity; it even insults personhood. A case manager, who has spent hours assisting many patients, wonders, "What are we other than our brains? Is there a part of me that can't be changed by a brain injury?"[254] A clinical neuropsychologist insists that character persists,[255] but a spouse sees what is before her eyes: "the Dave who woke up in the neuro-intensive care unit at Rush Hospital was not my husband."[256] A survivor says it best: "I'm not me anymore, but I'm still me."[257]

---

[254] Mason, *Head Cases*, 11; compare 213.

[255] Catherine Mateer, qtd. in Callwood, *The Man Who Lost Himself*, 199: ". . . personally I believe character is not a piece of your brain or a part of your heart. Maybe it's the soul that people talk about. Character lasts."

[256] Allison Pataki, *Beauty in the Broken Places: A Memoir of Love, Faith, and Resilience* (New York: Random House, 2018), 83; compare 106: "I loved so many things about Dave, but, most of all, I loved his brain. I loved his mind. I loved his wit. . . . How could I live without Dave's mind?"

[257] Qtd. in Mason, *Head Cases*, 212.

Each survivor is to us a mystery, and some, like Jen Barrick, are miracles. But it is so very easy to overlook the revelation, to assess it to death, to see only what is abnormal or subpar:

> Each member of the treatment team gave a report on Jen's progress. I felt like they were talking about someone else. "She can't follow a verbal command," one would say. "Jen is not responding as quickly as we would like." "She has a flat affect with no expression." . . .
>
> How I wished her therapists could see and hear Jen praying in the middle of the night rather than only during the daylight hours when her energy was gone. Those who sensed Jen's spiritual side knew how far she had come. Yes, physically and mentally she was extremely limited. But spiritually she was completely intact.[258]

"Your wife is pretty dissplintered," Pam said to me just last month. But I was allowed to witness her beautiful spirit laid bare; I was there when she worshipped, though she had no words.

Here we are all aphasic; we have no language adequate to the glory of personhood. Even theologians stammer and fall silent when they try to describe the image of God as it shines or flickers in human beings. Too many have confused it with a person's ability to jump through the hoops of tests designed by intellectuals.[259]

Some Christians today make much of a variant reading in a single verse: "For as he [a person—actually, in the context, specifically a miser] thinks in his heart, so is he" (Prov. 23:7, Ampl; see NIV text for alternatives). This is the very first text in Joyce Meyer's *Battlefield of the*

---

[258] Barrick, *Miracle for Jen*, 90. Compare 94: "Her mind and body were completely broken, yet her soul was uninjured. It was encouraging and devastating at the same time."

[259] See, e.g., Molly C. Haslam, *A Constructive Theology of Intellectual Disability: Human Being as Mutuality and Response* (New York: Fordham University, 2012).

Mind, and she returns to it several times: "The mind is the leader or forerunner of all actions"; "Thoughts are powerful, and . . . they have creative ability."[260] Similarly, Caroline Leaf quotes this verse often, and comments, "We must continually monitor what passes through our five senses. Whatever you think about will grow, and what you grow is what you do (Prov. 23:7)."[261]

As principles go, this is probably not a bad one. But the Bible is not really a book of principles, much less a tool for mental self-mastery. I cannot heal or remake my mind, any more than, by my own will or word or effort, I can save myself or forgive and love my neighbor. Only the grace of God can accomplish any of these things.

> I kept waiting to feel better. . . . Reading over my diary and letters written at the time, I am struck by how, being out of touch with the concept of recognizing one's limitations, I was sure that any day now I would return to normal, that it would all just go away. — Harrianne Mills[262]

How much more, when people have suffered brain injuries, do we weigh them down with a cruel and heavy yoke when we say, *Take control of your thoughts; monitor everything that passes through your mind.* The mind or intellect follows the heart, which God may call to go through pain. Moreover, Satan, who is to be crushed or bruised in the head, hates our heads and strikes at them, as he struck Jesus's head.[263]

---

[260] Joyce Meyer, *Battlefield of the Mind: Winning the Battle in Your Mind* (Tulsa: Harrison House, 1995), 11, 27, 29, 45.

[261] Caroline Leaf, *Think and Eat Yourself Smart: A Neuroscientific Approach to a Sharper Mind and Healthier Life* (Grand Rapids, MI: BakerBooks, 2016), 104; see also 124; and Caroline Leaf, *Switch On Your Brain: The Key to Peak Happiness, Thinking, and Health* (Grand Rapids, MI: Baker, 2013), 80, 99, 111, 124.

[262] Harrianne Mills, *A Mind of My Own: Memoir of Recovery from Aphasia* (Bloomington, IN: AuthorHouse, 2004), 311-12.

[263] Satan crushed: Gen. 3:15; Ps. 68:21; 74:13-14; Hab. 3:13-14. Satan striking: Matt. 26:67; 27:29-30; compare Mark 12:4; Isa. 50:6; 52:14.

We cannot balance ourselves. Earlier, we said that brain injury amplifies personality; aphasia exaggerates. What if the "exaggerated" and out of balance are a barometer and a challenge to our churches? "Much of what we do know about the brain's functions has come from the careful study of people who have had strokes";[264] cannot the body of Christ also learn from extraordinary people making remarkable adaptations? Helmut Thielicke charged us with "an inadequate theology of suffering";[265] what if we started, now, to feel the pain of the afflicted (1 Cor. 12:26); to value weak believers as "indispensable" (1 Cor. 12:22) to us, sent to reveal our own weakness and dependence on grace? What if we paid attention, expecting the power of Christ to be richly "manifest" in them (2 Cor. 12:9-10)? What if we listened to their stories, drawing and sharing biblical comfort, *parakleisis*: encouragement to press on?

Lacking such a ministry, people cope as best they can. A survivor concludes:

> Every day I have a choice. I can choose to focus on my limitations and thus stay limited, or I can choose life. I choose life.[266]

A spouse draws strength from the dictionary:

> I thought I *had* accepted Rich's accident, even though I kept putting myself in a place where it hadn't happened yet. . . . I thought that not accepting meant turning my face to the wall, unable to function. So now today I look up the word *acceptance* and the definition is "to receive gladly" and that doesn't sound right. I flip to the back, and look up its

---

[264] Stein, *Stroke and the Family*, 42.

[265] Qtd. in Philip Yancey, *I Was Just Wondering* (1989), revised edition (Grand Rapids, MI: William B. Eerdmans, 1998), 182.

[266] Shapiro, *Healing into Possibility*, 89.

earliest root, "to grasp," and discover this comes from the old English for "a thread used in weaving," and bingo, that's it. You can't keep pulling out the thread. You have to weave it in and then you have to go on weaving.[267]

Pam struggles with memory and language. She cannot return to work, and many days her vision does not permit her to drive. She crashes up against limitations every day. Although she spends hours with the audio Bible, letting the Scriptures renew her mind, still time hangs heavy. Some days she sleeps; occasionally, her frustration finds a voice, and she calls herself a retard who can no longer have friends. Grief often occupies her thoughts—grief, and a deep intercession; for she groans with all creation (Rom. 8:22-26).

FAITH AND MEDICATIONS

> Then Isaiah said, "Prepare a poultice of figs." They did so and applied it to the boil [Ampl "burning inflammation"], and [Hezekiah] recovered. — 2 Kings 20:7

For fifteen months, as I adjusted to the role of caregiver, I took an antidepressant. Even though I believe that it is God who "comforts *and* encourages *and* refreshes *and* cheers the depressed *and* the sinking" (2 Cor. 7:6, Ampl), each day I swallowed a pill. I thought of this not as turning from God, but as attempting to manage symptoms while I waited on Him. I hoped I was in the company of Paul's associate Timothy. He had certainly witnessed great miracles of healing in Jesus's name, yet the apostle urged him to supplement his drinking water with a little wine because of his "frequent ailments" (1 Tim. 5:23, NRSV).

---

[267] Thomas, *A Three Dog Life*, 123-24; emphasis in original. ". . . I can sometimes hold these two truths in my head at once: I wish he were whole, and I love my life" (124).

In Jesus's parable (Luke 10:34), the Samaritan applies the medicines of the day for wounds, "wine to cleanse, and oil to soothe."[268] Jesus Himself, in one of His miracles of healing, uses saliva (John 9:6), then believed to have healing qualities.[269] Yet this cure is no less miraculous than the rest; nor is the Samaritan condemned—indeed, it may show greater love to provide for a long convalescence, just as Jesus commends those who tend the sick (Matt. 25:36).

Not all believers take this view. In 1914, John G. Lake declared, "It is just as offensive for the Christian to take medicine as for the drunkard to take whiskey."[270] I don't condemn Lake; he was used by God in a great move of miraculous healings. But I am fairly sure that he would condemn me. As Paul says in Romans 14:3, the strong in faith tend to despise the weak, and the weak to criticize the strong. Sometimes we are not even sure which is which!

For me personally, the pills became an invitation to humility. It is humbling to take a psychiatric medication, and humiliating to admit as much on employment forms. I suspect that every Christian receives such invitations—perhaps in the form of a period of unemployment or a painful relationship. No doubt some of us need more schooling in humility than others. To all of us, though, the Bible says three times, "God opposes the proud but gives grace to the humble."[271]

The Lord supports the sinking mind. — Isaac Watts[272]

---

268 Vincent, 1:356.

269 Vincent, 2:182.

270 John G. Lake, "Divine Healing," Philadelphia, January 30, 1914; in Roberts Liardon, comp., *John G. Lake: The Complete Collection of His Life Teachings* (Tulsa: Albury, 1999), 123. Also available at *Healing Rooms Ministries*, accessed December 19, 2021, https://healingrooms. com/about/johnGLake/?document=69. In the same sermon, Lake compares consulting a doctor to committing adultery (118). It is difficult to see why Paul should call Luke "the beloved physician" (Col. 4:14, NRSV) if the entire profession is under a curse.

271 James 4:6 and 1 Peter 5:5, NIV84; Prov. 3:34.

272 Watts, "Psalm 146," in *Psalms and Hymns*, 467. Compare "Psalm 119 Part 17," 398: "When pain and anguish seize me, Lord, / All my support is from thy word."

Humility and faith coexist in odd ways. In Genesis 23, when Sarah dies, Abraham believes God's promise that all the land, as far as the eye can see, will belong to him and his descendants. Yet instead of claiming the promise, he pays an exorbitant fee, to people who don't share the promise, for a parcel of land to use as a burial plot. Is this a lack of faith? Or is it an example of humility giving faith the strength to believe and trust even when the fulfillment seems to lag?

It is not humility that hampers faith, but pride—specifically, my proud desire to exalt or elevate myself. This putting myself forward can masquerade as faith. Repeatedly, Jesus warns us that "everyone who exalts himself will be humbled, and he who humbles himself will be exalted,"[273] and the contexts indicate claiming a place or title or attitude of honor. Similarly, Paul says that his thorn in the flesh, probably a physical affliction, served to keep him from becoming elated or conceited (2 Cor. 12:7).

Yet we are also encouraged to trust that, "in due time," God will exalt us if we humble ourselves (1 Peter 5:6; James 4:10). "[Y]ou bestow glory on me and lift up my head," writes David; "you stoop down to make me great" (Ps. 3:3, NIV84; 18:35, NIV84).

Jesus is, of course, the great example: humbling Himself through long years to the lowest place, to be exalted to the highest place (Phil. 2:8-9). But we see the same pattern in Joseph (Ps. 105:17-21) and Solomon (1 Chron. 29:25), and most explicitly in Joshua:

> And the LORD said to Joshua, "Today I will begin to exalt you in the eyes of all Israel, so they may know that I am with you as I was with Moses." . . .
>
> That day the LORD exalted Joshua in the sight of all Israel; and they revered him all the days of his life, just as they had revered Moses. — Josh. 3:7; 4:14, NIV84

---

[273] Luke 14:11, NIV84; 18:14; Matt. 23:12.

Unlike Solomon, Joshua never suffered the humiliation of a fall from grace, and some of his most memorable words were spoken toward the end of his life (24:15).

When and how did Joshua humble himself? We first meet him as a military leader (Ex. 17), and later he was one of the twelve spies (Num. 13). In between, he was Moses's minister, servant, or aide (Num. 11:28). He endured the forty years of wilderness wandering. And, man of action though he was, we are told that he did not leave the tent of meeting (Ex. 33:11). He learned the discipline of waiting on God.

In the New Testament, particularly, exaltation is not individualistic, a promotion to honor, so much as it is a lifting up of the name of Jesus in His body, the church—paradoxically, by accepting responsibility and bending low to serve. Paul "conquers" by marching in Jesus's victory parade; he embraces weakness so that others may be strengthened.[274]

Humility is not grasping upward to seize but extending downward to pour out. Yet Jesus, who expressed humility in every word and gesture recorded in the Gospels, could speak of it as swallowing: "Shall I not drink the cup the Father has given me?" (John 18:11). According to Matthew 27:34, on the cross He even tasted a painkiller, but then refused it; musing on this, John Keble wrote, "Thou wilt feel all, that Thou mayst pity all."[275]

Zoloft is hardly the cup of God's wrath, but it is a start; there is a spiritual and psychological truth in the metaphor of eating humble pie. Humility may be incomplete without service to others, but it is rooted in waiting on God. In the end, whether or not we submit to medicine may not be very important. What counts is whether, at one of God's occasions, we find our way to the lowest chair, and sit in it.

---

[274] 1 Cor. 4:9-10; 2 Cor. 2:14; 4:12; see also Phil. 1:20.

[275] John Keble, "Fill High the Bowl" (Tuesday before Easter), *The Christian Year* (1827), 87; available at *Christian Classics Ethereal Library*, accessed December 19, 2021, https://www.ccel.org/ccel/keble/year. R. K. Harrison notes, "The anodyne offered to Christ during His crucifixion . . . was a diluted wine containing stupefying drugs": "Gall," *NBD*, 451.

In this, as in so many things, Pam is my teacher. Two years ago, she prayed:

> *Lord, thank You for putting me in this place. I know I am very limited, but I am with You.*

*   *   *

There are many incarcerations in Scripture, and the thought has occurred to me that God allows all the wrong people to be locked up. Put the apostle John in a cell; he'll be caught up in heavenly visions, or tickled that he is "beloved" by Jesus, and won't even be aware of his surroundings. Shut away Martha, and she'll clean the place; or Ezekiel—he'll either lie down on his side or tunnel through the wall. Matthew or Jeremiah's friend Baruch will simply keep writing.

But it's the doers and the people persons who get thrown in jail. And when Corrie ten Boom, suffering a series of strokes, lost the power of speech and became bedridden, her companion said that it was as if she was back in the cells and barracks of World War II; this was "another kind of imprisonment."[276]

In a heartbreaking passage, Paul asks Timothy, his son in the faith, not to be ashamed "of me, a prisoner for His sake," "chained like a criminal."[277] In the same vein, he writes to the church at Ephesus, "I ask you, therefore, not to be discouraged because of my sufferings for you, which are your glory."[278] I think this reflects, not just the frustration of an active man now shut away, but a church that (like our churches) hungered especially to hear of miracles and blessings, stories with happy endings. Peter had been delivered from prison (Acts 12); so had Paul in days past, in Philippi (Acts 16). Indeed, it's to the Philippians

---

[276] Moore, *The Five Silent Years of Corrie ten Boom*, 134, 44, 128; Moore, *Life Lessons from the Hiding Place*, 190.

[277] 2 Tim. 1:8, Ampl; 2:9; compare 1:12, 16.

[278] Eph. 3:13. Compare Ps. 69:6: "[M]ay those who hope in you not be disgraced because of me; . . . may those who seek you not be put to shame because of me."

that Paul tries, at some length, to explain that his present, unrelieved imprisonment "has actually served to advance the gospel,"[279] because now Christ is preached by many lips.

> I eagerly expect and hope that I will in no way be ashamed,
> but will have sufficient courage so that now as always Christ
> will be exalted in my body, whether by life or by death.
> — Phil. 1:20

Now, in later years, Paul isn't delivered—any more than John the Baptist was (Luke 7); any more than many of us are. They are off-camera, relegated to the sidelines. Paul seems to recognize this prolonged incarceration as part of his calling (Acts 20:23; 9:16); still, he worries about its effects on the faith of others. Apparently, even in those early days of the church, some believers criticized anyone who suffered. They may have said things like, "Oh, that Paul—he used to be really something, a great apostle, a man of faith, but now he seems to have lost it." It was too discomfiting to think that God might have contrasting plans for Paul in different seasons of his life: that at one time God might be glorified by displaying His mighty power to open prison doors; while at another time, His glory might shine through fruits of His Spirit—joy, perseverance, hope, and faith in the midst of dark times—displayed in the character of His child.

How sad when we are ashamed of these sufferers instead of honoring them, or discouraged rather than emboldened by their example. When we're urged to remember our leaders—"Consider the outcome of their way of life and imitate their faith" (Heb. 13:7)—the injunction includes the "outcome" of those "chained and put in prison" (11:36, NIV84). "Remember those who are in prison as if you were their fellow prisoner, and those who are ill-treated, since you also are liable to bodily sufferings" (13:3, Ampl). Yet how many believers, in all the various

---

[279] Phil. 1:12. Compare 2 Tim. 2:9, Ampl: "But the Word of God is not chained *or* imprisoned!"

prisons with which the devil tests us (Rev. 2:10), are left alone, to wonder and doubt (Matt. 11:2-3), in danger of taking offense at Jesus and falling away (11:6). However paradoxical it seems to us, we are to view these sufferers—in prisons, hospitals, refugee camps, insane asylums, homeless shelters, comas—as Christ's "ambassador[s] in chains" (Eph. 6:20). So Paul, after declaring to the Colossians, "I rejoice in what I am suffering for you, and I fill up in my flesh what is still lacking in regard to Christ's afflictions" (Col. 1:24)—after announcing that he yet labors with "all the energy Christ so powerfully works in me" (1:29)—says simply, "Remember my chains" (4:18).

God is glorified as we acknowledge our dependence on Him.[280] "He [Jesus] must become greater; I must become less," says John the Baptist (John 3:30). In this school, affliction is our best teacher. Paul writes of one period of crisis and distress that it "happened that we might not rely on ourselves but on God, who raises the dead" (2 Cor. 1:9). Nevertheless, later in the same letter he credits the persistent torment of his "thorn in the flesh" with preparing him to understand that he must dwell and walk in weakness if he wishes the power of Christ to rest on him and pitch a tent over him, as the heavenly tent that covers and swallows up his failing, mortal body.[281]

Limitations are like prison walls, and a stale routine like passing and impassive guards. We still await the coming of a promise from the Old Testament's last page:

---

[280] See the sermon on this theme by Jonathan Edwards: "The nature and contrivance of our redemption is such, that the redeemed are in every thing directly, immediately, and entirely dependent on God: They are dependent on him for all, and are dependent on him every way." "God Glorified in Man's Dependence" (1730, 1731), in Clarence H. Faust and Thomas H. Johnson, *Jonathan Edwards: Representative Selections, with Introduction, Bibliography, and Notes* (1935), revised edition (New York: Hill and Wang, 1962), 92; full text available at *Works of Jonathan Edwards Online*, accessed December 19, 2021, http://edwards.yale.edu/archive?path=aHR0cDovL2Vkd2FyZHMueWFsZS5lZHUvY2dpLWJpbi9uZXdwaGlsby9nZXRvYmplY3QucGw/cC4xNjoyMDUud2l2bbw.

[281] 2 Cor. 12:7-10, Ampl; 5:1, 4; 4:10-11; Vincent, 3:356.

> But unto you who revere *and* worshipfully fear My name
> shall the Sun of Righteousness arise with healing in His wings
> *and* His beams, and you shall go forth and gambol like calves
> [released] from the stall *and* leap for joy. — Mal. 4:2, Ampl

Shut up in the stall of its chrysalis, a caterpillar undergoes a kind of death. All the while, the chameleon runs free, and is ever changing—but the changes are only skin-deep, and, if you watch long enough, the colors repeat as conditions and circumstances return. It's in the hiddenness of the chrysalis that God works transformation, shaping and at the proper time releasing a new creation.

*   *   *

Pam sits before her pills. They stand like soldiers, ranged in companies and patrols, waiting to be deployed; she sits, submissive, ready to swallow. Christ, in furthest obedience, opened not His mouth (Isa. 53:7, Ampl), but she obeys by opening, receiving.

> Sympathy was a shortsighted emotion: it told you to make the
> pain stop *now*, and so you went with the quick fixes. Because
> you wanted your pain to stop, too. — Jessica Alexander[282]

We signal our dependence when we allow another to feed us. "The eyes of all look to you, and you give them their food at the proper time" (Ps. 145:15). This is trust; this is the faith of weakness and humility. We are a long time learning it, as Moses reminded Israel after forty years: "He humbled you, causing you to hunger and then feeding you with manna" (Deut. 8:3).

---

[282] Jessica Alexander, *Chasing Chaos: My Decade In and Out of Humanitarian Aid* (New York: Broadway-Random House, 2013), 310; emphasis in original.

I have always liked Martin Luther's definition of a sacrament as God's Word added to a (physical) element.[283] In baptism, God's promise is added to water; in communion, the words of institution are spoken over bread and wine.

When we have just a physical element, over which God has spoken no special word, we have only superstition. Luther would have pointed, for example, to his era's busy trade in relics, such as pieces of the true cross.

On the other hand, when we have only the Word and no element, our faith often falters, or we grasp after formulas and magic. The incarnation argues that our God loves to embody His words to us, to feed the whole person (including senses and emotions) rather than just the mind.

In this sense, sacraments are a great equalizer. In much of Protestant Christianity, we emphasize the sermon to the exclusion of all else—and so tend to intellectualize our faith. But when the Lord Jesus spreads His table or pours out His water, all who will may come. The cognitively impaired, or those afflicted with dementia, are not "less than"; they are full brothers and sisters in Christ, confessing Him as Lord with their very body language. From time to time the "strong" in faith want to spiritualize everything and bypass the sacraments; but the "weak" cling to them, finding grace in lowly matter.[284]

Medications are no sacrament, but they set forth, visibly and tangibly, the lowest place to which Jesus calls us. They embody the human

---

[283] See, e.g., Martin Luther, *Sermons on the Catechism* (1528), transl. John W. Doberstein, in John Dillenberger, ed., *Martin Luther: Selections from His Writings* (Garden City, NY: Anchor-Doubleday, 1961), 233. Luther cites Augustine, *Lectures or Tractates on the Gospel According to St. John* (ca. 416), 15.4.

[284] Therese Vanier tells the moving story of an intellectually disabled man named Robert who, as he received the elements from the Archbishop of Canterbury, broke the wafer in half and handed one piece back—a simple, profound demonstration of fellowship. *An Ecumenical Journey—l'Arche in the UK* (1989); qtd. in Kathryn Spink, *The Miracle, the Message, the Story: Jean Vanier and l'Arche* (Mahwah, NJ: HiddenSpring-Paulist, 2006), 148-49.

word of our doctors' diagnoses, and the God-stirred word of our cry to Him: the desperate prayer of this body of death, and the groaning of all creation in its humiliation. Sitting before our pillboxes, we echo "without a word" the bold statement of Daniel's band: The God we serve is able to save, and He will rescue us; but even if He does not, we will not turn aside, we will not deny or desert His name (Dan. 3:17-18).

Some days Pam is mostly silent. But some of her pills must be taken with food. She always pauses, at these moments, to offer a prayer of thanks.

Billy Sunday, a renowned evangelist of the early twentieth century, spoke for "strong" and "active" faith. He said in one of his sermons, "The only thing that pleases Jesus is winning souls."[285] Really? The *only* thing?! I find in Scripture a long list of things that are "well-pleasing" (*euarestos*) to God: "righteousness, peace and joy in the Holy Spirit" (Rom. 14:17-18); "to do good and to share with others," and through Jesus to "continually offer to God a sacrifice of praise" (Heb. 13:15-16). I also read that "a gentle and peaceful spirit . . . is very precious in the sight of God" (1 Peter 3:4, Ampl). We must beware of words, even from apostles, that serve to barricade little ones from Jesus (Mark 10:13-16).

Two days before the fifth anniversary of her stroke, Pam journaled this prayer:

> *Heavenly Father, Thank you for sending your only Son, Jesus, to save me, to teach me so many things then to die for me. Thank You for allowing Jesus to live forever. I'm so gratefull you sent the Holy Spirit to live here on earth with me and anyone one else who would ask Jesus into their hearts. I love you, Father, Son and Holy Spirit.*

Pam takes and eats what is set before her, and she blesses God.

---

[285] Qtd. in Douglas Frank, *Less Than Conquerors: How Evangelicals Entered the 20th Century* (Grand Rapids, MI: William B. Eerdmans, 1986), 255.

9

GRACE

DREAMS

Then Solomon awoke—and he realized it had been a dream.
— 1 Kings 3:15

When the LORD restored the fortunes of Zion,
we were like those who dream.
Then our mouth was filled with laughter,
and our tongue with shouts of joy;
then it was said among the nations,
"The LORD has done great things for them."
The LORD has done great things for us,
and we rejoiced.
Restore our fortunes, O LORD,
like the watercourses in the Negeb. — Ps. 126:1-4, NRSV

Love bade me welcome: yet my soul drew back,
Guiltie of dust and sinne.
But quick-ey'd Love, observing me grow slack
From my first entrance in,
Drew nearer to me, sweetly questioning,
If I lack'd any thing.

A guest, I answer'd, worthy to be here:
Love said, you shall be he.

I the unkinde, ungratefull? Ah my deare,
I cannot look on thee.
Love took my hand, and smiling did reply,
Who made the eyes but I?

Truth Lord, but I have marr'd them: let my shame
Go where it doth deserve.
And know you not, sayes Love, who bore the blame?
My deare, then I will serve.
You must sit down, sayes Love, and taste my meat:
So I did sit and eat. — George Herbert[286]

"Jahhh-ahhnn!"

I speak through the closed door, vainly hoisting the red flag: "Pooping."

Undeterred, she settles herself outside my bathroom. "I had a dream."

"Still pooping."

"There was a car—no, bus. BUS."

"Pooping POOPING pooping." Some aspire to know and be known, to plumb mysteries, or voyage out into the deep things of God. I am no longer one of them; I am more focused and more modest. Once before I die, I would like to defecate without a phone trilling or Pam calling my name. But she is well schooled, and comes boldly before the throne of grace.

Today she tells me that she has dreamed we were at a bus stop and, when the bus arrived, there was a woman seated beside the driver—except Pam couldn't tell whether she was a real person, or a manne-quin, or even a picture. She tried to draw my attention, but I wasn't seeing anything. So she stared intently, and at last the woman could

---

[286] George Herbert, "Love (3)," *The Temple* (1633; London: Methuen, 1899), 136; available at *Internet Archive*, accessed December 19, 2021, https://archive.org/details/temple00herb.

hold her inert pose no longer, and met Pam's eyes, and they both burst into laughter. As she recounts this, I hear her, squirming, swaying with delight, while I sit clenched and barren.

I'm jealous of my wife's dreams.

To be sure, she has her off nights, her nightmares about a rat, or human invaders.[287] But, almost every night, I thrash in restless anxiety dreams. I'm in a play, cast as a woman; there are no rehearsals, and I don't know my part. I'm playing the violin in a concert—or, as it changes, serving ineptly as the violinist's page turner; and I wake up protesting, "I can't help it if I don't know the music." I'm traveling, but I've forgotten to pack. I'm driving a truck, but I have to use reins to turn the steering wheel, because I'm floating high above. I'm lost, about to be late, getting interrupted; unprepared and out of control. It's as the philosopher says: "A dream comes when there are many cares" (Eccl. 5:3).

> Our dreams afford sufficient proof,
> The soul, without the flesh, can act. — John Newton[288]

Even my rare happy dream comes crashing down, often with her help. One morning I wake, groggily, to find Pam sitting up in bed; I put my right hand on her back and promptly drift off once more, to dream that I am at an outdoor barbecue or picnic. The food looks wonderful, and I load up a plate. I am just bringing my fork to my lips when, in real life, Pam grows bored, and moves to get up. My hand slides with her as, in the dream, someone yanks my fork away from my gaping mouth.

Pam's dreams are different. Some are extremely brief: she enters a room, and people respond by exclaiming, "Here she is!" Others suggest

---

[287] Perhaps this is not uncommon. Paul West writes of his early recovery, "I still could not speak a single word, although my dreams were being rapidly infiltrated by ghost voices over which I had no control." *The Shadow Factory*, 44.

[288] Newton, #2.98, in *Olney Hymns*, 475-76.

more of a process, a journey or at least a step of faith. In one, she observes a baby that is trying to nurse, and she has no milk. Then I make a cameo appearance, encouraging her to give it her finger to suck on; she tries this, and the baby goes to sleep, and Pam is filled with peace. How often God comes to us, saying, "What is that in your hand?" (Ex. 4:2); and how many times the little we have, given to Jesus, suffices to feed a hillside (John 6:9-13; 2 Kings 4:42-44).

Even her nightmares mostly recover. She sees a surge of water, and is fleeing, warning others, when someone tells her that it's the Holy Spirit, flowing everywhere. In another dream, she hears the words, "Open your mouth, and I will fill it." This is a paraphrase of Psalm 81:10 (most translations add the word "wide"). Waking, she concludes that God is telling her to speak up boldly, in faith, telling her story.

Most striking—and, on my jealous days, most irksome—have been a series of dreams about dogs that only Pam can see:

> ... I was in a church. A lot of people were there, I looked around and noticed two black Rotweiler's were walking toward me. Since I loved dog's I smiled and invited them to come closer so I could touch them. Peach and Joy unspeakable filled my heart. No one else seemed to notice these strong amazing guard Dog's stayed with me where ever I walked. The Anxietly I'd felt in the start of the wake up at first. Once I'd left my home and say these Rotweiler's I knew I'd continue to feel calm and safe.

> ... They are Angel's God sent. They are strong and have been sent by the Lord to protect me. They would stay with me for the rest of my life. Anywhere I go they will cover me with strength.

> Praise God for the Blood of the Lamb! Jesus is Alive! He will come back one day to bring me home and more will be revealed.

Despite the Magic 8-Ball language that concludes her journal entry, this dream has proved profoundly comforting and encouraging to Pam. She is not forgotten or left to cope alone. God walks with her, watching over her. A week later, she was still singing praise in her writing:

> *Deep + Wide, Deep and WIDE, There's a fountain flowing Deep and Will, Jesus Christ, Holy Spirit and Angels Rotweiler's that live in our live's at no cost.*

Because of the aphasia, it took about ten days for us to figure out that she was confused in her identification of the breed of the angelic dogs. In fact, they were not rottweilers, but jet-black greyhounds:

> *Last week I dreamed I'd walked into a church and saw 2 beautiful pure black grayhound dogs. They gently came over to me as they saw I had noticed them. I felt full of joy unspeakable yet full of glory. More people were in this church, other people were coming inside this church seeming to be in a hurry and I was amazed they didn't seem to notice these dog's. Then I woke up. Angel's = Grayhounds —*

The picture of faithful companions, silent but ever-present, has ancient and biblical roots. In Psalm 23, goodness (Hebrew *tob*) and mercy (*hesed*: the Lord's steadfast or unfailing love) will attend the psalmist "all the days of my life" as guardians, constant protectors; compare light and truth, mercy (*hesed*) and truth, righteousness and justice.[289] Or, as Pam has it, peace and joy.

Our culture has a fascination with angels; and why not? They are "ministering spirits sent to serve" (Heb. 1:14), and so it appears that we can acknowledge them and still remain the stars of our own shows. At least in popular imagination, they don't come with the fire of holiness,

---

[289] Ps. 23:6, NRSV; 43:3; 85:10; 89:14.

stilling us to trembling awe; they don't command, requiring our submission and obedience. Bland and affirming, their job is to make hope
easy and faith unnecessary.

Not so in Scripture, where the Angel of the Lord (the One, for
example, who wrestles with Jacob in Genesis 32) is "God Himself
appearing as a man";[290] and where even angels less directly identified
with God come directly from His presence.[291] They appear with glory,
or at least the strength and majesty of greyhounds; but they bear witness
to the fullness of His coming, humbly, as one of us. They stand on the
hills and point to the manger, directing our attention to *Immanuel*, God
who has come to dwell with us.[292] They do not preach the gospel—the
angel that stands before Cornelius directs him to send for Peter[293]—but
they herald it, visibly and audibly. They are too splendid to bear grace,
but they bear witness to it.

And Pam bears witness. In her dream of the bus stop, as she and the
not-quite-human woman laugh in mutual recognition, I am at last able to
see what Pam sees. Her new ability to discern spirits (1 Cor. 12:10) spills
over onto others. As is fitting, since every gift of the Holy Spirit is given
"for the common good" (v. 7). Some are downright inconveniences to
the recipient: my brother has one friend with a prophetic gifting that he
can't simply turn off; when he goes into the mall, intending only to buy
socks, he glances at people and knows at once sad truths about their lives,
and sometimes turns back, overwhelmed. The gift in some ways makes
him weaker, but it is a blessing to many. Grace has a way of multiplying,

---

[290] Edmund P. Clowney, *The Unfolding Mystery: Discovering Christ in the Old Testament* (1988),
25th anniversary edition (Phillipsburg, NJ: P & R, 2013), 75, 77-78.

[291] Luke 1:19; Dan. 9:21-23; Rev. 5:11.

[292] Luke 2:8-15; Isa. 7:14; Matt. 1:23.

[293] Acts 10:30-32. "God's method is to flesh out the Good News. He isn't interested in using
an angel to proclaim the gospel to humans. He wanted Cornelius to hear the message of divine
grace from a redeemed man who had experienced that grace for himself. He wanted him to
rub shoulders with another imperfect human being. He wanted members of two antagonistic
parties to come together in love through the gospel." Joseph C. Aldrich, *Gentle Persuasion:
Creative Ways to Introduce Your Friends to Christ* (Portland, OR: Multnomah, 1988), 205-06.

ripening, opening out, flooding. Just so, in one of Pam's later dreams, the greyhounds return: a woman accuses her of stealing them, but suddenly the two become five. With grace and spiritual gifts there can be no pride of possession, no competition; there is only abundance.

*   *   *

Grace (Hebrew *hen*, Greek *charis*) is an elusive concept. It is elegance, favor, acceptance; from one side yearning toward and seeking favor, and from the other inclining toward and showing favor.[294]

At least since B. B. Warfield, we have come to think of grace as "unmerited favor"—as "neither expected nor deserved."[295] Jim McClure points out that ancient notions of grace often emphasize reciprocity,[296] and we may add that some passages speak of merit. When Bildad advises Job that his supplication (*hanan*) or plea to God for grace will be heard so long as he is pure and upright (Job 8:5-6), he is only echoing the psalmists, who ask for grace on the grounds of their integrity (Ps. 26:11), and who declare that the Lord always shows grace to those who love (*'aheb*) His name (Ps. 119:132). Malachi 1:8-9 warns that God won't be gracious to a people whose offerings are poor.

Working mostly with the New Testament, James Ryle has redefined grace as the empowering presence of God. Ryle makes the point that "unmerited favor" is practically synonymous with mercy, so that, if we accept Warfield's definition, apostolic benedictions imparting "grace and mercy"[297] are redundant. Moreover, "unmerited favor" makes little sense in a number of passages, including a key verse: "He mocks proud

---

[294] *BDB*, 335-36; William F. Arndt and F. Wilbur Gingrich, *A Greek-English Lexicon of the New Testament and Other Early Christian Literature*, 4th edition (Chicago: University of Chicago, 1952, 1957), 885-86. (Hereafter Arndt and Gingrich.)

[295] *Vine's*, Old Testament section, 100 (*to be gracious, show favor*).

[296] Jim B. McClure, *Grace Revisited* (Geelong, Australia: Trailblazer Ministries, 2010), 39-40; see 48 on Warfield. Available at *Google Books*, accessed December 19, 2021, https://books.google.com/books/about/Grace_Revisited.html?id=UfwcPwF8PVgC.

[297] 1 Tim. 1:2; 2 Tim. 1:2; 2 John 3.

mockers but gives grace to the humble."[298] Surely proud mockers need unmerited favor at least as desperately as the lowly and afflicted do. But it is the humble, the crushed, who are in a position to welcome His empowering presence.[299]

McClure finds "empowering presence" helpful in defining grace, but still too narrow.[300] Particularly in the Old Testament, he calls *grace* "a most inadequate word" to describe either *hen* or *hesed*. At the heart of both, he believes, "is the concept of a kindly disposition."[301]

This is not very satisfactory. The God revealed in Scripture doesn't stop at dispositions; as He is, so He acts. When He "remembers" or calls to mind, He acts to intervene. In the same way, He gives or releases or sends forth (*natan*) grace (Ps. 84:11; Prov. 3:34); He "deals graciously" (*hanan*; Gen. 33:5, 11). Even on a human level, we are *gracious* particularly when we give.[302] So when human speech is called gracious,[303] one suspects that it is not simply characterized by elegance but unleashed "for the cause of truth and to defend the right" (Ps. 45:4, NRSV). Like *mercy* and *righteousness* and *peace*, *grace* is a doing word: God acting out or showing forth His love.

> How glorious was the grace
> When Christ sustained the stroke. — Isaac Watts[304]

----

[298] Prov. 3:34, NIV84; James 4:6; 1 Peter 5:5.

[299] James Ryle's definition is set forth in an undated audio series, *Amazing Grace: Experiencing the Fullness of God's Empowering Presence*, available also on DVD (http://isojourn.tv/store/amazing-grace-experiencing-fullness-gods-empowering-presence-video). See also Ryle's blog, accessed December 19, 2021, http://jamesryle.blogspot.com/2009_06_01_archive.html. On the other hand, John Piper distinguishes between *grace* as God's goodness to the undeserving and *mercy* as His goodness to the afflicted: *Future Grace: The Purifying Power of the Promises of God* (1995), revised edition (Colorado Springs: Multnomah, 2012), 73-76.

[300] McClure, *Grace Revisited*, 49.

[301] McClure, 46-47. But he goes on to emphasize the divine power associated with grace (56-65), and to make other helpful points.

[302] Ps. 37:21, 26; 112:5; Prov. 14:21, 31; 19:17; 28:8; Dan. 4:27.

[303] Ps. 45:2; Prov. 22:11; Eccl. 10:12.

[304] Watts, Hymn #1.142, in *Psalms and Hymns*, 695.

But, as we learn particularly in the New Testament, *grace* is something more than a great king wagging the finger of His immeasurable might, or paying my debt out of His inexhaustible storehouse. Grace is costly, even to God:

> For you know the grace of our Lord Jesus Christ, that though he was rich, yet for your sake he became poor, so that you through his poverty might become rich. — 2 Cor. 8:9; Msg "in one stroke he became poor and we became rich"

He has poured Himself out, taking on human flesh and human suffering—and this not for a brief span of time, but for eternity. Grace means that He has identified Himself with us; not only is He present with us, but He keeps us ever before Him, with Him, in His presence. And so grace is more than empowering, as the presence of Jesus brings hope, adoption, redemption, forgiveness, deliverance, mercy, truth, life from death:

> In love [the Father] predestined us for adoption to sonship through Jesus Christ, in accordance with his pleasure and will—to the praise of his glorious grace, which he has freely given us in the One he loves. In him we have redemption through his blood, the forgiveness of sins, in accordance with the riches of God's grace that he lavished on us. — Eph. 1:4-8

Though it is difficult to define, we instinctively recognize grace. William Barclay writes:

> What the ancient world longed for, as Seneca said, was a hand let down to lift us up. And that is precisely what Grace is. It is the hand of God to lift us out of frustration into victory, out of helplessness into power, out of defeat into triumph.[305]

---

[305] Barclay, *In the Hands of God*, 157.

The outstretched hand is brought vividly to life when Esther goes before the king, her husband. Already, because of an affectionate attraction (*'ahabah*), he has shown her grace (*hen*) and kindness (*hesed*) (Est. 2:17). Now, though she is so bold as to appear unbidden, she finds favor (*hen*) in his eyes—and the sign is that he extends to her the scepter in his hand (5:2), sparing her life (7:3; 8:3-6), and inviting her to draw near (5:2). So, too, Jacob the grasper wrestles with men and with God; he is still clasping the angel when he begs for grace, and grace appears through more extended hands, the angel's touch that hobbles or leashes him, and the embrace of his wronged brother Esau.[306] These stories prefigure the New Testament hands of Jesus, touching a leper, lifting up Peter, and the loving embrace of the prodigal's Father.[307]

Still, the great sign of grace is not a touch from God, but His continuous presence. Moses says as much just before and just after God's great revelation to him:

> For how shall it be known that I have found favor [grace, *hen*] in your sight, I and your people, unless you go with us? — Ex. 33:16, NRSV

> If now I have found favor [grace, *hen*] in your sight, O Lord, I pray, let the Lord go with us. Although this is a stiff-necked people, pardon our iniquity and our sin, and take us for your inheritance. — Ex. 34:9, NRSV

Repeatedly in Scripture, even on a human level, the sign of grace or favor is that you stay with me (Gen. 30:27; 1 Sam. 16:22). How much more we cry to God, "If I have found favor in your eyes, my lord, do not pass your servant by" (Gen. 18:3); "Turn to me and be gracious to me" (Ps. 25:16; compare 119:132); "Lord, be gracious to us; we long

---

[306] Gen. 32:26, Hos. 12:3-4, Gen. 33:4.
[307] Mark 1:41; Matt. 14:31; Luke 15:20.

for you" (Isa. 33:2). David, fleeing from his son Absalom, refuses to take the ark of God with him out of Jerusalem, but acknowledges that his flight is also a banishment: "If I find favor in the LORD's eyes, he will bring me back and let me see it and his dwelling place again" (2 Sam. 15:25). The blessing "God be gracious"[308] comprehends all blessings by inviting His presence.

The same Hebrew verb *hanan* that describes the giving or showing of grace is also used to express the seeking for it: crying, begging, pleading, groaning. When the Lord promises to pour out "a spirit of grace [*hen*] and supplication [*tahanunim*]" (Zech. 12:10), we see that He is already present, and grace is already present, in the crying out. Hunger itself is grace. This also helps us to understand why Proverbs 3:34 says that the Lord mocks the proud but gives grace to the humble: those who have received the grace of humiliation are already crying out and seeking. "Though the LORD is on high, he looks upon the lowly, but the proud [the haughty who are themselves lifted up on high] he knows from afar" (Ps. 138:6, NIV84). The heroes of faith are people who have pleaded and groaned[309]—as, in the New Testament, grace is displayed when Jesus cries out with and for us, the merciful Father pleads with us, and the Spirit of God groans in us.[310]

In Psalm 77:8-9, during a true dark night of the soul, the psalmist wonders whether the Lord's steadfast love (*hesed*) has ceased, whether He has forgotten to be gracious (*hanan*), and whether He has stifled His compassion (*rahamim*). Normally, though, the hope for grace, like that for mercy, is founded on the Lord's committed and unfailing *hesed* love. The Lord is with Joseph in prison, and shows His *hesed* by granting him favor (*hen*) with the warden (Gen. 39:21). In Psalm 51:1, a fallen David cries to God to be gracious (*hanan*) "according to" His unfailing love (*hesed*) and the multitude or abundance of His mercies

---

[308] Gen. 43:29; Num. 6:25; Ps. 67:1.

[309] Gen. 42:21; Deut. 3:23; Est. 4:8; 8:3; Dan. 6:11.

[310] Heb. 5:7; Luke 15:28; Rom. 8:26.

(*rahamim*). Though he is brought low in the pit of humiliation, his faith rises boldly, grace asking for grace: "Do not cast me from your presence or take your Holy Spirit from me" (Ps. 51:11).

> From his fullness we have all received, grace upon grace. —
> John 1:16, NRSV

Believers—the church—"administer" or "steward" God's grace (1 Peter 4:10; Eph. 3:2; 4:29), but "it is God alone who exercises it" or supplies it in the first place,[311] for He freely chooses to be present with us. So grace is emphatically not our work, ours to earn or take credit for.[312] We look away from ourselves to "the God of all grace" (1 Peter 5:10), we come empty-handed to "the throne of grace" (Heb. 4:16). We receive Jesus, wholly, daily, and from Him receive "grace upon grace" (John 1:16, NRSV). Truly, as J. I. Packer says, "rightly understood, this one word 'grace' contains within itself the whole of New Testament theology."[313]

Can we lose grace? Yes; paradoxically, we "miss" the grace of God (Heb. 12:15, NIV84) by aiming too high. We "fall from" grace (Gal. 5:4) when we try to use it as a stepping-stone to something greater: our own righteousness that we can brag about. Believers who do this aren't intending to refuse grace, but to add to it; and yet the New Testament is quite clear: if we return to trusting in our own strength, we set aside or frustrate grace (Gal. 2:21) and have received it in vain (2 Cor. 6:1); we desert the One who calls by grace (Gal. 1:6), and insult "the Spirit of grace" (Heb. 10:29). When we shoot for grace plus something, or Christ plus something, we end with nothing—in part because we are doing our best to stifle the hunger that is itself part of grace.

---

[311] J. I. Packer, *18 Words: The Most Important Words You Will Ever Know* (1981; Fearn, Scotland: Christian Focus, 2007), 95. First published as *God's Words*.
[312] Rom. 11:6; 4:4; Eph. 2:8-9; 2 Tim. 1:9.
[313] Packer, *18 Words*, 91.

And still He comes, seeking us. He "gives more grace" (James 4:6, RSV), the grace of His persistent, wooing, convicting, restoring presence. His grace abounds, superabounds, and overflows. More to the point: because He gives us Himself, His grace suffices.[314]

*　　　*　　　*

Once in a while, as I sleep, He does a drive-by. Mind you, these are not Pam dreams, and I am still jealous. But something more than anxiety is going on.

Not that I always know how to interpret the imagery. In one dream, I am simply presented with a gift cheese, wrapped in plastic and labeled, "Nice job!" A gift cheese?! Is that my heavenly crown?

Another night, I'm teaching an adult class. As usual, I'm unprepared and panicky; but somehow, this time, I get the participants to improvise dance routines. I may not have any wisdom to impart, but I'm given an opportunity to help them release their own creativity and skill.

There is also a waking vision. During a time of worship, I see a picture of a kite, and recognize it as my life: flimsy and inconsequential, yet allowing others to glimpse the wind of the Holy Spirit. I hear: "Don't worry about your life. Hold it lightly. Run after Me." Every day, Pam helps me to do that.

Finally, there's a dream in which I seem to be a journalist, interviewing a gang of dumpster-diving urchins (and not particularly enjoying the assignment). I ask whether this is all of them, and hear a bang from inside one of the dumpsters. Looking in, I see a little girl with fiery red hair and a fierce attitude which is somehow familiar. At that moment, in real life, Pam bumps the bed, waking me. I open my eyes, recognize her, grin, and go back to sleep. She will be heard.

*　　　*　　　*

---

[314] See Rom. 5:15; 2 Cor. 9:8; Rom. 5:20; 1 Tim. 1:14; 2 Cor. 12:9.

Pam crawls into bed beside me. I turn toward her, even though I know her game. She has come to steal my heat.

She is ALWAYS cold. I have suggested that she is naturally coldblooded; plus she keeps drinking ice water till it courses through her veins. And then there's the sore left foot that she still treats with icepacks—let that frozen extremity brush up against you in bed at night, and you'll wake up shrieking, convinced you're in the clutch of the Abominable Snowman.

This is our nightly ritual. I am up late, working; she stays near the audio Bible, and eventually falls asleep on the living room couch. In the wee hours, I slip past her quietly and go to bed. Sooner or later, she joins me.

A month after we came home, she told me she missed our evenings at National Rehab, when I would climb into her bed. We cuddled till visiting hours ended, and she fell in love with me again. She felt safe, and knew she wasn't alone.

So we made time to snuggle, and have ever since. During the day, when we are together, we hold hands; at night, we are eventually alongside. And when she comes stealing my heat, I know, chilled though she is, that she is seeking not warmth, but grace. She wants nothing less than the warm embrace of God. My inert carcass, and even visions of angelic dogs, are poor tokens and reminders. With her whole being she craves the presence that alone is love and life.

"I slept, but my heart was awake," says the beloved in Solomon's song (Song 5:2, NRSV). Pam also had a wakeful heart; even in a coma she cried out for grace.

> Upon my bed at night
> I sought him whom my soul loves;
> I sought him, but found him not;
> I called him, but he gave no answer. — Song 3:1, NRSV

O that his left hand were under my head,
and that his right hand embraced me! — Song 2:6; 8:3,
NRSV

Born of affliction, yet purged of bitterness; alert even in this somnam-
bular existence; she will not be denied. For the longing is already grace.

THE CUP

As the deer pants for streams of water,
so my soul pants for you, my God.
My soul thirsts for God, for the living God. — Ps. 42:1-2

Shall I not drink the cup the Father has given me? . . . I
thirst. — John 18:11; 19:28, Ampl

Grace means that Jesus accepts from His Father's hand the cup of wrath
drawn for us, and drains it, drinking a "cup of wasting astonishment
and horror and desolation" (Ezek. 23:33, Ampl) that causes even
Him, the Fountain of Living Water (John 4:10; Ps. 36:9), to thirst.
He entered the abyss of want, the maw of death, so that we who have
spurned grace and chosen a land of drought may "drink from [His]
river of delights" (Ps. 36:8).

And when this cup you give is filled to brimming
With bitter suffering, hard to understand,
We take it thankfully and without trembling,
Out of so good and so beloved a hand. — Dietrich
Bonhoeffer[315]

---

[315] Dietrich Bonhoeffer, "By Gracious Powers" (1944; transl. Fred Pratt Green, Hope Publishing Company, 1974), in Bert Polman, Marilyn Kay Stulken, and James Rawlings Sydnor,
eds., *Amazing Grace: Hymn Texts for Devotional Use* (Louisville, KY: Westminster John Knox,
1994), 42. Also available at *Hymnary*, accessed December 19, 2021, https://hymnary.org/text/
by_gracious_powers_so_wonderfully_shelte.

Yet still He queries us, "Are you able to drink the cup that I drink or be baptized with the baptism [of affliction] with which I am baptized?" (Mark 10:38, Ampl). It is another facet of grace that He inducts us into "the fellowship of sharing in his sufferings" (Phil. 3:10, NIV84).

There's a strange feature in Psalm 23. When it begins, David is saying great things about God, but they're all in the third person: "The LORD is my shepherd. . . . He makes me lie down . . . He leads me . . . He restores my soul." But in verse 4, it changes suddenly to the second person: "You are with me . . . Your rod . . . Your staff."[316] Something changes in the valley; there's a new intimacy with God. It may not be pleasant at first: David feels the rod of discipline rather than warm, embracing arms. Our first awareness that God is still with us may be that the Holy Spirit continues to convict us. But in time we come to hear His voice, and He doesn't need to prod us as much with His rod and staff. And the change is permanent; even on the other side of the valley, David is saying, "You prepare a table before me . . . you anoint my head" (Ps. 23:1-5). At least in this life, that intimacy is the highest peak of all.

> You prepare a table before me
> in the presence of my enemies.
> You anoint my head with oil;
> my [brimming] cup runs over. — Ps. 23:5, Ampl

The cup of grace overflows (Ps. 23:5) after we have drunk from the cup of affliction, and gasped thirst-stricken in the dust of death. But the cup of affliction becomes for us a cup of grace as Jesus holds it to our lips, as He ceases to be a distant *He* and is our *You*, our *Thou*.

*   *   *

---

[316] David Roper, *Psalm 23: The Song of a Passionate Heart* (Grand Rapids, MI: Discovery House, 1994), 108.

Why then is my cup so empty? John Milton struggled with this problem in his forties, as he was going blind, fearing that all his powers would prove "useless." He sensed an answer:

> God doth not need
> either man's work or His own gifts; who best
> bear His mild yoke, they serve Him best; . . .
> They also serve who only stand and wait.[317]

Waiting is indeed a more-than-minuscule part of our sojourn in the valley. The seed goes to ground and breaks apart to germinate through a long winter. We are not progressing ahead, but planted; we cannot chug the cup. As Moses says, He makes us hungry, and then—after that hunger and thirst have done their work in us—He feeds us (Deut. 8:3; compare Matt. 5:6). But God has promised that those who learn to wait with expectant faith, to hope, looking earnestly into the darkness for the approaching dawn, will not be put to shame; their strength will be renewed; they will inherit the land.[318] Hope is not easy: the Hebrew *qavah* originates in the tension of a stretched and straining cord.[319] Thirsting, we stretch out our hands to the Lord (Ps. 143:6), and our hearts. Even before He is stretched out, spread-eagled, on the cross, Jesus's agony (*agonia*) in Gethsemane (Luke 22:44) indicates profound and unbearable tension, the straining of every nerve (as we are to do also, Luke 13:24).[320]

My father had a favorite saying. Throughout his long years in Hong Kong, he witnessed many delays, particularly in transportation: crowded buses, late ferries, canceled trains. Almost always,

---

[317] John Milton, "Sonnet 19 (When I Consider How My Light Is Spent)" (1652-55); available at *Poetry Foundation*, accessed December 19, 2021, https://www.poetryfoundation.org/poems/44750/sonnet-19-when-i-consider-how-my-light-is-spent.

[318] Ps. 130:5-6; Isa. 49:23; 40:31; Ps. 37:9.

[319] *BDB*, 875.

[320] Arndt and Gingrich, 14-15.

the Chinese people affected, from businessmen to schoolchildren to coolies, settled placidly and even dozed, without comforts or even furniture, while westerners fumed and paced and tapped their watches and complained. He drew the cultural conclusion, "Americans can do anything but wait."

I am an American, impatient, unskilled at waiting. I recognize my calling to keep Pam company in the valley, but, the longer I do so, the more my cord of hope goes slack; I cease to peer ahead for the coming of God, and only observe her changes. Instead of chronicling the work of God, I am only aphasia's Boswell, recording the latest misfired phrase that still, somehow, strikes home. And I settle into unbelief, content just to crack wise; emailing a friend, "My cup runneth over, and my dish runneth away with the spoon."

Of all Jesus's parables, I most identify with the one about the barren fig tree:

> A man had a fig tree growing in his vineyard, and he went to look for fruit on it but did not find any. So he said to the man who took care of the vineyard, "For three years now I've been coming to look for fruit on this fig tree and haven't found any. Cut it down! Why should it use up the soil?"
>
> "Sir," the man replied, "leave it alone for one more year, and I'll dig around it and fertilize [KJV "dung"] it. If it bears fruit next year, fine! If not, then cut it down." — Luke 13:6-9

There aren't a lot of roles in this story, no great amount of interpretive wiggle room. I'm pretty sure that I'm the fruitless tree "cumbering" (KJV) the ground. The owner who's about ready to turn me into firewood is God the Father, but Jesus the vinedresser intercedes for a temporary stay of execution and then heaps poop on me. The part about the poop explains a great deal about my present circumstances, but it doesn't seem to be working. So I have these conversations with Jesus:

"Lord, I think maybe poop isn't my preferred learning style. What else Ya got?" But the poop keeps coming, and the fruit does not.

And yet . . . part of Milton's point seems to be that it doesn't so much matter whether I think I'm fruitful. The owner and the vinedresser know exactly what fruit they expect. The tree may not—just as it may not recognize, at first, that grace can look and feel and smell like poop.

Only God can supply the grace of His presence, but all believers administer grace; it becomes fruitful in us. The grace (*charis*) we receive releases in us spiritual gifts (*charismata*) with which to bless and encourage others (1 Peter 4:10; Rom. 12:6-8). And the gifts of God are irrevocable (Rom. 11:29). I began praying this promise over Pam while she was still in hospital, and she has often echoed it since:

> *Restore our memories of the gifts that You said are erivokable. Please add more gifts to bless other's with Your words!* [2012]

> *Your willing to Remove words and cast them as far as the East is 2 the West 2 be remember no more* [Ps. 103:12]. . . . *The Gifts are earevokable—* [2012]

> *Heavenly Father, I thank you for showing me why You placed me into a cofin in John Hopkin's. You reminded me of all the gift's You had reserved in my brain so I could know why? Lord, my gifts were erevokable, and, I would be needed here on earth to share the good new's Jesus die'd, and, brought back what the enemy—Satan—had stollen away from all who would ask Jesus into their hearts. I'd been praying to You, God, bring back the year's the locust had consumed* [Joel 2:25]. [2015]

Yet there is waiting. God Himself hungers to see our fruit, but He will not settle for bad fruit (Matt. 7:15-20), even with good presentation (7:21-23). He takes no pleasure in the product of our unredeemed, ambitious striving. He looks at the heart; in His kind recollection, Israel's youthful devotion refreshed His spirit "like finding grapes in the desert" or early figs.[321] But we are inconstant, and our hearts must change. Only the power of God can keep us from becoming barren and unfruitful, and the power of God is resurrection, life out of death.[322] Ultimately, we can only be fruitful in Jesus, the one true vine (John 15:1-6). The independent fig tree is waiting to die.

The object of biblical hope is the life that lies beyond nature's life. When Abraham paid an exorbitant price to buy a small parcel of all the vast territory promised to him by God, so as to have a burial site for Sarah, he was doing more than affirming his faith, and his willingness to wait for the fulfillment (that is, his hope). He was raising his eyes to a larger promise. "I am a stranger and a sojourner among you," he said to the Hittites (Gen. 23:4, RSV); and he always would be. He longed for a better, heavenly country (Heb. 11:16); whether he could have said so or not, something in him knew that the Lord who had brought life out of Sarah was not yet finished bringing life to her. Of the grace of God given to him, in his wealth, he poured out, as a willing exchange (in God's generous eyes, even a down payment) for the grace to be revealed. He declared himself content to wait.

> For the despondent, every day brings trouble; for the happy heart, life is a continual feast. — Prov. 15:15, NLT

Meanwhile, Pam finishes my biblical quotations as well, and as creatively, as all my other sentences. "A merry heart . . ." I begin; she concludes, ". . . gets the job done."

*   *   *

---

[321] Hos. 9:10; Jer. 2:2-3; compare Deut. 5:28-29.
[322] 2 Peter 1:3, 8; Heb. 11:19; Rom. 4:17-25; Eph. 1:18-20.

In the tales of King Arthur's knights, the cup of grace is a motif, appearing as the holy grail, the chalice Christ handed round at the Supper. The best of these stories look beyond a magic that lodges in the vessel, and hint at a grace of presence and pouring out.[323] One such narrative is central to the 1991 film *The Fisher King*.[324]

In the film, homeless Parry (played by Robin Williams) tells guilt-ridden Jack (Jeff Bridges) the story of a king who lies wounded, helpless, and alone. One day a fool wanders in and, filled with compassion, offers him a cup of water. The king is healed and, looking in his hands, discovers the holy grail which he has been seeking all his life.

> Everything on the Table and everyone around the Table becomes Gospel and is distributed to all who hunger and thirst after righteousness. — Eugene Peterson[325]

This film is a favorite with us. One day in 2012, I reminded Pam of the leading features of the plot, and she wrote this:

Jesus—Story John Tell's

There was a King who lived alone? Couldn't walk well? One day he was approached by a stranger who asked him for some water—? Odd? Wrong? He was the King the foolish man had approached—The fool didn't know he could be thrown away for even appraching the King. So, the King as the fool "Why did you

---

[323] Matthew Annis, "The Fisher King," part of *The Camelot Project* (2007), summarizes many versions, from Arthurian legend to T. S. Eliot to Pop Fisher in Bernard Malamud's *The Natural*. See *The Camelot Project*, accessed December 19, 2021, http://d.lib.rochester.edu/camelot/text/annis-the-fisher-king-essay-and-bibliography.

[324] *The Fisher King*, written by Richard LaGravenese, directed by Terry Gilliam; TriStar Pictures, 1991.

[325] Eugene H. Peterson, *Christ Plays in Ten Thousand Places: A Conversation in Spiritual Theology* (Grand Rapids, MI: William B. Eerdmans, 2005), 211.

*come in here? You have no right to be in here. So, why are you
in here*—[In margin: *Shame—Pam*]

*The fool replied "I was just thirsty and I was hungry—I saw you
there so I simply*

*Jesus did approch me thru John when I came out of the coma.
John was a stranger to me. I didn't remember anyone or
anything—I couldn't eat—John fed me. John was (still is) so
Christ like I got better. . . .*

*John—like God—know's all the horrible things I've done yet he
still loves me—*

Sometimes grace is just that simple. We love another, not perfectly,
but with our wounds; a cavity hollowed out in us by brokenness and
need fills with compassion. We stretch forth empty hands, and they are
fruitful; we determine to keep company, and, behold, a greater presence is with us. We wait, and the other rises.

> Arise, arise;
> And with his buriall-linen drie thine eyes.
> — George Herbert[326]

Grace is always more than natural. It is the smile of Jesus, which He
must be present to bestow. It is costly, lacerating His flesh and His
heart, as He kneels once more in the gravel, taut with His hopes and
our groaning, pouring Himself out to bathe and cool our errant feet.
There are in the bounty of God many flavors of healing and satisfaction, but only the steely blood-taste of grace assuages thirst. Grace
limps into a desert, dripping, and life springs up.

---

[326] Herbert, from "The Dawning," *The Temple*, 140.

LOVE LETTERS

I am writing to you, dear children,
because your sins have been forgiven on account of his
name. — 1 John 2:12

For I wrote you out of much affliction and anguish of heart
and with many tears, not to cause you pain but to let you know
the abundant love that I have for you. — 2 Cor. 2:4, RSV

"Grace is everywhere." So says the dying priest in Georges Bernanos's 1936 novel, *The Diary of a Country Priest.* His last words end the book. The priest is fictional, but the words were spoken, a few decades earlier, by Therese of Lisieux, a young nun dying of tuberculosis in 1897.[327]

"Grace is everywhere." At first the sentiment seems over-rosy and absurd. Better to say that pain is everywhere, or violence, injustice, sin. Only when Jesus, disfigured and radiant, has given us to drink of His living water, can we see aright. Then we know that eyes that discern grace are not clouded, blind to evil. Rather, they pierce the veils, spying God's frequent visitations and His refusal fully to absent Himself.

The earth, O Lord, is full of your steadfast love; . . .
— Ps. 119:64, NRSV

Life is tough sometimes, isn't it? And then you get a whisper of grace and it all seems bearable. Peter, trying to sum up a letter haunted by thoughts of suffering, in my imagination sweeps his thick arm spaciously as he declares, "*this* is the true grace of God; stand fast in it" (1 Peter 5:12, RSV; emphasis added). For grace comes to us embodied, and in unlikely ways.

*　　　*　　　*

[327] Georges Bernanos, *The Diary of a Country Priest* (1936), transl. Pamela Morris (1937; New York: Carroll & Graf-Avalon, 1983, 2002), 298; and Remy Rougeau, "Introduction" to Bernanos (2002), x, xiii. See also Kathryn Harrison, *Saint Therese of Lisieux*, Penguin Lives (New York: Lipper/Viking-Penguin, 2003).

Pam writes me letters. Some days she seems to see grace everywhere, or at least to try:

> *I feel like I'm being gypped, but I know that's not true.*

And sometimes she finds grace right there in the midst of our life together, and our story:

> *My Dearest John,*
>
> *Thank you 4 sharing your life with me. I did feel lost without you. How could I have forgoten who U were when I fell into that coma? . . . When I did meet you you were a stranger I met and fell in love again. That was as easy as you were the first time I met you year's ago. Remember how quickly I fell asleep when you met with me near KU. I trusted you.* [2012]

My lover spoke and said to me,
"Arise, my darling,
My beautiful one, and come with me.
See! The winter is past;
the rains are over and gone.
Flowers appear on the earth;
the season of singing has come." — Song 2:10-12, NIV84

> *I fell in love with you because you weren't in jail! That was the first time. You are amazing. You were a light in my darkness. Your words were so true. The Holy Spirit is in you. You weren't trying to get anything from me. We met at the Lied center, and you brought me a beautiful bouquet of flowers. It took my breath away. There was beauty all over you. I was impressed that you would spend so much on me. You love the Lord and he is very*

important to you. You put your arm around me and I fell asleep. You were so sweet that you let me sleep.

Then you went away for awhile. And I had a dream. And then we got married! At Church. Then we went out to eat! You're loving, and kind, and generous. I respect the time that you spend with the Lord every day.

I know how sweet you are because you take such good care of me every day. You are so gifted and so loving.

You helped me so much in the hospital by trying to understand what I was feeling. Everything was so confusing. But you even helped my dry eyes. You got me in music therapy. The Holy Spirit is there when we are together. And I know other people can see it. You have a beautiful voice. You know me, and you were helping others to respond to the me you knew. You let me be myself. You helped others work better with me. Comedy helped me and those around me get through. You were a breath of fresh air. . . .

Please take care of yourself. I am so grateful for you. I love you so much. We need each other. We understand each other so well. . . .

I am very much in love with you. We have our ups and downs. But everyone does. [2014]

But the letters are also for others. We see this, occasionally, just going through our day. Standing at the counter in Taco Bell, Pam kept changing her mind as I read her the menu choices; as usual, our decision-making was interspersed with banter and light insults. At last Pam turned to the high-school-age girl waiting behind the register, and with a smile asked, "Don't you wish you had someone to give a hard time to?"—and at once the girl exclaimed, "I want that!" We all laughed, and I commented that it's our mission to go about exciting envy. Later, Pam wrote:

> *How fun listening to the young girl telling us she wanted some-one like us. Happy, not sarcasm, dude.*

Then there was the day when she came to me with, "John, I have to tell you something. I feel bad." She had driven herself to an appointment at the hospital, around noon. She stopped by the cafeteria, saw that they were serving salmon, and bought two meals, one for each of us. She sat and ate hers there—and it was so good that she went on to consume mine as well.

They say that confession is good for the soul, but I have to say that this account didn't make me feel even slightly better. The next day we were both at the hospital, and Pam decided to follow up. Leading me into the cafeteria, she asked a young man, "Are you the cook?" He looked up as if caught in the act: "Who wants to know?" She pressed on, undeterred: "I was in here yesterday, and they had . . ." "Salmon," I supplied, adding sourly, "and she bought two, and then ate mine."

> Come, my Joy, my Love, my Heart:
> Such a Joy, as none can move:
> Such a Love, as none can part:
> Such a Heart, as joyes in love. — George Herbert[328]

Now the kid was intrigued, and even enthusiastic: "Oh, is that the one that they do with the really good glaze?" "I'll never know," I cried, raising my voice in mock indignation; "she ate mine!" Just then another server spoke up, grinning: "You two are adorable together!"

------

[328] Herbert, from "The Call," *The Temple*, 196.

Together or separately, we are letters from Christ (2 Cor. 3:2-3). Pam at least is clearly a love letter; people are drawn to her. She journaled:

> *God began to talk silently to me. He said I should fan into flame the gift the Lord had already given me by His grace.* [2 Tim. 1:6]

I think now that her main gift is simply her testimony, and she rekindles it each time she buttonholes a stranger and, telling it, relives the grace of God. How many more will come back to her, in this life or the next, declaring, "I remember you"?

Encouraging me to write this account, she said:

> *You explain to other's what you've heard how people have responed to my own weak word's I've shared with those stranger's.*
>
> *Jesus, God, H Spirit sent you that Gift of Righting so courageously—in a gift of love + encouragement that cannot be forgiven . . . no, I think I meant removed?*
>
> *We are the best story stranger's are drawn to.*

"I have written you only a short letter," says the author of the Letter to the Hebrews (Heb. 13:22, NIV84); and "I have written to you briefly," concludes Peter (1 Peter 5:12). Texts, even this book, come to an end; but stories of grace are an invitation to converse, a Dixie cup that beckons to a fountain, God Himself expressing thirst:

> Although I have much to write to you, I would rather not use paper and ink; instead I hope to come to you and talk with you face to face, so that our joy may be complete.
> — 2 John 12, NRSV

EASTER

When everyone had run away,
God sent an angel.
When hope was sealed up in a tomb,
God rolled away the stone.
When darkness reigned,
God lit a light that has never been extinguished.
When love had died,
it continued to be heard, even in hell.
When death squeezed out Jesus's final breath,
it was defeated and disarmed.
When evil triumphed,
God arose.

ACKNOWLEDGMENTS

Pam wrote to Cheri, after a grace-filled evening at Cheri and Pat's home: "I was touched by everything. And you were one of the everythings." Grace is everywhere, and we have many everythings to thank.

In Baltimore, Washington, and Lawrence, we received the assistance of some remarkable **doctors**, including Samuel, Brad, Carla, Blake, Thomas, Rawan, Jon, Mark, David, Penny, Kritis, Lisa, Kevin, Khylie, Matthew, Leslie, Stephan, Jennifer, Matthew, Sanjeev, John, Leslie, Cathy, Cleve, Thomas, Christina, Larry, John, Adrian, Tony, Tyler, Patrick, and John; **nurses** Claudia, Lynn, Lauren, Joe, Ken, Laura, Thelma, Kenneth, Rhea, Liz, Bethany, Erin, Mandi, Marie, Lordes, Diana, Lauren, Shantai, Christine, Palestine, Steph, Joyce, Leah, Stacy, Jacki, Kevin, Rita, Tamara, Kathryn, Maren, Olivia, Claudette, Carolyn, Raven, Sonia, Tina, Darlene, Sheri, and Ron; **therapists** Susan, James, Everette, Elias, Esmeralda, Wes, Trena, Jocelyn, Andrea, Jeremy, Erin, Joe, Jade, Kristi, Catherine, Mary Kay, Staci, Lauren, Kevin, Rita, Holly, Maria, Tamra, Beth, Lynn, Katie, Julie, McKenzie, Erin, Amanda, David, Janine, Lucille, Jasmyn, Karen, Cynthia, Morgan, and Pilar; **music therapists** Cynthia, Bill, Kara, Halle, Monica, Jennifer, Rachel, Leslie, Courtney, Mandy, Shelby, Ronette, Estarah, Shelby, Jordan, Kaitlin, Christine, Allison, Jenna, Anna, Daniela, Angie, Maddie, Tamieka, Carly, Stephanie, Elise, Ellen, Gabby, Riley, Anna, Morgan, Sarah, Olivia, Forrest, Anita, Tabitha, Weijie, Alison, Kassidy, Adison, and Zichan; **driving instructor** Walter; **social workers** Daniel, Cindy, and Renita; and **assistants and volunteers** Charles, Walter, Crystal, Elmira, Alisa, Courtney, Trena, Wanda, Nina, Keisha, Nikkia, Chelsea, Fiona, Kritis, Donnie, Shay, Kait, Rebecca, Josh,

Christopher, Quentin, Lance, and Tatiana. Pam's recovery would not have proceeded as smoothly nor progressed as far without your devoted efforts.

We also want to thank our *friends*, particularly Cheri and Pat, Pieter and Alice, Marc, Dana, Christy, Barb, Jim and Elizabeth, Jenny and Chris, Robin, Angie, Mike, Paul, Julie, Joe and Vicki, Robin, Vic, Steve and Sharon, Boniface and Leslie, Brent, Carl and Joyce, Brian and Norma, Julie and Gary, Dave and Darla, Ann and Walt, Connie, Judy, Julie, Carolyn, Peter and Tina, Eli, Seth, Rory, Dave, Tim, Mary-ann, Tim and Jen, Mark and Linda, Grace, Dick and Hua Chin, Larry, Walter, Rich, Lance, Earl, Paul, Chuck, Denny and Judy, Ben, Cindi, Renee, Will, Lisa and Hugh, Jon, Molly, Glenda, Dan and Maura, Lydia, Levi, Neil, Elaine, Bill and Noreen, Tom and Bridget, Khashtar, Rosa, Clarence, Marsha, D.D., Diana, Molly, Susan, Kendall and Steve, Mo and Steve, Jude, Michael, Mary Lou, Mike, Ann, Roy, Katie, Nick, 1 and 2 John, Vinay, Arthur, Humphrey, Elizabeth, Efanor, Tiffany, Angelique, Wendi, Susan, Mark, Chris, Lola, Andrea, Stephen, Joshua, Jop, Gregory, Beth, Leslie, Bob, Peter, Prodip, Harun, Maggie, Cathy, Brandis, Selina, Eng, Cuc, Becky, Shannon, Allie, and Jacinta; our *pastors and chaplains* Pieter and Alice, Paul and Barb, Eli, Thomas, Jeff, Ron, Bob, Timothy, Glenn, and Claudia; and *family members* Leslie and J.T., Koen, Asa, Griffin, Brian and Antigone, Georgia, Giulia, Michael and Melody, Ellie, Lydia, Samuel, George, Moriah, Meredith and James, John and Ruth, Deena and Michael, Lauren, Margo and Julian, Doug and Janet, Jayce, Danielle, Adam, Jeff and Sandi, Jeff Jr., Alysha, Shaun, Lincoln and Joyce, Nathaniel, Ethan, Kara, Rhema, Brenda and Tocher, Ginger, Ben, Doug and Linda, Jeanenne, Jim and Dagna, John and Mary, Gene and Eugenia, Ellen, Courtney, Jane and Jim, Amanda. Your love, prayers, and companionship have put to flight the spirit of heaviness, again and again; your many kindnesses have clothed us with the garment of praise.

Mark MacGougan valiantly and brilliantly traversed the entire dark valley of my first draft. He caught discordant phrases that had passed as music in my tin ear; he had the requisite tact and humor to persuade me to surrender numerous beloved digressions. Every reader is indebted to him for a shorter, clearer narrative, and every human being should bathe in the warm waters of Mark's own life-giving stories.

Some early jottings about disability, recovery, anger, and more appeared as essays posted at the *Relevant* magazine website, http://relevantmagazine.com/. I am grateful to editors Ryan Hamm, Tyler Huckabee, and Dargan Thompson.

Great thanks to Writer's Edge, which plucked this manuscript from the outer darkness of the slush pile, and to Andy Carmichael of Deep River Books, who found the listing on Writer's Edge and took a bold plunge. At Deep River I was ably shepherded by Tamara Barnet, Associate Director and Senior Editor, and Hannah Haas, Author Relations Coordinator. Special thanks go to my editor, Carolyn Currey, a fruitful vine even when I kept supplying her with more poop, and to Jason Enterline, who created the beautiful cover image.

I listen mostly to classical music, much of it instrumental; as Pam explained to one puzzled music store employee, "John listens to music without any sounds." I am grateful to Johannes Brahms, whose music with sounds, particularly his *German Requiem*, accompanied me as I wrote; and also to Franz Joseph Haydn, whose *Seven Last Words of Christ* carries me to sound's last breath.

A NOTE ON BOOKS

Our lives at times become like cramped apartments, and other people's stories appear as windows that restore to us a wider world. Pam and I are deeply grateful to all who have shared their pains and possibilities.

Memoirs Cited

Stroke: *See* Ackerman, Bauby, Byars, Douglas, Dunker, Garrison, Gillette, Hale, Hutton, Kerstetter, Lee,, McEwen, [Miller], Moore, Neal, Nutt, Pataki, Roland, Sarton, Shapiro, Sorbo, Talbot, Taylor, West, Wolf, Wulf

Traumatic brain injury: *See* Barrick, Bolzan, Callwood, Carpenter, Crimmins, Cuddy, Giffords, Mills, Osborn, Padgett, Spinney, Thomas, Woodruff

Aneurysm: *See* Kerstetter, Marks, Neal, Siles, Sorbo, Wolf

Aphasia: *See* Ackerman, Allen, Barrick, Bolzan, Douglas, Giffords, Hale, Lee, Marks, Mills, Moore, Neal, Roland, Taylor, West, Williams-Paisley, Woodruff, Wulf

Memory loss: *See* Ackerman, Allen, Barrick, Bolzan, Callwood, Carpenter, Crimmins, Kerstetter, Lee, Marks, Mills, Neal, Osborn, Pataki, Roland, Sacks, Story, Taylor, Thomas, West, Williams-Paisley

Ackerman, Diane. *One Hundred Names for Love: A Stroke, a Marriage, and the Language of Healing.* New York and London: W. W. Norton, 2011.

Allen, Laura, and Bruce Allen. *Brain Storm: A Journey of Faith through Brain Injury.* Bloomington, IN: Westbow-Thomas Nelson, 2012.

Barrick, Linda, with John Perry. *Miracle for Jen: A Tragic Accident, a Mother's Desperate Prayer, and Heaven's Extraordinary Answer.* Carol Stream, IL: Tyndale House, 2012.

Bauby, Jean-Dominique. *The Diving Bell and the Butterfly: A Memoir of Life in Death.* 1997. Transl. Jeremy Leggatt. New York: Vintage-Random House, 1998.

Bolzan, Scott, Joan Bolzan, and Caitlin Rother. *My Life, Deleted: A Memoir.* New York: HarperOne-HarperCollins, 2011.

Byars, Clay. *Will and I: A Memoir.* New York: Farrar, Straus and Giroux, 2016.

Callwood, June. *The Man Who Lost Himself: The Terry Evanshen Story.* Toronto: McClelland & Stewart, 2000.

Carpenter, Kim, and Krickitt Carpenter with Dana Wilkerson. *The Vow.* 2000. Revised edition. Nashville: B&H, 2012.

Crimmins, Cathy. *Where Is the Mango Princess?: A Journey Back from Brain Injury.* 2000. New York: Vintage-Random House, 2001.

Cuddy, Amy. *Presence: Bringing Your Boldest Self to Your Biggest Challenges.* New York: Little, Brown, 2015.

Douglas, Kirk. *My Stroke of Luck.* New York: Perennial-HarperCollins, 2002.

Dunker, Marilee Pierce. *A Braver Song to Sing.* Grand Rapids, MI: Zondervan, 1987.

Garrison, Julia Fox. *Don't Leave Me This Way: Or When I Get Back on My Feet You'll Be Sorry*. 2005. New York: HarperCollins, 2006.

Giffords, Gabrielle, and Mark Kelly with Harry Jaffe. *Enough: Our Fight to Keep America Safe from Gun Violence*. New York: Scribner-Simon & Schuster, 2014.

Giffords, Gabrielle, and Mark Kelly with Jeffrey Zaslow. *Gabby: A Story of Courage and Hope*. New York: Scribner-Simon & Schuster, 2011.

Gillette, Heidi E. *Midline Crisis*. Murrells Inlet, SC: Covenant, 2019.

Hale, Sheila. *The Man Who Lost His Language: A Case of Aphasia*. 2002. Revised edition. London and Philadelphia: Jessica Kingsley, 2007.

Hutton, Cleo (pseudonym). *After a Stroke: 300 Tips for Making Life Easier*. New York: Demos Medical, 2005.

Kerstetter, Jon. *Crossings: A Doctor-Soldier's Story*. New York: Crown, 2017.

Lee, Christine Hyung-Oak. *Tell Me Everything You Don't Remember: The Stroke That Changed My Life*. New York: Ecco-Harper Collins, 2001.

Marks, Lauren. *A Stitch of Time: The Year a Brain Injury Changed My Language and Life*. New York: Simon & Schuster, 2017.

McEwen, Mark, with Daniel Paisner. *Change in the Weather: Life after Stroke*. New York: Gotham-Penguin, 2008.

[Miller], Douglas James. *Stroke: The View from Within*. San Bernardino, CA: Xlibris, 2016.

Mills, Harrianne. *A Mind of My Own: Memoir of Recovery from Aphasia*. Bloomington, IN: AuthorHouse, 2004.

Moore, Pamela Rosewell. *The Five Silent Years of Corrie ten Boom.* Grand Rapids, MI: Zondervan-HarperCollins, 1986.

———. *Life Lessons from the Hiding Place: Discovering the Heart of Corrie ten Boom.* Grand Rapids, MI: Chosen-Baker, 2004, 2005.

Neal, Patricia, with Richard DeNeut. *As I Am: An Autobiography.* New York: Simon and Schuster, 1988.

Nutt, Amy Ellis. *Shadows Bright as Glass: The Remarkable Story of One Man's Journey from Brain Trauma to Artistic Triumph.* New York: Free Press-Simon & Schuster, 2011.

Osborn, Claudia L. *Over My Head: A Doctor's Own Story of Head Injury from the Inside Looking Out.* Kansas City, MO: Andrews McMeel, 1998.

Padgett, Jason, and Maureen Seaberg. *Struck by Genius: How a Brain Injury Made Me a Mathematical Marvel.* Boston and New York: Houghton Mifflin Harcourt, 2014.

Pataki, Allison. *Beauty in the Broken Places: A Memoir of Love, Faith, and Resilience.* New York: Random House, 2018.

Roland, David. *How I Rescued My Brain: A Psychologist's Remarkable Recovery from Stroke and Trauma.* Melbourne and London: Scribe, 2014.

Sacks, Oliver. *Musicophilia: Tales of Music and the Brain.* New York and Toronto: Alfred A. Knopf, 2007.

Sarton, May. *After the Stroke: A Journal.* New York and London: W. W. Norton, 1988.

Shapiro, Alison Bonds. *Healing into Possibility: The Transformational Lessons of a Stroke.* Novato, CA: New World Library, 2009.

Siles, Madonna. *Brain, Heal Thyself: A Caregiver's New Approach to*

Recovery from Stroke, Aneurysm, and Traumatic Brain Injuries. Charlottesville, VA: Hampton Roads, 2006.

Sorbo, Kevin. *True Strength: My Journey from Hercules to Mere Mortal and How Nearly Dying Saved My Life.* Cambridge, MA: Da Capo-Perseus, 2011.

Spinney, Lu. *Beyond the High Blue Air.* New York: Catapult, 2016.

Story, Laura, with Jennifer Schuchmann. *When God Doesn't Fix It: Lessons You Never Wanted to Learn, Truths You Can't Live Without.* Nashville: W-Thomas Nelson, 2015.

Talbot, David. *Between Heaven and Hell: The Story of My Stroke.* San Francisco: Chronicle Prism, 2020.

Taylor, Jill Bolte. *My Stroke of Insight: A Brain Scientist's Personal Journey.* 2006. New York: Plume-Penguin, 2009.

Thomas, Abigail. *A Three Dog Life.* Orlando, FL: Harcourt, 2006.

West, Paul. *The Shadow Factory.* Santa Fe, NM: Lumen, 2008.

Williams-Paisley, Kimberly. *Where the Light Gets In: Losing My Mother Only to Find Her Again.* New York: Crown Archetype, 2016.

Wolf, Katherine, and Jay Wolf. *Hope Heals: A True Story of Overwhelming Loss and an Overcoming Love.* Grand Rapids, MI: Zondervan, 2016.

———. *Suffer Strong: How to Survive Anything by Redefining Everything.* Grand Rapids, MI: Zondervan, 2020.

Woodruff, Lee, and Bob Woodruff. *In an Instant: A Family's Journey of Love and Healing.* 2007. New York: Random House, 2008.

Wulf, Helen Harlan. *Aphasia, My World Alone.* 1973. Detroit: Wayne State University, 1979.

OTHER CREDITS

Printed in the United States
by Baker & Taylor Publisher Services